PRINTED IN HOLLAND BY DRUKKERIJEN vh ELLERMAN HARMS nv, AMSTERDAM
Copyright © 1968 by Tantivy Press   U.S. Library of Congress no. 64-1076.

International
Film Guide
1969

EDITOR: Peter Cowie

TANTIVY PRESS, 7 SEDLEY PLACE, LONDON W.1.

A.S. BARNES & CO. INC., NEW YORK, U.S.A.

THE SOURCE
FOR FILM CLASSICS

JANUS FILMS

Janus Films · 24 West 58th St. · New York, N.Y.

4

INTERNATIONAL FILM GUIDE Choice of Films '67-'68:

1. *The Red and the White* (Jancsó)
2. *Rosemary's Baby* (Polanski)
3. *Playtime* (Tati)
4. *Belle de Jour* (Bunuel)
5. *Bonnie and Clyde* (Penn)
6. *2001: A Space Odyssey* (Kubrick)
7. *Je t'aime, je t'aime* (Resnais)
8. *Monsieur Hawarden* (Kümel)
9. *Ole dole doff* (Troell)
10. *Indian Summer* (Menzel)

Best Animated Film: *Yellow Submarine* (Dunning)

INTERNATIONAL FILM GUIDE Liaison:

Australia: John Baxter
Austria: Goswin Dörfler
Canada: Gerald Pratley
France: Peter Graham
West Germany: Peter F. Gallasch
Hungary: György Fenyves
India: Chidananda Das Gupta
Italy: Lucio Settimio Caruso
Japan: Donald Richie
Poland: Ryszard Koniczek
Portugal: Vasco Granja
Spain: William Dyckes
Switzerland: Felix Bucher
U.S.A.: Margot S. Kernan
Editorial Assistance: Allen Eyles

INTERNATIONAL FILM GUIDE Directors of the Year:

1964	1965	1966	1967	1968
Visconti	Fellini	Kurosawa	Franju	Widerberg
Welles	Satyajit Ray	Rosi	Losey	Ivens
Truffaut	Bunuel	Demy	Polanski	Lumet
Wajda	Malle	Brooks	Frankenheimer	Nemec
Hitchcock	Kubrick	Haanstra	Torre Nilsson	Antonioni

6

CONTENTS

INTERNATIONAL FILM TV-FILM AND DOCUMENTARY MARKET

APRIL and OCTOBER

2 GRAND AWARDS FOR TELEFILMS

MIFED - the International Film, TVfilm and Documentary Market - was founded in 1960 at the time of the thirty-eighth Milan Fair. Since then the Lombard capital has become a great world centre for business transactions associated with the film industry. MIFED is held twice a year: in APRIL to coincide with the Milan Fair, and in OCTOBER.

MIFED offers several international film awards at its two annual sessions. Among these are the «Five Continents Trophy» and «TV Pearl». The first goes to the best entertainment feature; the second is presented in two Grand Prix Awards for the best full-length or serialized film, and for the best short film produced for TV transmission.

Interested persons are cordially invited to attend.

Information from: MIFED
Largo Domodossola 1
Milano (Italy)
Telegrams: MIFED - Milano

8

DIRECTORS OF THE YEAR

1. SERGEI BONDARCHUK

SEVERAL Soviet directors have made an impact on the West these past dozen years — Kalatazov, Chukhrai, Paradjanov, to mention some of the younger generation. But Sergei Bondarchuk has the added advantage of being known as an actor; he has directed only two films, *Destiny of a Man* and *War and Peace*, but both have been enormously successful, from a commercial and a critical standpoint.

SERGEI BONDARCHUK was born in 1920 in a Ukrainian village. His generation is usually dubbed "October's contemporaries"; it grew up with the Revolution and also fought in World War Two. While he was still very young, Bondarchuk moved with his parents to Taganrog, an ancient town of craftsmen and workers. Here he took part in amateur dramatics, and resolved that he would become an actor one day. After graduating at school, he entered the Rostov Theatrical College, but it was only in the front line, during the war, that he was able to make his stage début — in an army ensemble. In 1946 he joined the Institute of Cinema Art.

Bondarchuk's first film appearance came when he was 28. It was the role of the Communist, Valko, in Sergei Gerasimov's *The Young Guards*. All the parts were played by Gerasimov's students at the Institute, and Bondarchuk impressed critics and professionals by his portrait of a man nearly twice his age. While he was still a student, he received further offers to play leading roles from directors, Igor Savchenko and Yuli Raizman among others. As a result, Bondarchuk took the name part in Savchenko's *Taras Shevchenko*. The character of Shevchenko, both poet and rebel, one of the most tragic figures in Russian history, demanded much from Bondarchuk, and in this film he proved conclusively that he had the stuff of a great tragedian in him.

As the years went by, Bondarchuk's name appeared in one film after another, usually at the top of the cast. He played a runaway serf, one of Pugachov's brothers-in-arms *(Admiral Ushakov)*, the writer Garmash *(This Must Not Be Forgotten)*, the engineer Yershov *(Unfinished Tale)*, the title role of *Ivan Franko*, and many other parts that showed his ability to project the primordial forces latent in a man's personality.

It was surprising when he appeared as Dr. Dymov in the screen version of Chekhov's *The Grasshopper* in 1955. The image of Bondarchuk as a powerful, resolute actor was modified. One suddenly realised that there existed quite another

Bondarchuk, a quiet man with a gentle voice and deep, inhibited feelings. A combination of these traits of temperamental energy and heartfelt sincerity was discernible in his portrayal of Othello in Yutkevich's film of the Shakespeare play. Here was a Moor who was perhaps closer than any other to modern man in his psychological make-up, a man caught in the meshes of fate and unwilling to abandon his ideals of humanity and justice.

Then, in 1958, Bondarchuk embarked on his career as a director. He had read Mikhail Sholokhov's story, *Destiny of a Man*, in *Pravda*, and, after working in close harmony with the author, he completed a picture that was shown subsequently in some 60 countries. It is a study of an ordinary man's fate, a "man in the street" caught up in the crucible of war. Andrei Sokolov (played by Bondarchuk) is a village carpenter who endures the privations of the front line and the horror of a Nazi concentration camp only to find at the end of the war that his house has been burned down and his family killed. And so, his world reduced to ashes, he stumbles along the road and meets a 5 year old orphan boy. Gently, but persuasively, he tells the boy that he is his father — and the child accepts the pretence. Sokolov has been physically crushed, but his soul remains dignified and somehow, beautiful. Bondarchuk seems to have taken Gorky's remark as his watchword in this film: "Man is made for happiness as a bird is made for flight", and the strongest images of *Destiny of a Man* are the ones that express sublime pleasure (the unforgettable helicopter shot that wheels above Sokolov as he lies spreadeagled in a wind-swept wheatfield after his escape from the camp).

It was as a direct result of the success of this film that Bondarchuk was asked by Rossellini to play the part of a Russian prisoner of war who had escaped from a concentration camp in *Era notte a Roma*. Bondarchuk was dressed in exactly the same tunic as he had been in his own film. This was Sokolov to the last detail, except that here he had made a successful escape in Italy together with two other POWs, an Englishman and an American.

For more than half the sixties, Bondarchuk worked on his vast production of *War and Peace*, the most ambitious film ever made in the Soviet Union, and probably the most successful from a box-office point of view. Obviously Tolstoy's novel holds a capital place in Russian culture, but Bondarchuk brought to it the epic sweep that had eluded King Vidor in his 1956 version. And yet, says Bondarchuk, "What bothered us least of all was the scope of the work, its visible effects. The main, the only purpose that we set ourselves was to reproduce Tolstoy on the screen as completely and precisely as possible. We strove, with the aid of modern cinematic means, to reproduce Tolstoy's thoughts, emotions, philosophy, and ideals." The original 4-part film is so rich that pages would be needed to analyse it in detail. But it can be fairly said that Bondarchuk is happiest when dealing with the battle scenes, and more prone to over-emphasis and excessive solemnity in the intimate sequences. The clashes between French and Russian troops at Shengraben, Austerlitz, and Borodino are brought alive with the full power of the 70mm screen. For the hour-long Borodino sequence, 60 cannons were cast to the exact models of old French and Russian artillery pieces, and tens of thousands of cubic metres of earth were

Bondarchuk as actor in his own DESTINY OF A MAN.

moved to construct two fortifications alone, the battery commanded by Rayevsky and the *flèches* of Bagration. A huge burial mound was erected to make it look precisely like the real landscape of Borodino. Even the tall pine tree described by Tolstoy was provided to complete the picture.

Altogether some 158 scenes were shot for *War and Peace*. More than 160 locations were used. 6,000 military uniforms, and 2,000 civilian outfits were made for the cast. The uselessness of war becomes the overriding sentiment of the film, and the camera glances hither and thither in despair, as Pierre (played by Bondarchuk with a blend of childlike ingenuousness and kindness) wanders over the field of Borodino after Andrzej has been killed.

As in all his work, Bondarchuk lays stress on the noble impulses in man, in his capacity for unostentatious bravery. There is not a single negative character among the many that he has played or created in the cinema, and one wonders just where his sympathies will lie in his forthcoming production, *Waterloo*, which will be shot next summer in the Soviet Union, in conjunction with Dino De Laurentiis.

Bondarchuk Filmography

Bondarchuk appeared in the following films as an actor; *The Young Guards* (as Valko, directed by Gerasimov, 1948); *The Story of a Real Man* (as Gvozdev, directed by Stolper, 1948); *The Path of Glory* (as a District Party Secretary, directed by Buneev, Rybakov, and Shvetser, 1949); *The Bearer of the Gold Star* (as Sergei Tutarinov, directed by Raizman, 1950); *Taras Shevchenko* (as Shevchenko, directed by Savchenko, 1951); *Admiral Ushakov* (as the serf, Prokofiev, directed by Mikhail Romm, 1953); *Warships Assault Fortresses* (again as Prokofiev, directed by Romm, 1953); *It Should Not Be Forgotten* (as Garmash, directed by Lukov in 1954); *The Unfinished Story* (as a shipbuilding engineer, directed by Ermler, 1955); *The Grasshopper* (as Dr. Dymov, directed by Samsonov); *Ivan Franko* (as Franko, directed by

(Continued on pages 34 and 35).

2. MILOŠ FORMAN

MILOS FORMAN'S gift for describing young people without rancour or captiousness makes his comedies the most pleasing aspect of the new Czech cinema. Forman is not preoccupied with the last war, unlike most of his countrymen. There is no glamour in his cinema; nor is there squalor and depression. Instead, Forman studies people in their daily lives, and returns again and again to the stresses and strains of the generation gap. "All the most important and immediate conflicts in life," he says, "are between different, equally well-intentioned people's conceptions of what the best is." But even though Forman's films have recognisable affinities, each of them seems to penetrate sociological dilemmas more acutely.

MILOS FORMAN was born on February 18, 1932, in Cáslav, and graduated at the Academy of Music and Dramatic Art in Prague, having studied dramaturgy under Professor Milos V. Kratochvíl. He began writing scripts and also worked as a radio commentator. Some of his screenplays, such as *Leave It to Me* and *Puppies*, were turned into films. He co-operated for several years with Alfréd Radok, first as assistant on the film *Old Man Motorcar* and then as a director of *Magic Lantern* (the programme shown at the Brussels World Fair in 1957). But he had to wait until 1963 to shoot his first film, which was begun, like so many significant works in the postwar cinema, on 16 mm. It was called *Audition*, and was shortly afterwards bracketed with another medium-length study, *If It Wasn't For Music*, to form a feature. As Antonín Novak has said, "Forman requires no more than an anecdote to depict the social and human universe within its seemingly narrow confines." The anecdote in *If It Wasn't For Music* contrasts the vagaries of two young bandmasters as they practise for an important local competition. The twist in the story comes when neither boy turns up on the actual day. They watch a motorcycle race instead. The accent here, and in *Audition*, is on young folk, and Forman observes how their behaviour differs from their elders' expectations. Already as a writer-director he is able to express a whole type of person through one individual, while his skill as a documentarist is all-pervasive in *Audition*, as thousands of girls compete for a

Milos Forman and the quirks of facial expression. Top, PETER AND PAVLA; middle and below, A BLONDE IN LOVE.

singing assignment at the Semafor Theatre. This kind of setting gives the youngsters of Forman's world a communal identity; each is hiding from his emotional problems, but each is part of a larger membership.

Forman's style may spring from the *cinéma-vérité* approach, yet it is really very personal in its choice of characters and environment. One has the illusion that what happens on the screen in a Forman film *is* reality; one senses that this is life refracted through one man's consistent vision of things, whereas in *cinéma vérité* the interviews are cold, objective, and (in Vilgot Sjöman's work) self-conscious. This is why "warm" and "personal" are the two adjectives most readily used to classifiy Forman's cinema.

Peter and Pavla is to some degree a sequel to *If It Wasn't For Music*. Jan Vostrcil is once more the representative of the older generation, conducting a brass band at weekends and administering stern reproofs to his son, Peter, while the mother looks on solemnly. Peter has a job in a self-service store, looking for shop-lifters, but he finds it disconcerting and rather illogical. Forman sums up his personality in a single shot towards the end. After reporting a man who he previously suspected of stealing, he relaxes with an air of satisfaction and stares idly at a stout housewife as she hides several bags of sweets in her bag. Peter is the archetypal Forman hero — the youngster bewildered by adult life. He is always being confounded by those more experienced than himself. When he goes to a dance, he practises earnestly in a corner, and drinks some alcohol to give him courage. But by the time he returns to the floor, his girl-friend has been whisked away by a rival. Later, his father concludes an attenuated and embarrassed discussion about a textbook on "The Body" with the withering remark, "I read that ages ago. Good night."

Relationships in Forman's world are struck up clumsily, hesitantly, or with a kind of bland resignation. In *A Blonde in Love*, Andula, like Peter, is cautious and diffident up to a point. She works in a factory and sleeps in a hostel with a group of girls. When she decides to trust a lover, a young dance musician (played with antic mournfulness by Pucholt), she discovers that life only brings tears if one takes it too seriously. The film contains two brilliant anthology scenes: the first at a local dance, where three soldiers try to pick up some girls (Andula among them) until the fundamental differences in personality pull apart the evening's plans; the second at the boy's home, when Andula arrives unexpectedly with her belongings and stubbornly endures the parents' suspicious reaction. The tug of emotion at the close of a Forman sequence is not artificially engendered; nor does it pretend to be high tragedy. Andula will recover and laugh again. Her troubles teach her tolerance, and Forman's mischievous camera communicates this growth of understanding with a keenness born of candour and sincerity.

It is more than long lenses that enable Forman to record and emphasise such intimate details within a spectacular, "public" framework, like the dance-hall scenes in *Peter and Pavla* and *A Blonde in Love*. It is an innate sense of timing, a facility for isolating the one really expressive facial reaction in a thousand. *Like A House On Fire* takes this to virtuoso extremes, for the major part of the film is set in the hall where the local fire brigade is celebrating its annual ball. The old man in charge of the tombola sees his table of prizes slowly depleted and dishevelled; the search for a beauty queen, who will present an award to the aged Brigade Commander, drifts inexorably into chaos. The suggestion is that people only expose their true attitudes in a public crisis. They are "acting" in front of their colleagues, and so they cling doggedly to a set course of action instead of adapting their decisions to circumstances. *Like A House on Fire* is a tragi-comedy about old men, old men who are just as confused and naïve as Andula or Peter in the earlier films. Thus, for Forman, life is a cycle; we begin and end at the mercy of a complex code of social behaviour. When we are in our prime, says Forman, "We pursue our professions, go after money, after women, after position, and we mercilessly spin the wheel of society which carries both old and young in its whirl, whether they like it or not, because they cannot protect themselves against it — they have neither the sense nor the strength necessary." That is why, in *Like A House on Fire*, it is so wrenching a moment when the weary but stiff-backed Brigade Commander opens his presentation box and sees that the gilt axe has been stolen. A brief scene like this, or the one when Andula simply abandons her composure and weeps against the bedroom door in *A Blonde in Love*, is surely ample refutation of the charge that Forman is a shallow director, a man whose films amount to light-hearted trivia. On the contrary Forman demonstrates unobtrusively that comedy has been invented by men to delay the moment of despair, to offset the waste of emotion. "Truth as such is not enough," he says, "It must be a truth that surprises."

Forman Filmography

Forman wrote the scripts of Martin Frič's *Leave It to Me* (1955), and Ivo Novák's *The Puppies* (1957).

1963 KONKURS/AUDITION (comprising two musical *feuilletons, Audition* and *If It Wasn't For Music*). Script: Miloš Forman and Ivan Passer. Direction: Forman. Photography: Miroslav Ondříček. Music: Jiří Slitr and Jiří Suchý. *Players:* Jan Vostrčil, F. Zeman, Vladimír Pucholt, V. Křesadlová, Jana Brejchová. For Filmstudio Barrandov. 90 mins.

1964 CERNY PETR/PETER AND PAVLA/BLACK PETER. Script: Miloš Forman and Jaroslav Papoušek. Direction: Forman. Photography: Jan Němeček. Editing: Miroslav Hajek. Music: Jiří Slitr. Art Direction: Karel Cerný. Players: Ladislav Jakim *(Peter)*, Pavla Martinková *(Pavla)*, Pavel Sedlaček *(Lada)*, Jan Vostrčil *(Peter's Father)*, Bozena Matušková *(Peter's Mother)*, Vladimír Pucholt *(Cenda)*. For Srebo. 85 mins.

1965 LASKÝ JEDNÉ PLAVOVLASKY / A BLONDE IN LOVE / THE LOVES OF A BLONDE. Script: Miloš Forman, Jaroslav Papoušek, Ivan Passer. Direction: Forman. Photography: Miroslav Ondříček. Editing: Miroslav Hajek. Music. Evžen Illín. Art Direction: Karel Cerný. Players: Hana Brejchová *(Andula)*, Vladimír Pucholt *(Milda)*, Vladimír Mensík *(Vacovsky)*, Antonín Blazejovsky *(Tonda)*, Milada Jezková *(Milda's Mother)*, Josef Sebánek *(Milda's Father)*, Jana Novaková *(Jaruska)*. For Sebor-Bor, Filmstudio Barrandov. 82 mins.

1967 HORI, MA PANENKO / LIKE A HOUSE ON FIRE. Script: Miloš Forman, Jaroslav Papoušek, Ivan Passer. Direction: Forman. Photography: Miroslav Ondříček (Eastmancolor). Editing: Miroslav Hajek. Music: Karel Mareš. Art Direction: Karel Cerný. Players: Václav Stöckel *(Previous Brigade Commander)*, Josef Svět *(Old Man)*, Jan Vostrčil *(Chairman of the Ball Committee)*, Josef Kolb *(Josef)*, František Debelka *(First Committee member)*, Josef Sebánek *(Second Committee member)*, Karel Valnoha *(Third Committee member)*, Josef Rehořek *(Fourth Committee member)*, Marie Jožková *(Josef's Wife)*, Anina Lípoldová, Alena Květová, Míla Zelená *(Candidates for Beauty Queen title)*. For Filmstudio Barrandov (Prague)/Carlo Ponti (Rome). 73 mins.

3. MIKLÓS JANCSÓ

THE success of *The Round-Up* not only made Miklós Jancsó a director of international repute; it paved the way for the *cinéma des auteurs* in Hungary. It has stimulated Jancsó, András Kovács, and a still younger generation (István Gáal, Péter Bacsó, Pál Sándor) to try to formulate their own film idioms and to react against the traditional "collective" formula of communist cinema.

MIKLÓS JANCSÓ was born in 1921, in Vác. He studied law at Kolozsvár, and then ethnography and the history of art at university, receiving his first diploma in 1944. Six years later he graduated at the Academy of Dramatic and Film Art, and began making newsreels. Between 1954 and 1961 he completed some 16 shorts and documentaries. "I belong," he says, "to the generation of Hungarian film directors — those aged between 40 and 50 today — for whom it was perhaps the hardest to find a means of artistic self-expression . . . For us politics and private life were so closely linked at that time as can hardly be imagined by people who are 30 or 20 years old today."

Apart from *Cantata*, all Jancsó's feature films unfold in the sour and weary aftermath of war. In *The Bells Have Gone to Rome*, schoolchildren are ordered to dig trenches in a pathetic attempt to forestall the Soviet troops advancing on the Nazi headquarters in a provincial town. Students are dragged to the front line and only Tibor, their teacher, has the courage to foil this ghastly programme. "War is evil in all its forms, death is evil in all its forms," remarks Jancsó, "and yet there are causes in life for which we must die, or for which it is worthwhile to die."

Cantata (taken from the composition by Bartók and an illustration of the fable at the music's prologue) may not be Jancsó's most perfectly realised film, but it is surely humane where his recent works have been chill and aloof. A surgeon, Ambrus Járom, is dissatisfied with his profession. He is egocentric and dogmatic; he despises the older generation, personified by a senile colleague who insists on operating unaided. Simultaneously he grows tired of his intellectual friends and their avant-garde whimsies.

But a day in the country at his family farm causes him to ponder the benefits of progress. He finds himself attracted by the peace and rhythm of rural life. His self-confidence evaporates; he realises that his career has been built on callous and indifferent behaviour. Jancsó's gift for character analysis, so impressive here, seems to have moved into the background these past few years, and Zoltán Latinovits's Ambrus remains one of the most minutely and sympathetically composed portraits in the postwar Hungarian cinema. But *Cantata* is still a parochial film, and Jancsó has now turned away from the provincialism that has hampered the growth of many Hungarian artists since the poet Attila József.

Jancsó has been widely compared to Eisenstein. Certainly both directors are attracted by the human face and by the cruelty to which man is prone. If Jancsó's range is more limited than Eisenstein's, his technique is more fluent and mesmeric. One learns to appreciate the self-denial of his style, as one appreciates the poet who

*The contemplative cinema of Miklós Jancsó: above, CANTATA; below (left)
the Polish star of THE RED AND THE WHITE, and (right) the two young
soldiers in MY WAY HOME.*

works in the sonnet form, or the composer who resorts to the tightly strung concision of a quartet.

My Way Home takes place in early 1945. A young Hungarian student emerges from a sullen cluster of refugees, deserters, and deportees, as Soviet troops flush out the last of the Nazis. He is taken prisoner, driven to an internment camp, discarded, and captured yet again. Then the Russians leave him under the eye of a soldier who cares for a herd of cows in the hills. Slowly — and despite the impenetrable language barrier — a rough and taciturn friendship wells up between the two men. When the Russian succumbs to an inflamed stomach wound, the hero is alone and vulnerable once more. He is thrown back on his own resilience and, like nearly everyone in Jancsó's militaristic world, he finds life a horrifying puzzle.

The photography in *My Way Home* is outstanding. The camera moves ominously over the slopes and plains. Soldiers spring from nowhere into the frame, creating a mood of apprehension and menace. Jancsó's supple and ingenious *mise en scène*, at its most effective in *The Round-Up* and at its most abstract in *Silence and Cry*, already here precludes any real empathy with the personalities on screen. The young Russian guard has many engaging traits, and one feels a pang when he drifts so quickly to death. But Jancsó, constantly beware of sentimentality, shifts one's attention to the Hungarian student as he heads once more for home.

In *The Round-Up*, Jancsó found a subject and a milieu precisely in accordance with his own cinematic vision. A group of brigands is herded into a stone enclosure set in the vast Hungarian Plain. They are the remnants of the anti-Habsburg revolutionaries of 1848. Now they must pay for Kossuth's bravery, and Jancsó watches their resolution crumble before a series of insidious questions and confrontations. The guards are inscrutable; the film's groundswell of tension derives from their fiendish subtlety and also from the prisoners' fear of their own weakness. Each man here is indeed an island, as is stressed by the single wooden cells constructed in the enclosure. The first execution is startling. As the victim shuffles away hastily into the idle landscape of the plain, the camera stays behind the officer, watching through the door. Suddenly a shot explodes off-screen, and the man seems to pause in his walk before falling backwards like a plank of wood. The sly movements of Jancsó's camera encompass the topographical signs of distress — the spotless white buildings, designed to harbour beasts more than men, the black cloaks of the inquisitors, the unnerving absence of walls or fences (when one man tries to flee, he is swiftly, scornfully outflanked by guards on horseback).

The Round-Up was made, says Jancsó, as "an appeal to face our illusions, which go back over a thousand years; to realise that our history is by no means so pleasant and flattering as our great narrators (Mór Jókai, for example) could easily make us believe." *The Red and the White* (a co-production with Mosfilm) reflects a similar disenchantment with the Magyar character. It evolves in central Russia in 1918. Some Hungarians who have fought in the internationalist brigades of the Red Army are systematically and sadistically captured by the Whites. Man is deprived of hope in these circumstances. He obeys orders without resistance. He is trapped in a pitiless environment where even the buildings (as in *The Round-Up*) prove

18

to be hostile prisons rather than shelters. The film was shot mainly in the ancient Russian town of Kostroma, and in the surrounding countryside.

Jancsó works in an epic film language. Although he relies considerably on the impact of close-ups, he is most masterful when ordering figures in a landscape. This gives his scenes a visual grandeur; on the other hand it diminishes one's contact with the people involved. At the close of *The Red and the White* the Red troops sing "La Marseillaise" as they advance downhill in impeccable formation towards the enemy lines, knowing as surely as the spectator does that they will be massacred. One admires the authority of the direction more than one pities the doomed soldiers. As in all Jancsó's war films, the Hungarians are treated with contempt by their captors. They are often given the illusion of liberty — for instance, in that hideous scene when the nurses are made to dance in a forest glade before the White Guards, the *look* of serenity is matched by the *sense* of humiliation.

Pursuit and humiliation are also at the root of *Silence and Cry*. István, a raw soldier of the Red Army, is isolated after the fall of the Hungarian Republic of Councils in 1919. He hides at a farmer's small-holding in the Great Hungarian Plain, avoiding the patrols that prowl through the area in search of victims and scapegoats. He is shielded by the complaisance of the local gendarmerie commander, who has known him since childhood, and by the farmer's wife and sister-in-law. But events force István to admit his identity. He proves more courageous and unselfish than other men in Jancsó's world, and in the remarkable final shot he whirls round and shoots his commander instead of committing suicide to prescription. It is the one display of emotion in the most dispassionate of films. There is no sentiment in the kisses, no latent verve in the statuesque poses of the farmer and his family. They exist only for their plastic, abstract significance. They are manipulated within the field of the telephoto lens like ballet dancers by a choreographer. The camera circumscribes the characters as they approach each other, restless, overwrought, and yet still responding to an ingrained code of discipline. "If it were an order, I would kill even my own father," says a guard laconically. Like death itself, the fate of Jancsó's men is inevitable but nevertheless terribly fascinating.

Jancsó Filmography

Short films:
1950 WE TOOK OVER THE CAUSE OF PEACE/KEZUNBE VETTUK A BÉKE UGYÉT. Directed by Jancsó in collaboration with Dezsó Koza and Gyula Mészáros.
1951 SOVIET AGRICULTURAL DEPUTATION/SZOVJET MEZÓGAZDAS-ÁGI KULDÖTTSÉG. Directed by Jancsó in collaboration with István György.
1952 THE EIGHTH FREE MAY DAY/A 8. SZABAD MÁJUS 1.
1953 BEFORE ELECTION/VÁLASZTÁS ELÓTT.
HARVEST IN THE CO-OPERATIVE "DOZSA"/ARAT AZ OROSHÁZI DÓZSA.
ON A COMMON PATH /KÖZÖS UTON. Directed by Jancsó in collaboration with Oszkár Berek and László B. Nagy.
1954 AT THE RIVER GALGA/GALGAMENTÉN.
AUTUMN IN BADACSONY/ÓSZ BADACSONYBAN.

LIFE-BRINGING WATER/ÉLTETŐ TISZAVIZ.
DON'T ALLOW IT!/EMBEREK, NE ENGEDJÉTEK! Directed by Jancsó, in collaboration with Károly Wiedermann and István Tímár.
PICTURES AT AN EXHIBITION/EGY KIÁLLITÁS KÉPEI.
1955 THE YOUTH OF "THE LAND OF ANGELS"/ANGYALFÖLDI FIATALOK.
WORLD YOUTH FESTIVAL IN WARSAW/A VARSÓI VIT.
AN AFTERNOON IN THE VILLAGE/EGY DÉLUTÁN KOPPÁNYMONOSTORBAN.
YOUNG PEOPLE, REMEMBER/EMLÉKEZZ, IFJUSÁG.
1956 ZSIGMOND MORICZ/MÓRICZ ZSIGMOND.
1957 IN THE OUTSKIRTS OF THE CITY/A VÁROS PEREMÉN.
THE LANDSCAPES OF SOUTHERN CHINA/DÉL-KINA TÁJAIN.
COLOURFUL CHINA/SZINFOLTOK KINÁBÓL.
PALACES OF PEKING/PEKINGI PALOTÁK.
WE HAVE BEEN THE GUESTS OF CHINA/KINA VENDÉGEI VOLTUNK.
1958 DERKOVITS/DERKOVITS.
1959 IMMORTALITY/HALHATATLANSÁG.
ISOTOPES IN MEDICAL SCIENCE/IZOTÓPOK A GYÓGYÁSZATBAN.
1960 THE ART OF REVIVAL/AZ ÉLEDÉS MŰVÉSZETE. Directed by Jancsó in collaboration with Márta Mézsáros.
1961 THE WHEELS OF TIME/AZ IDÓ KEREKE.
DUSKS AND DAWNS/HAJNALOK ÉS ALKONYOK.
INDIAN STORY/INDIÁN TÖRTÉNET.
1963 LIVING TREE.../HEJ TE ELEVEN FA.....
1965 THE PRESENCE.
1966 CLOSE-UP: THE BLOOD/KÖZELRÓL: A VÉR.

Feature films:
1958 THE BELLS HAVE GONE TO ROME/A HARANGOK RÓMÁBA MENTEK. Script: Lajos Galambos and Lajos Szilvásy. Direction: Miklós Jancsó. Photography: Tamás Somló. Editing: Vera Selmecy. Music: Iván Patachich. Art Direction: Tivadar Bertalan. Players: Miklós Gabor *(Tibor)*, Ferenc Deák *(his younger brother)*, Vilmos Mendelényi *(Hawk-Eye)*, Gabi Magda *(Jana)*, József Fonyó, Istvan Holl, János Pásztor. Produced by Budapest Film-studios. 90 mins.
1960 THREE STARS/HÁROM CSILLAG. Jancsó directed the first part of this feature film. Script: Lajos Galambos. Photography: István Hildebrand. Editing: Zoltán Farkas. Music: Ferenc Farkas. Art Direction: Tivadar Bertalan. Players: Miklós Gábor *(Imre)*, Eva Ruttkay *(The Girl)*, Lajos Básti *(The Colonel)*.
1963 CANTATA/OLDAS ES KOTES. Script and Direction: Miklós Jancsó. Photography: Tamás Somló. Editing: Zoltán Farkas. Music: Bálint Sárosi. Art Direction: Tivadar Bertalan. Players: Zoltán Latinovits *(Dr. Ambrus Járom)*, Miklós Szakáts *(Head Surgeon)*, Andor Ajtay *(Professor Adám)*, Béla Barsi *(Járom Snr.)*, Edit Domján *(Marta)*, Gyula Bodrogi *(Gyula)*, Mária Medgyesi *(Etus)*, Gyöngyvér Demjén *(Blonde)*. Produced by Budapest Filmstudio. 99.5 mins.
1964 MY WAY HOME/IGY JÖTTEM. Script: Gyula Hernádi, from the novel by Irme Vadasz. Direction: Miklós Jancsó. Photography: Tamás Somló. Editing: Zoltán Farkas. Music: Zoltán Jenei. Art Direction: Tivadar Bertalan. Players: András Kozák *(Jóska, the student)*, Sergei Nikonenko *(Kolya, the Russian)*, János Görbe *(Man in peaked hat)*, Sándor Siménfalvi *(Old man)*, László Csurka *(Man with binoculars)*, Vilmos Izsóf *(Aircraftsman)*, Judit Mesz-léry *(Girl)*, József Madaras, Zoltán Gera, Lajos Tándor *(Prisoners of war)*, Lajos Oze, Arpád Gyenge, János Koltai *(Returning Jews)*. Produced by Studio IV, Mafilm. 109 mins. (English version: 82 mins.)
1965-6 THE ROUND-UP/SZEGÉNYLEGÉNYEK. Script: Gyula Hernádi. Direction: Miklós Jancsó. Photography: Tamás Somló. Editing: Zoltán Farkas. Music: none. Art Direction: Tamás Banovich. Players: János Görbe *(Gaidor)*, Tibor Molnár *(Kabai)*, András Kozák *(Kabai's son)*, Gábor Agárdy *(Torma)*, Zoltán Latinovits *(Veszelka)*, István Avar *(First In-terrogator)*, Lajos Oze *(Second Interrogator)*. Produced by Studio IV, Mafilm. 94 mins.
1967 THE RED AND THE WHITE/CSILLAGOSOK, KATONAK. Script: Georgi Mdivani, Gyula Hernádi, and Miklós Jancsó. Direction: Jancsó. Photography: Tamás Somló. Editing: Zoltán Farkas. Music: none. Art Direction: N.I. Tshobotariev. Players: Tatyana Konyukova

(Yelizaveta), Krystyna Mikolaiewska *(Olga)*, Mikhaïl Kozakov *(Nestor)*, Viktor Avdiushko *(Sailor)*, Bolot Beisenalyev *(Tshingiz)*, Sergei Nyikonyenko *(Cossack Officer)*, Anatoli Yabbarov *(Tshelpanov)*, József Madaras *(The Commander)*, Tibor Molnár *(András)*, András Kozák *(László)*, Jácint Juhász *(István)*. Produced by Studio IV, Mafilm (Budapest)/Mosfilm (Moscow). 92 mins.

1968 SILENCE AND CRY/CSEND ÉS KIÁLTÁS. Script: Gyula Hernádi and Miklós Jancsó. Photography: János Kende. Editing: Zoltán Farkas. Music: none. Art Direction: Tamás Banovich. Players: András Kozák *(István)*, Zoltán Latinovits *(Kémeri, the commander)*, József Madaras *(The Farmer)*, Mari Törőcsik *(His wife)*, Andrea Drahota *(His sister-in-law)*. Produced by Studio IV, Mafilm. 79 mins.

4. ARTHUR PENN

ONLY once in his career can any film director hope to score a really resounding success with public and critics alike. Bergman achieved it with *The Silence*; Fellini with *La Dolce Vita;* Antonioni with *Blow-Up*. But after the commercial disaster of *Mickey One* and the tepid response by nearly everyone to *The Chase*, one felt that Arthur Penn's talent would slip away unnoticed. *Bonnie and Clyde* has given his reputation a powerful impetus, however, and has suddenly brought into focus a number of recurrent themes in his cinema.

ARTHUR PENN was born on September 27, 1922, at Philadelphia. He studied horology, but his real interest was the theatre and during his military service at Fort Jackson in South Carolina, he formed a small stage group. In 1951 he entered television as a floor-manager for NBC, and was assistant director of the Jerry Lewis-Dean Martin show in Hollywood. Within two years he was directing a series of plays himself. On Broadway he has been responsible for many notable productions — *The Miracle Worker, All the Way Home, Toys in the Attic, Two for the Seesaw, In the Counting House,* and *Home before Dark* — and he is the principal stage director at Stockbridge, Massachusetts.

Penn has quickly proved himself capable of recreating a past era on film. He prefers to describe the 19th century West and the America of the early Thirties through ordinary folk. "Outstanding characters belong to no epoch," he says. Billy the Kid and Bonnie and Clyde have that elemental, mythical quality that makes for legends. (At the end of *Bonnie and Clyde*, for instance, C. W. Moss lets his heroes drive off towards the ambush; he cannot conceive that anyone could really touch this pair that he worships so intensely.)

In *The Left Handed Gun*, Billy is befriended by a Scotsman named Tunstall. When the Scotsman is murdered, Billy embarks on a tour of revenge. But this William Bonney is not depicted by Penn as the fearless young outlaw who killed 21 men by the age of 21; in the film he is a confused and complex-ridden adolescent, betrayed by his friend Pat Garrett. Like Helen Keller in *The Miracle Worker* and Clyde in *Bonnie and Clyde*, Billy resorts to violence as a means of response to what seems a drab and regimented world.

21

The Miracle Worker is the only one of Penn's films that suffers from its director's long experience in the theatre. William Gibson's play about the determined education of the blind and dumb Helen Keller by Annie Sullivan is intelligently written but, apart from Patty Duke and Anne Bancroft, the characters are formulated too melodramatically to survive for the full extent of the film. Against this must be set the persuasive flashbacks to Annie's youth, and Penn's ubiquitous sense of persecution, which frustrates Helen as much as it does Billy the Kid or Mickey One. The central, physical battle between the two girls is the outward expression of the clash of wills on which the film turns. As usual in Penn's film community, hysteria masks an inferiority complex and a profound loneliness.

Mickey One is far too symbolist a work to impress on the level of *Bonnie and Clyde*. It apes a score of fancy camera tricks without assimilating them into its confused story of a cabaret entertainer (Warren Beatty)) who feels himself hunted for debts he owes to previous employers. He jumps from a train into Chicago's scrofulous West Side, grows anonymity with a social security card he pinches from a man in the street, and is baptised "Mickey One" by his boss in a dustbinmen's co-operative. Has he really experienced the drunken, orgy-filled past he dreams of? Only when he meets a weird night-club owner (Hurd Hatfield), who inhabits a blazing white, op-art bathroom for his conferences, does it look as if Mickey One's fears are justified. But Penn allows the symbols to proliferate within an already confused narrative structure. The Japanese who grins like a Greek chorus at odd intervals throughout the film reminds Mickey of hope and invention, one assumes. Images of destruction are more eloquent — a car-crushing plant where cranes bear down dangerously on Beatty; and a man's sewn-up throat in a wrecked café. As Albert Johnson has written, "The symbolic position of the entertainer-as-outsider, the tragic jester to whom life is a succession of irresolute audiences, crafty agents, and vacuous producers — this lies at the basis of *Mickey One*."

Sam Spiegel's rather ponderously-edited production of *The Chase* is only occasionally recognisable as a Penn film. For all its attempts to be headline-fresh, the film looks as if it were made in the mid-Fifties, when the Deep South setting — this particular story presents E. G. Marshall as a patrician banker whose power buys some of the townsfolk and eats up others with jealousy — was at its most fashionable. The director admits that Lillian Hellman's screenplay lacked an effective finishing punch, and this led him to introduce the big scene in the car cemetery as well as the final murder "à la Kennedy". The film's intentions are blurred for the first hour or so, from the opening credits, which promise a glossy thriller, to the wild parties that reek of infidelity and corruption. Even the colour problem is dragged in, rather implausibly. Only in the second half of *The Chase* do Brando's banked-up power and flint-sharp comments predominate over the theatrical acting of most of the cast (Angie Dickinson as his wife always excepted). Yet despite the violence and vicious blood-letting which links *The Chase* to *Bonnie and Clyde* and *The Left Handed Gun*, there is a fine sense of taste and calm in Penn's approach to the theme of the town's disdain for an impotent legal establishment.

In fact all Penn's principal characters have to sidestep the law to save themselves

Warren Beatty and Faye Dunaway in BONNIE AND CLYDE.

or to make any kind of impact on a hostile society. Clyde Barrow and Bonnie Parker are outsiders just as Billy the Kid and Mickey One are outsiders. If, as the film seems to say, life is nothing much to lose, then crime pays; it brings a peculiar intoxication and paints everyone else in the world as crass and slow-thinking. In essence, *Bonnie and Clyde* is a film about frustration, about the dismal, tattered years of the Depression. Barrow and Parker plunge recklessly into the business of robbing banks and securing their groceries at gun-point. Together with Clyde's brother, his wife, and a laconic garage hand (played by Michael J. Pollard), they constitute a formidable and soon notorious gang. They take outrageous risks. They kill clumsily as if from a guilty conscience. Bystanders envy their escape from the grey idleness that has engulfed the South. This dangerous gaiety derives from the same intense and often unacknowledged inner loneliness that plagues Billy the Kid, Mickey One, and the young Helen Keller.

Bonnie and Clyde breaks new ground in the gangster film field. It romanticises where the more familiar model is sordid; it humours where other gangster movies condemn; and it inspires Warren Beatty and Faye Dunaway to act with a heart-rending brilliance never found in the performances of Muni, Raft, or Robinson. The sole tie with the great tradition of Hollywood black cinema is the violence, and, as Albert Johnson says, "the gore is part of folk-balladry and legend, and that is exactly what the film is about — the *legend* of Bonnie and Clyde, not the truth about them."

Penn notes that in the Depression, "Young people felt excluded from a society that seemed to be destroying itself economically." This is the major reason for the enormous popularity of the film among the young generation of today, which finds itself faced by a crisis of similar dimensions.

Penn will shortly begin a new picture about the American Indians between 1840 and 1874. "It will be a fictional film," he emphasises, "not a documentary. In a didactic way." In a fictional film, too, the impetuous behaviour that so obsesses Penn can be presented in a more moving and "involving" manner.

Penn Filmography

1957 THE LEFT HANDED GUN. Script: Leslie Stevens from a play by Gore Vidal. Direction: Arthur Penn. Photography: J. Peverell Marley. Editing: Folmar Blangsted. Music: Alexander Courage. Art Direction: Art Loel. Players: Paul Newman *(William Bonney)*, Lita Milan *(Celsa)*, John Dehner *(Pat Garrett)*, Hurd Hatfield *(Moultrie)*, James Congdon *(Charlie Boudre)*, James Best *(Tom Folliard)*, Colin Keith-Johnston *(Tunstall)*, John Dierkes *(McSween)*, Bob Anderson *(Hill)*, Wally Brown *(Moon)*, Martin Garralaga *(Saval)*, Denver Pyle *(Ollinger)*. Produced by Fred Coe for Haroll/Warner Bros. 102 mins. On 16mm: Warner-Pathe (G.B.)

1962 THE MIRACLE WORKER. Script: William Gibson from his play. Direction: Arthur Penn. Photography: Ernest Caparros. Editing: Aram Avakian. Music: Laurence Rosenthal. Art Direction: George Jenkins. Players: Anne Bancroft *(Annie Sullivan)*, Patty Duke *(Helen Keller)*, Victor Jory *(Capt. Keller)*, Inga Swenson *(Kate Keller)*, Andrew Prine *(James Keller)*, Produced by Fred Coe for Playfilms/United Artists. 106 mins. On 16mm: United Artists (G.B.)

1964 MICKEY ONE. Script: Alan Surgal. Direction: Arthur Penn. Photography: Ghislain Cloquet. Editing: Aram Avakian. Music: Eddie Sauter. Art Direction: George Jenkins. Players: Warren Beatty *(Mickey)*, Alexandra Stewart *(Jenny)*, Hurd Hatfield *(Castle)*, Franchot Tone *(Ruby Lapp)*, Teddy Hart *(Berson)*, Jeff Corey *(Fryer)*, Kamatari Fujiwara *(The Artist)*, Donna Michelle *(The Girl)*. Produced by Arthur Penn for Florin-Tatira/Columbia. 93 mins.

1965 THE CHASE. Script: Lillian Hellman from the novel and play by Horton Foote. Direction: Arthur Penn. Photography: Joseph LaShelle (Panavision, Technicolor). Editing: Gene Milford. Music: John Barry. Art Direction: Richard Day, Robert Luthardt. Players: Marlon Brando *(Calder)*, Jane Fonda *(Anna Reeves)*, Robert Redford *(Bubber Reeves)*, E. G. Marshall *(Val Rogers)*, Angie Dickinson *(Ruby Calder)*, Janice Rule *(Emily Stewart)*, Miriam Hopkins *(Mrs. Reeves)*, Martha Hyer *(Mary Fuller)*, Richard Bradford *(Damon Fuller)*, Robert Duvall *(Edwin Stewart)*, James Fox *(Jake Rogers)*, Diana Hyland *(Elizabeth Rogers)*, Henry Hull *(Briggs)*, Jocelyn Brando *(Mrs. Briggs)*. Produced by Sam Spiegel for Horizon-Lone Star/Columbia. 133 mins. (122 mins. in G.B.)

1967 BONNIE AND CLYDE. Script: David Newman, Robert Benton. Direction: Arthur Penn. Photography: Burnett Guffey. Editing: Dede Allen. Music: Charles Strouse. Art Direction: Dean Tavoularis. Players: Warren Beatty *(Clyde Barrow)*, Faye Dunaway *(Bonnie Parker)*, Michael J. Pollard *(C. W. Moss)*, Gene Hackman *(Buck Barrow)*, Estelle Parsons *(Blanche)*, Denver Pyle *(Frank Hamer)*, Dub Taylor *(Ivan Moss)*, Evans Evans *(Velma Davis)*, Gene Wilder *(Eugene Grizzard)*. Produced by Warren Beatty for Tatira-Hiller/Warner Bros. 111 mins.

5. JACQUES TATI

JACQUES TATI is one of the most painstaking of directors. A perfectionist in the field of film comedy, he has created his own world — and that is perhaps the highest compliment any comedian can be paid. His Monsieur Hulot is a universal comic because he is a normal being in a sphere of abnormality, the ordinary, unpretentious man with whom we all like to identify. "I'm the opposite of a Chaplin or a Keaton," he maintains. "In the old days, the comic used to come on and say 'I am the funny man in this film. I know how to dance, sing, juggle, do the lot.' But Hulot . . . he's life. He doesn't need gags. He only has to walk . . ."

JACQUES TATI was born on October 9, 1908, at Pecq (near Saint Germain-en-Laye). His real name is Tatischeff, and he has Russian, French, Dutch, and Italian blood. His first intention was to study art and join his father's business of restoring pictures. But he was also a sportsman in his youth and played rugby for Racing Club de Paris's top team at one period. By 1932 he was known as a mimic and for his excellent pantomime work on the music hall circuit. His talent had emerged during his army service, and in the same year he entered the cinema by making *Oscar, champion de tennis*. Other shorts followed: *On demande une brute* (with Tati as a wrestler), *Gai Dimanche, Soigne ton gauche* (in which he played a country valet skilled in boxing), and *Retour à la terre*.

It was only after the war, however, that the personality of Monsieur Hulot started to grow from these *jeux d'esprit*. *L'Ecole des Facteurs* (1947) has been called a first draft for *Jour de Fête*, and it sketches some of the gags that were to appear in the later feature films. François, the blundering postman in *Jour de Fête*, is unable to cope with incidents (the arrival of the mosquito/wasp, for example) that ordinary folk would brush aside without a moment's thought. For François, riding a bicycle is as perilous a procedure as negotiating Niagara Falls in a barrel. Like all the great silent comedians, Tati looks perpetually misplaced in his environment. This masterly combination of mimicry and situation comedy was probably inspired by Tati's own life in the village of Sainte-Sévère after the Liberation.

Jour de Fête was a major triumph at the box-office. But Tati's next film did not appear until 1953. *Les Vacances de Monsieur Hulot (Mr. Hulot's Holiday)* is one of the finest screen comedies ever made. Tati is the author, director, and leading actor. His character of Monsieur Hulot is an unusual mixture of the servile and the innocent. He is seen first in his coughing hen-house of a car, bound for the staid resort of St. Marc-on-Sea. The hotel staff are soon perplexed by this mysterious stranger who leaves doors open so that the resulting gusts of wind create havoc in the entrance lounge, and who plays raucous music when everybody else is quietly cheating at cards. His tennis serve is ferocious, and quickly denudes the court of opponents. At the climax of the holiday, he is trapped in a beach hut full of fireworks — at night — and chaos is complete. Tati the director is always in evidence, compiling a soundtrack rich in humorous noises, and imparting to objects like a canoe the latent menace that paves the way for a Hulot catastrophe.

Impending catastrophe: the Arpels' garden in MON ONCLE.

When *Mon Oncle (My Uncle)* arrived in 1958, Tati seemed to have veered away from his provincial settings. Monsieur Hulot is now confronted by the terrifying gadgets of urban civilisation (and in *Playtime* this impression persists of a man lost in the computer age, dwarfed by its massive buildings, and flabbergasted by its confused bureaucracy). But the film itself is seen through the eyes of a little boy, and so Hulot is surrounded by an aura of responsibility. His gentle, inoffensive disposition seems hopeless in dealing with all the paraphernalia of a modern kitchen. He has a knack of provoking trouble without actually *causing* it. Hulot's presence — elastic walk, mumbling speech, pipe and umbrella protruding like weapons as he moves — inclines other people to trip over their own petty conventions. His attic room, perched awkwardly but snugly at the top of an ancient building, serves as a contrast with the Arpels' villa, where a fish-shaped fountain spouts water whenever the front gate opens, and an electrically operated garage can turn into a dungeon.

Playtime, shot in 70mm and colour, is arguably the first international film — the first film to switch between French, English, and German with complete familiarity and success. The different languages symbolise a failure of communication and co-operation; they also symbolise the noisy muddle that inevitably accompanies high-speed living. People in *Playtime* embark on some action and then, harassed, abandon it and turn to something else. Here the tiny details of life are given gigantic emphasis, and one suddenly realises just how ridiculous — or just how important? — they are in comparison with the complex structures created by science. The last hour of the film, which takes place in a brand new restaurant, is one of the most extraordinary sequences ever attempted in cinema. There is a miraculous sensation of organised confusion, hovering just the right side of anarchy. At times the spectacle is like a ballet, in which each character moves in a pre-ordained pattern (except, of course, for Monsieur Hulot, who shifts from one corner of the fray to another with unpredictable charm). *Playtime* makes brilliant use of the 70mm format. All corners of the screen seem to be filled with jokes. The huge camera eye is logical, says Tati, for "it corresponds to the dimensions of the modern world. They no longer build little roads, only motorways; no longer small houses, only vast blocks."

The essentially visual wit of Tati's films recalls the heyday of the silent cinema. The gags burn slowly and surreptitiously until suddenly what appears to be a normal situation looks hysterically funny. Hulot's slightest gesture is like a distress signal. He is forever poised on the balls of his feet as if ready to break into flight. His absent-mindedness is a joy to watch — and to share. For Hulot/Tati is a modest figure in a brash and pompous world. "I am lucky to have been able to make four films," he says. "Really, anybody is lucky to be able to make one film."

Tati Filmography

Tati has made acting appearances in: *Sylvie et le Fantôme* (Autant-Lara, 1945), and *Le Diable au Corps* (Autant-Lara, 1946).

Short films:
1932 OSCAR, CHAMPION DE TENNIS. Script and Direction: Jacques Tati. Player: Tati.
1934 ON DEMANDE UNE BRUTE. Script: Jacques Tati and Alfred Sauvy. Direction: Charles Barrois (with assistance from René Clément). Players: Tati and a wrestler.
1935 GAI DIMANCHE. Script: Jacques Tati and Rhum, the clown. Direction: Jacques Berr. Players: Tati and Rhum. Produced by Atlantic-Films (O.M. de Andria). 33 mins.
1936 SOIGNE TON GAUCHE. Script: Jacques Tati. Direction: René Clément. Music: Jean Yatove. Player: Tati. Produced by Fred Orain for Cady-Films.
1938 RETOUR A LA TERRE. Script and Direction: Jacques Tati. Player: Tati.
1947 L'ÉCOLE DES FACTEURS. Script and Direction: Jacques Tati (with assistance from Henri Marquet). Photography: Louis Félix. Music: Jean Yatove. Player: Tati. Produced by Fred Orain for Cady-Films. 18 mins.

Feature films:
1949 JOUR DE FÊTE. Script: Jacques Tati and Henri Marquet, with contributions from René Wheeler and members of the cast. Direction: Tati. Photography: Jacques Mercanton. Editing:

Marcel Moreau. Music: Jean Yatove. Art Direction: René Moulaert. Players: Jacques Tati *(François, the postman)*, Paul Frankeur *(Marcel, the showman)*, Guy Decomble *(Roger, his associate)*, Santa Relli *(the show woman)*, Maine Vallée *(Jeanette)*, Roger Rafal *(the hairdresser)*, Beauvais *(the café proprietor)*, Delcassan *(the old gossip)*, with the inhabitants of Sainte-Sévère (Indre). 88 mins. On 16 mm (G.B.):

1953 LES VACANCES DE MONSIEUR HULOT. Script: Jacques Tati and Henri Marquet, with assistance from P. Aubert and Jacques Lagrange. Direction: Tati. Photography: Jacques Mercanton and Jean Mousselle. Editing: Suzanne Baron, Bretoneiche, and Grassi. Music: Alain Romans. Art Direction: R. Briancourt and Henri Schmitt. Players: Jacques Tati *(Monsieur Hulot)*, Nathalie Pascaud *(Martine)*, Louis Perrault *(Fred)*, Michèle Rolla *(the aunt)*, Suzy Willy *(the Commandant's wife)*, André Dubois *(the Commandant)*, Valentine Camax *(English woman)*, Lucien Frégis *(Hotel proprietor)*, and Marguerite Gérard, René Lacourt, Raymond Carl, Michèle Brabo, Georges Adlin. Produced by Cady-Films. 86 mins.

1958 MON ONCLE. Script: Jacques Tati, with assistance from Jacques Lagrange and Jean L'Hote. Direction: Jacques Tati, with assistance from Henri Marquet and Pierre Etaix. Photography: Jean Bourgoin (Eastmancolor). Editing: Suzanne Baron. Music: Frank Barcellini and Alain Romans. Art Direction: Henri Schmitt. Players: Jacques Tati *(Monsieur Hulot)*, Jean-Pierre Zola *(Monsieur Arpel)*, Alain Bécourt *(little Gérard)*, Lucien Frégis *(Richard)*, Dominique Marie *(the neighbour)*, Betty Schneider *(the concierge's daughter)*, J.-F. Martial *(Walter)*, André Dino *(the sweep)*, Max Martel *(the drunkard)*, Yvonne Arnaud *(the Arpels' maid)*, Claude Badolle *(the rag picker)*, and Nicolas Bataille, Régis Fontenay, Adélaide Danielli, Denise Péronne, Michel Goyot, Francomme, Dominique Derly, Claire Rocca, Jean Rémoleux, Mancini, René Lord, Jean Meyet, Nicole Regnault, Suzanne Franck, Loriot, with the inhabitants of old Saint-Maur. Produced by Specta-Films, Alter-Film (Paris)/Film del Centauro (Rome). 116 mins.

1967 PLAYTIME. Script: Jacques Tati, with assistance from Jacques Lagrange. (English text: Art Buchwald). Direction: Tati. Photography: Jean Badal and Andréas Winding (Eastmancolor, 70mm). Editing: Gérard Pollicand, with assistance from Denise Giton, Sophie Tatischeff, and J. F. Gallaud. Music: Francis Lemarque. Art Direction: Eugène Roman. Players: Jacques Tati *(Monsieur Hulot)*, Barbara Dennek *(a tourist)*, Jacqueline Lecomte *(her friend)*, Valérie Camille *(M. Lacs's secretary)*, France Rumilly *(spectacles salesman)*, Erika Dentzler *(Mrs. Giffard)*, Yvette Ducreux *(Cloakroom attendant)*, Laure Pailette and Colette Proust *(two women with the lamp)*, Rita Maiden *(Mr. Schulz's friend)*, Billy Kearns *(Mr. Schulz)*, Jack Gaulthier *(the guide)*, Henri Piccoli *(the V.I.P.)*, Léon Doyen *(porter)*, Reinhart Kolldehoff *(German executive)*, Grégoire Katz *(German salesman)*, André Fouché *(Manager of the Royal Garden Restaurant)*. Produced by Specta-Films (Bernard Maurice), and René Silvera. 140 mins.

Interview with JOHN FRANKENHEIMER

This conversation was recorded in Budapest earlier in the year when John Franken-heimer was shooting THE FIXER there. Questions were asked by Gerald Pratley, the distinguished film critic from CBC Toronto and our correspondent in Canada.

Question: What was there about Bernard Malamud's book that prompted you to make a film of it?

Frankenheimer: Well, basically, the whole theme of the book is the indomit-ability of the human spirit, the strength of man, which is what I wanted to tackle. Yakov Bok is not a very lucid person who can express his feelings all the time. This is a man who acquires a strength he never realised he had. I think there is a tremen-dous identification with this character for every person who sees the film. At least I hope there is. It has nothing to do with the fact that he's a Jew. It could be any-time, anywhere.

Q: One of the films you made at the beginning of your career was also about a man in prison, *Birdman of Alcatraz*. In a way this film and *The Fixer* are like "brackets", enclosing an important period in your work. In the years between, and the films between, how do you feel you have changed as an artist, as a director?

F: I think that if I were to do *Birdman of Alcatraz* again I'd do it quite differently. I'm not saying I would do it better, but I would do it differently. I would certainly shoot it in a real prison. One of the things that damaged the film was shooting it in a set. Personally I find it much easier to shoot in a natural location because I don't have to worry about where to put the camera. As to how I've changed — well, I work much more thoroughly on a film than I did a few years ago. In those days I was a kind of hired director, so that the script was written before I was hired. Now I can change a script when I feel it is called for.

Q: Do you feel that you can achieve the same sort of style in colour as you did so successfully in black-and-white?

F: I think that today you virtually *have* to make a film in colour, and I'm not just talking about television sales. We've found ways of making colour work for us now. Here, for instance, we are forcing the film a good deal. The ASA rating on *The Fixer* in reality is 50/35 and we're going up to 65 and 70 with it, and really forcing the negative as far as it will go. We're using no back light whatsoever, just side light and front light. But I find it more difficult to work in colour than in black-and-white because there are so many more things to worry about. In black-and-white something comes out either black, white, or grey. Here, one curtain on a window can spoil an entire scene. You have to have a much more conclusive idea of what your finished film should look like.

In reference to the question you asked before as to how I have changed. Luckily I have reached a point where I have the right of final cut on my films. I find that I shoot a lot more film and I'm no longer afraid of someone's taking the picture and re-editing it after I have finished with it. I find that by doing more coverage of scenes, in the final analysis you edit them much better and you're not having to devise camera tricks to prevent a scene being mis-cut behind your back. But I must say I never really had much interference, except on my very first film (*The Young Stranger*) which was totally re-cut at RKO. I experienced no problems working with Hecht in the early days, nor with United Artists.

Q: What are the principal considerations you give to deciding on what film you're going to make? Is it a question of what the audience might like? Or what you yourself like? Or a combination of both?

F: I think to make worthwhile films you yourself must be interested in the subject. I don't believe in making films for an audience. I think you have to make them because you believe in them, and because you want to do them. My next picture, *The Gypsy Moths*, is not a film about parachute jumping despite what the publicity releases say. It's an extremely personal and intricate story — the story of a relationship. And I think what interests me more than anything else is the relationship between people that one has a chance to examine in the cinema. After that I'll be making Harold Pinter's *The Homecoming*, which completely knocked me over when I saw it on stage. I know this is going to be a controversial film, but I happen to be one of those who love the play, and we'll be making it precisely as he wrote it.

Q: How do you feel about the current audience reaction to violence on-screen?

F: I don't believe in violence for the sake of violence. I believe that if you

have a point to make with it then you should use it. It would be impossible to do *The Fixer*, for example, without showing violence. You cannot have a man incarcerated in prison for three years without being touched, because they try literally every method to make him confess. And you have to show some of it. But as to what degree of violence you show, that is indeed a matter of taste. I remember there was a point in *The Manchurian Candidate* when we had to show the man shooting his father-in-law and his wife. It was terribly difficult. He just pulled the trigger and there was no choice. Unless you abandoned the movie. Violence is a very risky thing. It's become almost a Madison Avenue slogan — "This film is too violent."

Q: Did you find it hard to make the break from television into feature films?

F: I was extraordinarily lucky, and it was not really difficult at all. But after my experience with *The Young Stranger* I turned down a great many film offers. I stayed in television until live tv ended. But moving to feature films was not something I really wanted to do. I certainly enjoy live television very much.

Q: What was it about motor-racing that made you want to film *Grand Prix*?

F: I used to be a racer. It's very simple. It's something I have always wanted to do. It had nothing to do with political conditions or anything like that. I just really wanted to make a film about race driving, and it had been a kind of childhood dream. Making that film was like being paid for all your Walter Mitty fantasies.

THE FIXER. *Script:* Dalton Trumbo, from the novel by Bernard Malamud. *Direction:* John Frankenheimer. *Photography:* Marcel Grignon (Metrocolor). *Editing:* Henry Bergman. *Art Director:* Bela Zeichan. *Players:* Alan Bates, Dirk Bogarde, Georgia Brown, Jack Gilford, Hugh Griffith, Elizabeth Hartman, Ian Holm, David Warner, Carol White. *Produced by* John Frankenheimer and Edward Lewis *for* M-G-M.

GUIDE TO TITLE CHANGES

OTHER COUNTRIES	U.S.A.	BRITAIN
1	Breathless	Breathless
2	Yesterday Girl	Yesterday Girl
3 Adua e le campagne (Italy)	Love à la carte	Hungry for Love
4 Alleman (Netherlands)	The Human Dutch	The Human Dutch
5	The Appaloosa	Southwest to Sonora
6	Bend of the River	Where the River Bends
7	Chance Meeting	Blind Date
8	The Guest	The Caretaker
9 Cerny Petr (Czechoslovakia)	Black Peter	Peter and Pavla
10	The Concrete Jungle	The Criminal
11	The Defiant Ones	The Defiant Ones
12 Donzoko (Japan)	The Lower Depths	The Lower Depths
13	Edge of the City	A Man is Ten Feet Tall
14	Experiment in Terror	The Grip of Fear
15	The Fearless Vampire Killers	Dance of The Vampires
16	Will o' the Wisp	A Time to Live and a Time to Die
17 Co-prod. with Mexico	Republic of Sin	Swamp of Lust
18	The Fortune Cookie	Meet Whiplash Willie
19	From Here to Eternity	From Here to Eternity
20 Gycklarnas afton (Sweden)	The Naked Night	Sawdust and Tinsel
21	High Noon	High Noon
22	Hud	Hud
23 Las Hurdes (Spain)	Land without Bread	Land without Bread
24	Knave of Hearts	Knave of Hearts
25	Kind Hearts and Coronets	Kind Hearts and Coronets
26 Kvinnodröm (Sweden)	Women's Dreams	Journey into Autumn
27 Kumonosu-jo (Japan)	Cobweb Castle	Throne of Blood
28	The Lavender Hill Mob	The Lavender Hill Mob
29	The Last Laugh	The Last Laugh
30 Ljubavni slucaj (Yugoslavia)	Love Affair	Love Dossier or The Switchboard Operator
31	Madigan	Madigan
32	A Degree of Murder	A Degree of Murder
33 Mr. Arkadin (Spain)	Mr. Arkadin	Confidential Report
34	My Darling Clementine	My Darling Clementine
35 Nattvardsgästerna (Sweden)	Winter Light	Winter Light

OF FILMS IN 4 COUNTRIES

FRANCE	GERMANY	DIRECTOR & DATE	
A Bout de Souffle	Ausser Atem	Jean-Luc Godard. 1959	1
Anita G or Une Fille sans Histoire	**Abschied von gestern**	Alexander Kluge. 1966	2
Adua et ses campagnes	Adua und ihre Gefahrtinnen	A. Pietrangeli. 1960	3
Tous les Hommes	12 Millionen	Bert Haanstra. 1963-64	4
L'Homme de la Sierra	Südwest nach Sonora	Sidney Furie. 1966	5
Les Affameurs	Meuterei am Schlangenfluss	Anthony Mann. 1952	6
L'Enquête de l'Inspecteur Morgan	Die tödliche Falle	Joseph Losey. 1959	7
Le Concierge	Der Hausmeister	Clive Donner. 1962	8
L'As de Pique	Der schwarze Peter	Milos Forman. 1964	9
Les Criminels	Die Spur führt ins Nichts	Joseph Losey. 1960	10
La Chaîne	Flucht in Ketten	Stanley Kramer. 1957	11
Les bas-fonds	Nachtasyl	Akira Kurosawa. 1957	12
L'Homme qui tua la peur	Ein Mann besiegt die Angst	Martin Ritt. 1956	13
Allo, Brigade Spéciale	Der letzte Zug	Blake Edwards. 1962	14
Le Bal des Vampires	Tanz der Vampire	Roman Polanski. 1967	15
Le Feu Follet	Das Irrlicht	Louis Malle. 1963	16
La Fièvre monte à El Pao	Für ihn verkauf ich mich	Luis Bunuel. 1959	17
La Grande Combine	Der Glückspilz	Billy Wilder. 1966	18
Tant qu'il y aura des hommes	Verdammt in alle Ewigkeit	Fred Zinnemann. 1953	19
La Nuit des Forains	Abend der Gaukler	Ingmar Bergman. 1953	20
Terre sans Pain	Erde ohne Brot	Luis Bunuel. 1931	21
Le plus sauvage d'entre tous	Der Wildeste unter Tausend	Martin Ritt. 1963	22
Le Train sifflera trois fois	12 Uhr Mittags	Fred Zinnemann. 1952	23
Monsieur Ripois	Liebling der Frauen	René Clément. 1953	24
Noblesse Oblige	Adel verpflichtet	Robert Hamer. 1949	25
Rêves des Femmes	Frauenträume	Ingmar Bergman. 1954	26
Le Château de l'Araignée	Das Schloss im Spinnennetz	Akira Kurosawa. 1957	27
De l'Or en Barres	Einmal Millionär sein	Charles Crichton. 1951	28
Le dernier des hommes	Der letzte Mann	F. W. Murnau. 1924	29
Une Affaire de Coeur	Ein Liebesfall	Dusan Makavejev. 1967	30
Police sur la Ville	Nur noch 73 Stunden	Don Siegel. 1967	31
Vivre à tout prix	**Mord und Totschlag**	Volker Schlöndorff. 1967	32
Dossier secret	Herr Satan persönlich	Orson Welles. 1955	33
La Poursuite Infernale	Tombstone or Faustrecht der Prärie	John Ford. 1946	34
Les Communiants	Licht im Winter	Ingmar Bergman. 1962	35

OTHER COUNTRIES	U.S.A.	BRITAIN
36 **Ningen no joken** (Japan)	The Human Condition	No Greater Love
37 **Nära livet** (Sweden)	Brink of Life	So Close to Life
38	Gang War	**Odd Man Out**
39 **Los Olvidados** (Mexico)	The Young and the Damned	The Young and the Damned
40 **Ostre sledované vlaky** (Czechoslovakia)	Closely Watched Trains	Closely Observed Trains
41	Purple Noon	Purple Noon **or** Blazing Sun
42 **Pociag** (Poland)	Baltic Express	Night Train
43 **Szegenylegenyek** (Hungary)	The Round-Up	The Round-Up
44	**Ride the High Country**	Guns in the Afternoon
45	**The Searchers**	The Searchers
46 **Sommarlek** (Sweden)	Illicit Interlude	Summer Interlude
47	**Stagecoach**	Stagecoach
48 **Syskonbädd** (Sweden)	My Sister My Love	My Sister My Love
49	This Sporting Life	**This Sporting Life**
50	**Touch of Evil**	Touch of Evil
51 **Vaghe Stelle dell'Orsa** (Italy)	Sandra	Of a Thousand Delights
52 **El Verdugo** (Spain)	Not on your Life	The Executioner
53	**Vertigo**	Vertigo
54	The Devil's Envoys	Les Visiteurs du Soir
55	My Life to Live	It's My Life
56	**Wagonmaster**	Wagonmaster
57	**A Woman of Paris**	A Woman of Paris

Bondarchuk Filmography, continued from page 12

Levchuk, 1956); *Othello* (as the Moor, directed by Yutkevich, 1956); *Two from the Same Block* (directed by Gurin and Ibragimov, 1957); *Pages of the Story* (as a stage reader, directed by Kryzhanovsky, 1967); *There Went Soldiers* (as Matvey Krylov, directed by Trauberg, 1957); *Destiny of a Man* (see below); *Serezha* (as Korostelov, directed by Danelya and Talankin, 1960); *Era notte a Roma* (as Fyodor, directed by Rossellini, 1961); and *War and Peace* (see below).

Feature Films

1959   SUDBA CHELDOVIEKA/DESTINY OF A MAN or FATE OF A MAN. Script: Y. Lukin and F. Shakhmagonow, from a story by Mikhail Sholokhov. Direction: Bondarchuk. Photography: Vladimir Monakhov. Editing: T. Likhacheva. Music:

FRANCE	GERMANY	DIRECTOR & DATE	
La condition humaine	Barfuss durch die Hölle	Masaki Kobayashi. 1957	36
Au seuil de la vie	Am Anfang des Lebens	Ingmar Bergman. 1958	37
Huit heures de sursis	Ausgestossen	Carol Reed. 1947	38
Pitié pour eux	Die Vergessenen	Luis Bunuel. 1950	39
Trains rigoureusement controlés	Liebe nach Fahrplan	Jiri Menzel. 1966	40
Plein Soleil	Nur die Sonne war Zeuge	René Clément. 1959	41
Train de Nuit	Nachtzug	Jerzy Kawalerowicz. 1959	42
Les sans espoir	Die Hoffnungslosen	Miklós Jancsó. 1965	43
Coups de Feu dans la Sierra	Sacramento	Sam Peckinpah. 1961	44
La Prisonnière du désert	Der schwarze Falke	John Ford. 1956	45
Jeux d'été	Einen Sommer lang	Ingmar Bergman. 1950	46
La chevauchée fantastique	Ringo or Hollenfahrt nach Santa Fé	John Ford. 1939	47
Ma Soeur Mon Amour	Geschwisterbett	Vilgot Sjöman. 1965	48
Le Prix d'un Homme	Lockender Lorbeer	Lindsay Anderson. 1963	49
La Soif du Mal	Im Zeichen des Bösen	Orson Welles. 1958	50
Sandra	Sandra	Luchino Visconti. 1965	51
Le Bourreau	Der Henker	Luis Berlanga. 1963	52
Les sueurs froids	Aus dem Reich der Toten	Alfred Hitchcock. 1958	53
Les Visiteurs du Soir	Die Nacht mit dem Teufel	Marcel Carné. 1942	54
Vivre sa Vie	Die Geschichte der Nana S.	Jean-Luc Godard. 1962	55
Le Convoi des Braves	Westlich St. Louis	John Ford. 1950	56
L'Opinion Publique	Die Nächte einer schönen Frau	Charles Chaplin. 1923	57

V. Basner. Art Direction: I. Novoderyozhkin and S. Voronkov. Players: Sergei Bondarchuk *(Sokolov)*, Zinaida Kirienko *(Irina, his wife)*, Pavlik Boriskin *(Vaniushka)*, P. Volkov *(Ivan Timofeyevich)*, Y. Averin *(Müller)*, K. Alexeyev *(A German Major)*. Produced by Bondarchuk for Mosfilm. 77 mins.

1962-1966 VOINA I MIR/WAR AND PEACE. Script: Sergei Bondarchuk and Vassili Soloviev from the novel by Leo Tolstoy. Direction: Bondarchuk. Photography: Anatoly Petritsky. Editing: T. Likhacheva. Music: Vyacheslav Ovchinnikov. Art Direction: Mikhail Bogdanov and Gennady Myasnikov. Players: Lyudmila Savelyeva *(Natasha Rostova)*, Sergei Bondarchuk *(Pierre Bezoukov)*, Vyacheslav Tokhonov *(Prince Andrei Bolkonsky)*, Victor Stanitzin *(Count Rostov)*, Kira Ivanova-Golovko *(Countess Rostova)*, Oleg Tabakov *(Nikolai Rostov)*, Nikolai Kodin and Seryozha Yermilov *(Petya Rostov)*, Irinia Gubanova *(Sonia)*, Anatoly Ktorov *(Prince Nikolai Bolkonsky)*, Antonina Tchuranova *(Princess Maria)*, Anastasia Vertinskaya *(Princess Lisa)*, Irina Scobtseva *(Helen)*. Produced by Mosfilm. Originally 4 parts. but condensed into two parts and released in the U.S.A. by the Walter Reade Organisation and Satra. 373 mins.

Film Societies in Britain

As film becomes more widely established as an art form in Britain, the role of the film society becomes increasingly valuable. There are vast areas outside the major cities where the public would be starved of serious cinema but for their local film society.

There are now well over 500 bona-fide societies in Britain and the number gradually increases each month. The size and character of each society differs greatly depending mainly on location. Those in the major cities well served by either art house or regional film theatre tend to operate on a highly specialised policy varying from a concentration on wholly silent films to a group that confine their activities to a study of horror movies. Otherwise up and down the country a large group of societies continue to fulfil a very necessary need by screening the latest continental films to reach Great Britain and the occasional "difficult" and non-commercial British and American film that would otherwise pass by unseen.

One of the basic aims of the movement is to inculcate a genuine care and respect for and enjoyment of, all aspects of cinema. Societies always seek a high standard of presentation and a number of societies offer members programme notes of a quality only equalled in one or two European art cinemas. The social atmosphere of the film society is quite unique for it offers a regular meeting place for film enthusiasts and discussions, lectures, and visits by film-makers are often provided for those members wishing to do more than merely view films.

The British Federation of Film Societies, a self-governing voluntary association, is now administered by a paid secretary — the British Film Institute Film Society Liaison Officer. Through the Federation all the 500 plus societies can keep in close contact with each other through the monthly Newsletter as well as being informed of latest film distribution news. Various week-end film events are held in most regions of the country throughout the year and all such events are open to and enjoyed by societies' members.

The leading publication of the Federation is **Film** (6s. or $ 1 per year, three issues appearing quarterly during the season). **Film News** (14s. or $ 2 for four issues a year) is directly aimed at film selection committees and keeps abreast of festival and distributors' new releases from the point of view of film society suitability and is particularly concerned with controversial and neglected features (especially those which have not had a commercial opening). It also offers the fullest coverage of shorts.

All inquiries about any of the above details or any advice about how to start a film society can be obtained from Barrie Wood, Secretary, Federation of Film Societies, 102 Dean Street, London, W.1.

CENSORSHIP — The Point of Resistance

When Mr. Trevelyan, the secretary of the British Board of Censors, agreed to be present at a press showing of the Swedish film *Hugs and Kisses (Puss och Kram)*, cinema history was made. For this was the first time any censor had appeared in public to interpret a decision of the Board concerning a cut to a film. His appearance at the press show was indicative of the Board's awareness of a widely held opinion that the time was ripe for a thorough reappraisal of film censorship. Unfortunately, Mr. Trevelyan's exposition on this occasion did little to clarify the mystique surrounding the duties of the censor. Although he had found the particular scene unobjectionable, the law on obscenity was uncertain. Actually there was no law, only a vague technical ruling of the courts whereby any member of the public could prosecute distributors and cinema owners on the grounds of obscenity. This in turn would rebound on the Board of Censors for having passed the film. That *Hugs and Kisses* had already been licensed by the City of Newcastle in its entire version and shown without raising any public outcry, could not affect the judgment of the censor in London. Only a test case in a court could perhaps determine a precedent for the future.

Why had we at Contemporary decided to make a stand, and fight the decision of the censor? *Hugs and Kisses*, the first film by the Swedish director, Jonas Cornell, is an unsentimental, ironic study of the relationship between three young people — a married couple and the friend of the husband who comes to live with them. For a brief fifteen seconds at the beginning of the film, the wife before going to bed stares at her naked reflection in the mirror, and the reflection clearly shows her pubic hair. This, the censor explained, was quite out of the question. We would have to make a cut.

Not a very serious cut perhaps, but the sequence had been shot in such a way as to make it impossible to remove any frames without mutilating an entire sequence carefully conceived by a serious and talented young director. Were we in the twentieth century to be ruled by hypocritical attitudes steeped in the nineteenth? Further, it seemed to us, to deny the human body in its natural state was in itself obscene.

Thus, as we considered the problem further, the whole question of film censorship came under our re-evaluation. With the public being daily exposed in the cinema to the most vile brutality far more morally damaging than anything this innocent sequence could do, why should we submit to this illogical decision?

Because the cinema, by its very nature, has been geared as entertainment for the masses, it has suffered by rarely receiving the consideration and respect paid to other forms of culture such as the theatre and art. It is commercial interests that often decide what the public are to be exposed to. Good taste and artistic merit are rarely considered. Yet throughout its history, the cinema has proved its right to be treated as a serious artistic media. Might there not be some connection then between the right to exercise censorship and the conception of the cinema as mere entertainment? It would follow then that with the wider realisation of film as an art form, a re-appraisal of censorship would automatically take place.

After the show, the opinion of the press was on our side. Everyone agreed on the complete absurdity of the cut, that is all except a few of the more popular newspapers who expressed their disappointment that a film showing a woman with pubic hair could be so innocent and unerotic. They had still not understood the issue. And what about the censor who did not have the courage to act on his own convictions? What a pity he couldn't endorse the plea of one critic who said: "Let's have more love, less war" — **Kitty Cooper.**

THE MULTISCREEN AUDIENCE

by George Dunning

In May 1968, TVC London arranged a Festival of Multiscreen Films in London, consisting mainly of entries at Expo 67 in Montréal. Some were dull and uninventive; but others, like Don Levy's Sources of Power *and Bill Sewell's* Canada is My Piano *afforded an exciting glimpse of this new format's potential. George Dunning, producer of* Canada is My Piano, *and the leading British advocate of multiscreen, gives here some thoughts on the communication between image and audience.*

The eye is a great acceptor of things. The mind is greedy. This makes a good combination for a multiscreen presentation. If the audience sees a picture which occupies only a quarter of the screen space, it 'accepts' this straight away and looks inside the picture for the content.

As well as absorbing the synchronised stereophonic soundtrack, the mind is still greedy and wants to know other things. What else is happening, perhaps in other places or other aspects of the meaning of that image.

A simple three-screen presentation: on the left side an expert speaking on camera on the subject of pollution of a lake, on the right hand screen a picture of a swimmer emerging from the water covered in muck, on the middle screen throughout was a picture of the surface of the lake with the sun sparkling on the waves. Three simple pictures — very good material for the greedy mind.

In another three-screen film which included a sequence called *Hide and Seek* the highest interest point was where three kids finally arrived at their hiding places and simultaneously hid themselves in three totally different situations and the two eyed audience took in the three images with complete ease because of the degree of story interest.

The presence in our lives of simultaneous action the whole time is something which perhaps television brought 'home' to us in the first place. Everything happening at once, cameras being thrust down people's throats to 'see what is in' the stomach and other people examining what is on the opposite side of the moon, keeps informing us all of the presence of many things simultaneously or a sort of multi presence in our ordinary daily life.

We learned a great deal about this same thing making the first cartoon three-screen film *(Canada is My Piano)*.

The story ought to be the thing which fuses the three or several images. Whether the images be opposed, or relative views, or parallel action; the field is open.

39

Australian Commonwealth Film Unit

Australian Commonwealth Film Unit
Eton Road, Lindfield, New South Wales 2070

British and U.S. inquiries through
Australian News and Information Bureau

Canberra House	**636 Fifth Avenue**
10-16 Maltravers Street	**New York**
The Strand, London W.C. 2	**N.Y. 10020**

and at official Australian posts in over 50 countries

WORLD PRODUCTION SURVEY

Australia

World Production

general survey   **by John Baxter**

On paper, the Australian film scene remained substantially similar to that of previous years. With a population of 12 million people to serve and 1,100 theatres (125 of them drive-ins) to supply, the local film distributors were forced to rely heavily on foreign features, 477 of which were imported during the year. Government help for the establishment of an indigenous feature industry has still not been forthcoming, but there are encouraging signs that a film community for long lethargic is finding a new spirit.

A number of independent features are in the planning stage, and one has been completed — on schedule and inside budget. *Two Thousand Weeks*, directed by Tim Burstall, a Venice award-winner with his 1960 short, *The Prize*, promises to be a milestone in the industry. Following the pattern of previous years, co-productions are proving a useful means of organising local production. A U.S.-Australian company has just finished *It Takes All Kinds*, a thriller with an international cast and Sydney settings, while Nautilus-Powell International Films, heartened by the success of *They're A Weird Mob*, has produced *Age of Consent*, adapted from the novel by Norman Lindsay and starring James Mason.

Short and experimental productions are booming, much of the credit going to a new interest throughout Australia in "underground cinema". Ubu Films, a Sydney film-makers' co-operative formed by experimentalists Albie Thomas, David Perry, and Andrew Read, has electrified the field with its road-show screenings of local and imported experimental shorts. Screening and renting on a profit-sharing basis, they have provided Australian short film-makers with their first market, and also introduced local audiences to such foreign directors as Bruce Conner, Carson Davidson, and Don Levy. Ubu's productions are likewise influential. *Man and his World* was one of the hundred 50-second films singled out for commendation at Expo 67, and the later *Bolero* earned praise at Knokke-le-Zoute.

Hopeful signs of a new attitude go beyond production. *Cardin in Australia*, the documentary noted in IFG 1968, received the Australian Film Institute's Gold Award for the best documentary of the year, and its young director, Peter Thompson, left for Europe soon afterwards on a study scholarship. In a decision which may prove to have far-reaching significance, the Customs Department lifted censorship restrictions on the Sydney and Melbourne Festivals, thus bringing both events into line with international practice. More interest in serious cinema among distributors, an increase in the number of art cinemas, and general liberalisation of censorship all hint at a hopeful future for Australian filmgoers.

Commonwealth Film Unit news

During 1968 the Unit maintained its annual output of approximately 50 documentary and information films for world circulation. *Desert People*, the ethnographic film reviewed in IFG 1968, continued to win acclaim, gaining prizes at the Padua, Prades, and Edinburgh Festivals. This film, now available through Contemporary Films (New York) or Australian official posts, was also included in a programme of Australian anthropological films circulated throughout North America during the year.

Recently the Unit has been using less familiar forms of information film. Dramatised documentary has been employed in three films where actors, elaborate sets and feature film production values are used on subjects like telephone etiquette (*Heaven Help Us!*), weather forecasting (*Is Anybody Doing Anything About It?*), and one of Australia's most scenic areas (*Will the Great Barrier Reef Cure Claude Clough?*). Other new films include documentaries on national development (*Papua and New Guinea 1967*, *The Northern Territory*), safety and economy in industry (*Operation Picul Stick*), and creative drama teaching in schools (*Drama Lesson*), while the recent sailing film *Eighteen Footers* won first prize at the 9th International Review of Maritime Documentaries, Milan, 1968.

Commonwealth Film Unit productions may be borrowed from the London and New York offices of the Australian News & Information Bureau, or Australian official Posts in more than 50 countries. Hire charges, where levied, are modest. Catalogues are available from all Posts, and the excellent periodical Newsletter is obtainable from Box 46, Lindfield, NSW, 2070, Australia.

recent films

AGE OF CONSENT. *dir:* Michael Powell. *phot:* Hannes Staudinger. *players:* James Mason, Jack MacGowran, Helen Mirren. 110 mins. *In its day (1938), Norman Lindsay's novel was a protest against conventional morality embodied in the story of an erotic idyll between an artist and his nubile teenage model. Powell's modernising includes re-location on the Great Barrier Reef and a rather more uninhibited climax to the unconsummated love affair of the original.*

DRAMA LESSON. *dir:* Joe Scully. *prod:* Richard Mason (Commonwealth Film Unit). 22 mins. "*Creative drama*", *as taught in Australian schools, is as much a system for freeing the imagination as a means of dramatic training. With teachers in mind, Drama Lesson outlines the method, its application and potential.*

GREAT BARRIER REEF. *prod:* Richard Mason. *underwater phot:* Ron Taylor. 27 mins. Commonwealth Film Unit. *An exhaustive study (in colour) of the Great Barrier Reef, its bird, animal and marine life. Rare footage includes sequences of plankton, coral growth, brilliantly coloured fish, and the life cycle of the turtle.*

Left: TWO THOUSAND WEEKS — Will Gardiner (Mark McManus) handing a pair of spectacles to his dying father in hospital. Right: Max Meldrum as Alexander Graham Bell in HEAVEN HELP US! An Australian Commonwealth Film Unit production.

IT TAKES ALL KINDS. *dir. and prod:* Eddie Davis. *phot:* Mick Bornemann. *players:* Vera Miles, Barry Sullivan, Robert Lansing. For Goldsworthy Productions in conjunction with Commonwealth United Entertainments. *A thriller shot in and around Sydney about a group of international criminals out to steal a rare stained glass window from an art gallery.*

SHADES OF PUFFING BILLY. *dir. and script:* Antonio Colacino. *phot:* Reg Pearse. *mus:* Don Burrows. *prod:* Malcolm Otton (Commonwealth Film Unit). 11½ mins. *The Ferntree Gully narrow-gauge railway runs between two mountain towns in Victoria, and is a great favourite with children. This light-hearted film shows a typical journey. Prize for Best Children's Film, Brussels Festival, 1967. Eastmancolor.*

TWO THOUSAND WEEKS. *dir. and script:* Tim Burstall. *phot:* Robin Copping. *players:* Jeanie Drynan, Mark McManus. *prod:* Patrick Ryan for Eltham Films. 100 mins. *At thirty, a man has forty years to live — just two thousand weeks. A realisation of this precipitates writer Will Gardiner into a re-organisation of a life which has become cluttered with wife, mistress, friends and rivals. Burstall shot this modern drama on location around Melbourne.*

API (Air Programs International), one of the largest producers of animated cartoon films in the world, is currently at work on 39 half-hour colour shorts dealing with the adventures of "Arthur", based on the legend of King Arthur and the Knights of the Round Table. The series is well-advanced and is sold world-wide. Distribution for Europe is handled by Associated British-Pathé, London, and for the U.S.A., South America, and Pacific areas by Four Star Entertainment of New York.

In the planning stage at API is a new set of animated half hours for production from the beginning of 1969, and the company also anticipates production of a package of feature movies and at least one filmed "live" series in 1969. Executive producer is Walter J. Hucker and director of animation is Zoran Janjic.

38 MARTIN PLACE, SYDNEY, AUSTRALIA
RADIO ● TELEVISION PRODUCTIONS

api

Austria

the current situation   ## by Goswin Dörfler

Last year we reported that "Austrian film production and cinema attendances are in a state of crisis." As far as 1968 is concerned, this crisis has been resolved — the patient having died peacefully . . . In practice there is no more national film production. The Austrian cinema has reached its year zero, thus giving hope for a new start. Both the state and private enterprise have given serious thought to this, and there are vehement discussions at various levels for the reconstruction of the home industry. The king is dead; long live the king!

Statistics reflect the situation: attendances numbered only 57.65 million in 1967, compared with 65.8 in the previous year. A further 14 cinemas closed in Vienna, so that the capital, with its population of 1.7 million, now has only 165 cinemas, most of them owned by the city authorities. In sharp contrast to this, the number of television receivers exceeded one million at the beginning of 1968, and that in a country whose total population barely exceeds 7 million.

The number of films in distribution fell slightly from 490 in 1966 to 472 in 1967. Most of these (174) came from the U.S.A., from West Germany and Italy (65 each), from Britain (56), and France (45). Whereas in 1966 some 18 Austrian films (even if half were co-productions with foreign countries) were premiered, only 12 reached the screens in 1967, the best of which were again co-produced.

The Federation of Austrian Film Critics, affiliated to FIPRESCI, selected Lelouch's *Un Homme et une Femme* as the Best Film in 1967. Austria's leading film critic, Professor Hans Winge, who had spent many years in Hollywood and abroad, died in April 1968. This was a great loss to the domestic film scene. The only annual film festival in Vienna, known as the "Viennale", has been forced through lack of suitable material to abandon its theme of "humorous cinema", and to adopt the slogan "Films which failed to reach us". Weeks of Soviet and Hungarian films also took place during 1968. The art cinema Studio 1 has been showing a number of foreign films in their original version under the title of "Studio Avant". The more established Burgkino in Vienna also shows this type of picture. So, with all these developments, one still hopes that 1968 will be the year in which Austrian cinema took a turn for the better.

élisabeth films
BRONKA RICQUIER

34, rue de la Tulipe / Brussels 5
Phone: 11.28.28 or 12.36.36
Cable: Elisabethfilm

formed at the end of 1966, the young Belgian filmcompany produced:

1967: **LE DÉPART**

Director: Jerzy Skolimowski

Golden Bear and Award of the International Critics Union at the 1967 Berlin Festival

1968
co-produced with Studio Barrandov PRAGUE:

we may eat of the fruit of the trees of the garden

Director: Vera Chytilova

(This feature will be completed at the beginning of 1969)

Several projects for 1969

46

Belgium

the current scene   by Walter van Uytfangh

Belgium is one of the European countries where the industry and the production of feature films are still in their infancy. Only 5 or 6 pictures are completed each year. Shorts are more popular and some 100 of these are produced annually. One of the most famous and successful of these short film-makers is Raoul Servais, who made *Chromofobia*, a prize-winner at Venice, Leipzig, Moscow, Montreal, Teheran, and Bilbao in 1967. Now Servais has made a feature, called *Sirene*, which will be

Director Vera Chytilová and (at left) cameraman Jaroslav Kucera (her husband) have been shooting WE MAY EAT OF THE FRUIT OF THE TREES OF THE GARDEN for Elisabeth Films of Brussels.

screened at the Belgian Film Festival in Antwerpen in February 1969.

The winning of the Golden Bear at Berlin in 1967 with *Le Départ* was a great spur to Elisabeth Films, who are now engaged on the production of Vera Chytilová's *We May Eat of the Fruit of the Trees of the Garden*, with Ester Krumbachová as co-writer of the screenplay and Jaroslav Kucera as director of photography. Other pictures are already finished: *Monsieur Hawarden*, for example, directed by Harry Kümel and noted pictorially in our Netherlands section, with photography by Eddy van der Ende and music by Pierre Bartholomée; *Adieu Filippi*, directed by Rik Kuypers, and set in the circus world created in her novel by Blanka Gyselin. The cast includes Wies Andersen, Benny Scheffer, Robert Marcel, Alberto Althoff Jr., Johan Kaart, Robbe de Hart and others. Walter Smets is director of photography.

A commercial success in the Belgian film world has been *Cash? Cash!*, first shown at the Utrecht Cinemanifestatie in February 1968. It has run several weeks in Antwerp and months in cinemas all over Holland. The stars are Jan Verbist, Brigitte Kowaltchuck, Annemiek Sauwen, and Joris Collet. Paul Collet is the producer and director.

There are now about 1,000 cinemas open in Belgium. Prior to 1960 there were around 1,750, but the coming of television and the five-day week has proved too much for several theatres which have had to close as a result. About 200 features are imported each year, although the specialised titles tend to be screened only in Brussels and at film societies.

Brazil

the current situation   by Jaime Rodrigues

The entire cinema field in Brazil has been transformed by the formation of the National Institute of Cinema (formally established on November 18, 1966, but only working since May 1967). Many incentives to production and film in general were created, such as a prize of about 15% of their earnings to films of acknowledged quality, and a contribution averaging around 10% towards all domestic productions. Firms wanting to import cinema equipment have been aided, largely from money recovered from taxes on foreign films.

The new generation — men like Glauber Rocha, Walter Hugo Khoury, Nelson Pereira dos Santos, Roberto Santos, and Julio Bressane are trying to develop low-budget productions with a considerable artistic content. The National Institute also encourages the production of short films, and by issuing "Special Classification" certificates, it ensures that the films of these new directors are exhibited for at least 28 days a year.

new and forthcoming films

BRAZIL ANO 2.000 *(Brazil Year 2,000)*. *dir:* Walter Lima Jnr. *players:* Annecy Rocha, José Lewgoy, Eugenio Kusnet, Delorges Caminha.
AS ARMAS *(The Guns)*. *dir:* Benedito Astolfo de Araújo.
PARATI. *dir:* Eliseu Visconti Cavalleiro. *players:* Maria Della Costa, Rute Escobar, Itala Nandi, Carlos de Aquino.
O BRADO RETUMBANTE *(The Resounding Cry)*. *dir:* Carlos Diégues.
TRILOGIA DO TERROR *(Three Tales of Terror)*. *dir:* Ozualdo Candeias, José Mojica Marins, Luís Sérgio Person.
O HONEM QUE COMPROU O MUNDO *(The Man who Buys the World)*. *dir:* Eduardo Coutinho. *players:* Flávio Migliaccio, Marília Pera, Jardel Filho, Cláudio Marzo.
ATE QUE O CASAMENTO NOS SEPARE *(Until Marriage Separates Us)*. *dir:* Flávio Tambellini. *players:* Vera Barreto Leite, Mário Benvenuti, Anna Christie.
O CANTO LIVRE *(The Free Song)*. *dir:* Luís Carlos Barreto. *players:* Nara Leão, Caetano Veloso.
OS MARGINAIS *(The Margin)*. *dir:* Carlos Alberto Prates Corrêa, Moisés Kondler, Paulo Leite Soares. *players:* Paulo José, Dina Sfat, José Lewgoy.
A MADONA DE CEDRO *(The Virgin of Cedar)*. *dir:* Carlos Coimbra. *players:* Leila Diniz, Anselmo Duarte, Leonardo Vilar, Sérgio Cardoso.

Valeria Vidal in A MARGEM (The Border), directed by Ozualdo Candeias.

ANTES O VERAO *(Before the Summer)*. *dir:* Gerson Tavares. *players:* Norma Bengell, Darlene Glória, Jardel Filho, Jofre Soares.

FOME DE AMOR *(Hungry for Love)*. *dir:* Nelson Pereira dos Santos. *players:* Leila Diniz, Paulo Porto, Arduíno Colassanti, Irene Stefania.

A DOCE MULHER AMADA *(The Sweet and Beloved Woman)*. *dir:* Rui Santos. *players:* Arduíno Colassanti, Irma Alvarez, Grande Otelo.

OS CARRASCOS ESTAO ENTRE NOS *(The Killers Are Among Us)*. *dir:* Adolpho Chadler. *players:* Karin Rodrigues, Adolpho Chadler, Larry Carr.

CAPITU. *dir:* Paulo César Saraceni. *players:* Isabela, Othon Bastos, Marília Pera.

A LEI DO CAO *(The Law of the Dog)*. *dir:* Jece Valadão. *players:* Esther Mellinger, Jece Valadão, Paulo Frederico, Adriana Prieto, Wilson Viana.

O DIABO MORA NO SANGUE *(Evil Lives in the Blood)*. *dir:* Cecil Thiré. *players:* Cecil Thiré, Ana Maria Magalhães, Maria Pompeu, João Benio.

COMO MATAR UM PLAY-BOY *(How to Kill a Playboy)*. *dir:* Carlos Hugo Christensen. *players:* Agildo Ribeiro, Anna Christie, Mílton Carneiro.

Canada

the current situation   by Gerald Pratley

It was no doubt inevitable that following the jubilation and achievements of Centennial Year there would be something of a slow-down during 1968. Part of this was due to a curb on spending, by both government and private industry, which spent liberally during 1967. However, as 1968 draws to a close, there is every reason to feel optimistic about future developments in production. The Canadian Film Finance Corporation is now (at long last) at work and considering the many scripts and proposals being submitted to it. The Corporation has made it clear that it will only put money into what would appear to be good commercial subjects, and is interpreting the Act under which it administers loan funds in the widest possible sense to encourage the production of movies here by American, British and other interests. John Terry, managing director of Britain's NFFC, visited Canada in an "advisory position" to the Corporation and said that co-productions would be "a healthy thing for both sides during this initial period of development."

From Montreal came the sad news of the demise of the International and Canadian film festivals. Whether this will be for one year or for ever is still not known. The festival was closed mainly as a result of protests from film-makers in Quebec who felt that any money which the federal and provincial governments grant to the festival would be better spent on financing production. In view of the large amount of international publicity the festival brought to Montreal and its determined film-makers, this seems like a narrow view. Vancouver's international film festival, which has struggled through almost ten years of mis-management yet always offered good programmes, also missed this year. On the positive side, the annual Canadian Film Awards, which has seen 19 years of somewhat ineffective celebrating (ineffective in the sense that the award-winning films remained largely unknown to the public) has been completely reorganised and taken over by the film-makers' guilds and programmes of winning films will be shown across Canada. An indication of the continuing strength and vitality of short film-making and of the growing number of feature length films being made is seen in the number of entries submitted to the Awards Committee: 12 features and over 170 shorts ranging from 15 minutes to an hour in length.

On the international scene it was Canada's year at Berlin, where the festival opened with Don Owen's *The Ernie Game* and included Eric Till's Montreal-made, American-financed first feature, *A Great Big Thing*, both films being similar in content as they relate the wanderings of lost youths. Also shown was Christopher Chapman's multiple image 70mm short subject made by the Ontario Government

for its Expo Pavilion called *A Place to Stand*, which has achieved an enormous international success and been widely shown in theatres throughout North America. Also at Berlin, the Week of Young Cinema was devoted to a programmes of Quebec-made movies: Michel Brault's *Entre la mer et l'eau douce*, Jean-Pierre Lefebvre's *Le revolutionnaire* and *Il ne faut pas mourir pour ça*, Arthur Lamothe's *Poussière sur la ville*, Gilles Groulx's *Le chat dans le sac*, Gilles Carle's *Le viol d'une fille douce* and Larry Kent's *High*. All except the last-named are in French.

The Dominion Bureau of Statistics' latest film-trade figures are: paid admissions, 87,635,059; tickets sold, $ 83,171,556; number of theatres, 1,420; number of feature films imported, 510.

National Film Board news

The Board received the expected amount of enraged criticism, along with the CBC, for its features *The Ernie Game* and *Waiting for Caroline*, which went so far over-budget without becoming masterpieces that it's a wonder the Board ever wants to hear the term "feature film" mentioned again. Nothing daunted, it has two more in production. This is the only way to establish a basis for regular production, and one day its efforts will be rewarded with a winner. In the meantime, *Waiting for Caroline*, which cost over $ 600,000, was sold to UA world-wide for $ 100,000! The Board received no praise at all for an excellent one-hour dramatised story of an aging trade union official, called *Do Not Fold, Staple, Spindle or Mutilate* with Ed Begley, written by Millard Lampell and directed by John Howe. And undoubtedly, one of its major achievements is Norman McLaren's beautiful *Pas de deux*, a remarkable experiment in which two dancers from Les Grand Ballets Canadiens are seen first as single forms then followed by endless reflections of themselves. *Get Wet (d* William Canning) is a colourful, pleasing, and fast-moving compilation of swimmers enjoying themselves; *The Sea Got in Your Blood (d* David Millar), a pleasant evocation of seafaring days in Lunenburg and the building of the old and the new "Bluenose"; *Satan's Choice (d* Donald Shebib), not quite Canada's Corman or *Hell's Angels* but a fascinating study of Toronto's motor-cycle club and how its members think; *The Changing Wheatbelt (d* Joseph Koenig), a classroom study of life in Western Canada, not bad; *The Game (d* George Kaczender), successor to *Phoebe* and *You're No Good*, a brave study of teenagers playing the game of seducing girls in their cars, but uncertain, murky and miserable; *Ghosts of a River (d* Pierre Patry and Jacques Kasma), a last and impressively photographed look at the beautiful mountain region West of the Great Divide before the Columbia River is dammed and all is flooded; *The Long Haul Men (d* Michael Rubbo), a lively glimpse of long-distance truck drivers travelling from Mexico to Alberta, good material for a feature; *Fisherman's Fall (d* Robert Nichol), an imaginative and attractively filmed study showing concern over conservation and pollution; *Sudden Departure (d* Georges Dufaux), a moving and delicate look at young children separated from their parents, what happens to them, and how their emotional needs are not fully understood; and *Ride for your Life (d* Robin Spry), the life of a motor racing driver and his family, shorn of all the false glamour — thoughtful and intelligent. All of the Boards' shorts are now enjoying unprecedented playing time in Canadian cinemas, a source of great encouragement to their makers who are at last finding larger audiences.

reviews   by Gerald Pratley

ISABEL. *script, prod.* and *dir:* Paul Almond. *phot:* Georges Dufaux (Eastmancolor). *music:* Harry Freedman. *players:* Geneviève Bujold, Marc Strange, Gerard Parkes. 108 mins. *A young girl returns to her home in the lonely Gaspe region and becomes aware of strange influences at work around her. Beautifully photographed, sensitively acted and directed, splendidly brooding and atmospheric, this first feature by former CBC-TV director Paul Almond turns, unfortunately, into a tedious tale of virtually nothing.*

ENTRE LA MER ET L'EAU DOUCE. *dir:* Michel Brault. *phot:* Bernard Gosselin, Jean-Claude Labrecque, Michel Brault. *players:* Geneviève Bujold, Claude Gauthier, Louise Latreverse, Paul Gauthier, Robert Charlebois. 90 mins. *A sincere but dreary tale of a young man who goes to Montréal, finds fame as a folk singer, and loses the girl he loves. Although this slight and familiar story takes on a new life for being set against little-known Quebec backgrounds, and a restless society, Brault's direction renders it all bleak, slow, and monotonous with few moments of humour or pathos. We never penetrate the characters or share their emotional experiences.*

THE ERNIE GAME. *script* and *dir:* Don Owen. *phot:* Jean-Claude Lebrecque (Eastmancolor). *music:* The Kensington Market. *players:* Alexis Kanner, Judith Gault, Jackie Burroughs. 86 mins. *A dull fellow playing a dull game. A fragmentary non-story film about a shiftless young man in Montréal precariously close to insanity and unable to face life. He survives by imposing on two girls, by using people, by talking of the things he plans to do but is incapable of carrying out. But we never really know him. The two girls are the Donna and Gail of Owen's earlier, shorter movie,* Notes for a Film about Donna and Gail.

WAITING FOR CAROLINE. *dir:* Ron Kelly. *script:* Kelly and George Robertson. *phot:* Denis Gillson (Eastmancolor). *music:* Eldon Rathburn. *players:* Alexandra Stewart, Robert Howay, Françoise Tasse, Sharon Acker. 86 mins. *Ron Kelly, who established a good reputation with his interesting work in documentary and television, over-steps himself here and fails badly with a beautifully-made, expensively-mounted piece of melodrama in the Hollywood style concerning a girl and her love for two men, one from Quebec, the other from British Columbia. Between the snows of one province and the mountains of the other, audiences are likely to be bored to extremes while she decides on her choice.*

Czechoslovakia

introduction **by Peter Cowie**

The Oscar awarded to Jiří Menzel's *Closely Observed Trains* in 1968 was a reminder of the world success of the Czech cinema, just as the Oscar for *The Shop on the Main Street* two years previously had announced its achievements to the English-speaking countries. Only a proportion of Czech films are seen abroad, and more than half the national production consists of comedies, detective stories, adventure films, and films for children. Although most pictures are made for under 100,000 dollars, no film can recoup its budget from its domestic release, and so the foreign market is needed and respected.

The breakthrough came in the years 1963-1965, when some 15 new directors emerged. Non-professional actors were widely used, because the professionals tended to sneer at the slim scripts offered them and were altogether too busy to film on tight time schedules. This led to the natural, unforced expressiveness of so many characters in the new Czech cinema. Not surprisingly, the success of these directors has brought tempting offers from outside Czechoslovakia. Passer is planning to shoot in England, Forman in Italy and America, while Chytilová has been making a co-production with Elisabeth Films of Brussels. Alain Robbe-Grillet's *L'Homme qui ment* was also a co-production with Czechoslovakia, and Yves Ciampi has been at work this year in Prague too.

The Czech cinema has a considerable production capacity. The big Barrandov studios in Prague, the Kudlov studios in Gottwaldov, Moravia, and the Koliba studios in Bratislava, Slovakia; six puppet and cartoon film studios; and modern laboratories in Prague and Gottwaldov.

O SLAVNOSTI A HOSTECH (The Party and the Guests)

Script: Ester Krumbachová and Jan Němec; *Direction:* Němec; *Photography:* Jaromir Šofr; *Editing:* Miroslav Hájek; *Music:* Karel Mareš; *Players:* Ivan Vyskočil, Jan Klusák, Jiří Němec, Zdenka Škvorecká, Pavel Bošek. For Filmstudio Barrandov. 71 mins.

"How pleasant it is to take part in all the parties life offers. To sit down at a well-laid table and leave behind the cares and worries you cannot do anything about in any case; to live, and above all, to survive, that is the credo of people and societies, never formulated but all the more vigorously put into practice." So Nemec comments on his extraordinary fable, which was only released to the world at Cannes 1968, after two years of languishing in official disfavour, probably because the villainous Host and his psychopathic brother bear a close resemblance to communist leaders of our time. Because Nemec has modelled so many scenes on well-known reactions and settings (like the Nobel Prize banquet), one is constantly aware of the allusiveness of events in the film, which seems like a nightmare and yet is only a slightly distorted picture of modern civilisation and *moeurs*.

The Party and the Guests is shot from start to finish in ferocious close-ups, creating a palpable atmosphere of claustrophobia and helplessness, and marvellously suggesting the myopic stupidity that restrains all but one of the guests from leaving the sinister gathering. Harsh tones in the photography give menace to every stone and tree; the slow descent of dusk on the forest is a reminder of the Satanic control that the Host gradually exerts over his guests. The pleasant music accompanying the feast underlines the film's fundamental premise; that tyranny can exist in a congenial, almost a family context. The individual who leaves his table abruptly is branded as a traitor, not because he abandons his newly-wedded wife, but because (in the words of scenarist Ester Krumbachová) he "declines to play the game and thereby threatens the structure of inter-collaboration, guilt, and indifference" — **Peter Cowie.**

TRI DCERY
(Three Daughters)

Script: Alfonz Bednar and Stefan Uher, from a story by Bednar; *Direction:* Uher; *Photography:* Stanislav Szomolanyi; *Music:* Ilja Zeljenka; *Art Direction:* Anton Krajcovic; *Players:* Alzbeta Strkulová, Stanislava Strobachová, Dusan Blasković, Milan Fabiane.

Stefan Uher, probably the most important Slovak director (already distinguished by films like *The Sun in a Net*, *The Organ*, and *The Miraculous Virgin*) now comes forward with his fourth feature, a ballad of our times called *Three Daughters*. The plot concerns a greedy father who soon after World War Two sends his three daughters to a convent, so as to keep his farm and to make as much out of it as possible. But under the new government he loses his land and begins to search for his "lost children". One has left the convent, married, and does not want to put up with her father; another is working in a hospital and has no room for the old man; the third lives among some nuns who are busy in a "Collective", which would like to abandon the religious women.

The whole film is a precisely worked account of the beginning of the Communist régime, and is saturated with black humour. The errors, the profiteering, and the commercial selfishness (even with the "Collective") are all pointed out. Uher also brings the rift between Church and State into the open, and this adds tension to an already absorbing film — **Felix Bucher.**

Surprise and confusion in Milos Forman's LIKE A HOUSE ON FIRE.

HOŘÍ, MÁ PANENKO
(Like A House On Fire)

Script: Miloš Forman, Jaroslav Papoušek, Ivan Passer; *Direction:* Forman; *Photography:* Miroslav Ondříček (Eastmancolor); *Editing:* Miroslav Hajék; *Music:* Karel Mareš; *Art Direction:* Karel Cerný; *Players:* Václav Stöckel, Josef Svět, Jan Vostrčil, Josef Kolb. For Filmstudio Barrandov (Prague) / Carlo Ponti (Rome). 73 mins.

Like A House On Fire stills any fears of Forman's using his commercial success to produce trite entertainment; on the contrary, he is more than ever alert to the anguish that can lurk behind every chuckle. The new film deals with the failure of good intentions, in much the same manner as *A Blonde in Love.* The slow disintegration of the array of tombola prizes is funny because of Forman's timing, his cutting between situation and reaction; but the humour becomes darker as one realises how important decorum and peace of mind are to the old man guarding the table. The evening's formalities go so astray that the brigade looks positively relieved when someone arrives with the news that a house is ablaze. At last the men are in their element, able to justify their existence and to demonstrate that they are more than mere querulous parasites. But again Forman uses irony to isolate them, for when they return to the village hall they find that all the tombola prizes have been stolen. The 86 year old Commander has to suffer the worst indignity; after innumerable abortive attempts, he is presented with a gilt fireman's axe to honour his 40 years of service. But when he opens the box, the axe is missing. Like many of one's objectives in life, it has disappeared after being so close for so long — **Peter Cowie.**

documentaries for hire

The following films are on free loan from Educational & Television Films Ltd., 2 Doughty Street, London W.C.1. British applications only, please. Most titles have English commentary.

Distance Twenty-Five (Black-and-white, 400 ft.)
Stone Age Cave Culture (Colour, 500 ft.)
Valley of Two Faces (Colour, 450 ft.)
Naïve Art (Colour, 400 ft.)
The Bell Founder (Black-and-white, 500 ft.)
The Excursion (Black-and-white, 600 ft.)
Movement and Time (Colour, 550 ft.)
Edinburgh Symphony (Black-and-white, 900 ft.)
War Cameraman (Black-and-white, 600 ft.)
A Suite in Baroque (Colour, 3 parts.)
Old Valassko (Colour, 550 ft.)
The Czech Philharmonic (Black-and-white, 800 ft.)
A Concert for Italy (Black-and-white, 450 ft.)
The Last Years (Black-and-white, 750 ft.)
Metamorphic Rocks (Colour, 900 ft.)
A Greek of the Danube (Black-and-white, 550 ft.)
Where No Birds Fly (Colour, 1,300 ft.)

ROZMARNÉ LÉTO
(Indian Summer)

Script: Vaclac Nyvlt and Jiří Menzel, from a novel by Vladislav Vančura; *Direction:* Menzel; *Photography:* Jaromír Šofr; *Music:* Jiří Šust; *Art Direction:* Oldřich Bosák; *Players:* Rudolf Hrušinský, Vlastimil Brodsky, Míla Myslíková, František Rehák. For Film Studio Barrandov.

This little masterpiece is the second feature by Jiří Menzel, who won official recognition (which was disputed before the recent wave of "liberalisation") for the young Czech cinema with his Oscar for *Closely Observed Trains*. Menzel has adapted with great fidelity and convincing clarity the major novel by Vladislav Vančura, the most significant Czech poet of the 20th century whose *Markéta Lazarová* has been made into an impressive film by František Vlácil. The story is simple and almost banal: a small circus arrives at a village. There is a tightrope dancer (played by Menzel) and his assistant (Jana Drchalová), who quickly bewitches three far from youthful gentlemen and draws them under her spell. Thus these three, the swimming master, the retired Major, and the canon, try to approach this glorious creature — and naturally their efforts run aground. The circus moves on once more, and the trio of men remain behind, the look on their faces showing that they now realise that there is something even more tantalising and remote than the events in their village.

The story, which takes place at the turn of the century, is given a peculiar charm because Vančura allows his characters to speak in flowery and bombastic language — and as if it were quite the done thing. Menzel has captured completely the atmosphere and charm of the village and its inhabitants, while his players understand perfectly how to emphasise the oddities of the dialect and yet remain relaxed and uninhibited. *Indian Summer* could be misinterpreted by the public abroad, if subtitles fail to convey the idiomatic subtleties of the dialogue; superficially it could be seen as a pleasing trifle — and it is definitely more than that — **Felix Bucher.**

Denmark

introduction

In proportion to the size of her population (4,5 millions), Denmark is a large film producing country. About 20 features are completed annually plus a considerable number of shorts and documentaries. The country contains approximately 400 cinemas. Some 300 Danish and foreign films are released each year, together with a growing number of re-releases of high quality films.

During the first decades of the century Danish film production held a central position in the European film market; but its chances of competing internationally were drastically reduced when talking pictures arrived. With a few notable exceptions such as the work of Carl Th. Dreyer, Danish films enjoyed considerably less popularity outside Scandinavia in the ensuing years.

Many of the features produced now are unpretentious entertainment pictures, but during the past two years some talented directors have embarked on more ambitious projects. The creation of the Danish Government Film Foundation ("Filmfonden") in 1965 has helped to provide favourable conditions for the domestic film industry. The activities of the Foundation are financed by a 15% royalty on tickets and licence fees paid by cinema owners. In 1967 the Film Foundation had a total income of 21,5 million Kroner, of which 15 million derived from royalties and 6 million from licence fees from cinema-owners. A film academy has been created under the auspices of the Foundation. Secondly, the production of film is supported by guarantees for loans of up to 45% of the budget. The Foundation also has a system of awards for films of high quality, and prizes are also given to film distributors, directors, and actors. The foundation gives financial support to the Danish State Film Centre (distribution, acquisition, and production of educational shorts) and to the Danish Film Museum (see our Film Archives section).

Danish
film

**For information on Danish films,
please write to
The Danish Government Film Foundation
Store Sondervoldstraede, Copenhagen K.**

recent films

I LOVE BLUE. *dir:* Sven Methling. *phot:* Ole Lütken. *players:* Ulla Lemvigh-Müller, Jørgen Kiil, Peter Bunke. For Saga.

THEY ALL DO IT. *dir:* Knud Leif Thomsen. *phot:* Jørgen Skov. *players:* Tina Wilhelmsen, Judy Gringer, Jesper Langberg, Per Bentzon Goldschmidt. For Nordisk Films.

IN A GREEN FOREST. *dir:* Palle Kjaerulff-Schmidt. *phot:* Claus Loof. *players:* Yvonne Ingdal, Peter Steen, Ellen Winther, Morten Grunwald, Jesper Langberg. For Nordisk Films.

MARTHA. *dir:* Erik Balling. *phot:* Jørgen Skov. *players:* Ove Sprogøe, Karl Stegger, Hanne Borchsenius, Poul Bundgaard. For Nordisk Films.

LIFE WITH DADDY. *dir:* Finn Henriksen. *phot:* Ole Lütken. *players:* Ghita Nørby, Morten Grunwald, Bodil Udsen, Marguerite Viby. For Palladium.

DAYS IN MY FATHER'S HOUSE. *dir:* David Nagata. *phot:* Jerry Hirschfield. *players:* Poul Bastek, Gunnar Lauring, Preben Neergaard, Hanne Borchsenius. For Asa Film Studio.

ONE SATURDAY EVENING . . . *dir:* Erik Balling. *phot:* Jørgen Skov, Claus Loof. *players:* Daimi, Morten Grunwald, Claus Nissen, Ove Sprogøe. For Nordisk Films.

THE HANDSOME ARNE AND ROSA. *dir:* Sven Methling. *phot:* Ole Lütken. *players:* Morten Grunwald, Judy Gringer, Poul Bundgaard, Carl Ottosen. For Saga Film.

DR. GLAS. *dir:* Mai Zetterling. *phot:* Rune Ericsson. *players:* Per Oscarsson, Lone Hertz, Ulf Palme, Nils Eklund, Bente Dessau, Bent Rothe, Helle Hertz. For Laterna Film.

PEOPLE MEET AND SWEET MUSIC FILLS THE HEART. *dir:* Henning Carlsen. *phot:* Henning Kristiansen. *players:* Harriet Andersson, Preben Neergaard, Erik Wedersøe, Eva Dahlbeck, Lone Rode, Georg Rydeberg. For Henning Carlsen, Nordisk Films, Sandrews.

Astrid Henning-Jensen was born in Copenhagen in 1914. She was an actress at the "intimate theatre", Riddersalen, in the thirties, and then assisted her husband/director, Bjaerne Henning-Jensen, at Nordisk Film. Later she made independent productions herself for Nordisk and also for Norsk Film (Oslo) between 1950 and 1952. Since then she has worked as a free-lance director, at the United Nations and elsewhere. Here features include *Palle alone in the World* (1949), *Paw* (1959), *Unfaithful* (1966), *My Grandfather is a Stick* (1967), and *Nille* (1968).

Niels Larsen in THOMAS ON THE RUN.

THOMAS ER FREDLOS
(Thomas on the Run)

Script and Direction: Sven Gronlykke; *Photography:* Jesper Hom (colour); *Music:* Patrick Gowers, Blossom Toes; *Players:* Niels Larsen, Poul Dissing, Bent Christensen, Peter Belli, Birger Jensen. For ASA Film Studio.

Fantasies are all too tempting for most makers of children's films. But the various hero/villain figures of this picture are so gently and lyrically introduced that they mould into the pastoral environment without effort or embarrassment. Thomas, the 10 year old schoolboy, plays truant with his favourite horse, and his adventure books spring to life. Tuaregs, Red Indians, policemen, supermen, even Hitler are there to menace and pursue him. Dream and reality merge in a comedy that is full of action and yet hardly farcical; idyllic and yet not too sweet. Eventually Thomas is joined by a little girl from his class, and they escape on a raft with a top-hatted violinist whining away beside them. This adroitly made film, only one hour in length, shows the Danish landscape at its most enchanting, and also communicates some dimension of the adolescent's world of wish-dreams — **Peter Cowie.**

Dr.Glas

Laterna film

Just over a year ago Mogens Skot-Hansen bought the former Flamingo Studio at Naerum, north of Copenhagen, for his production company, LATERNA FILM. The studio has now been completely re-built and re-equipped, with the result that although one of the smallest in Denmark it is at the same time one of the most modern.

In addition, the fact of its being situated at Naerum makes for an ideal radius of action covering the chaming small towns, villages and countryside of North Zealand as well as the fascinating milieu provided by the city of Copenhagen itself. »Doctor Glas«, the official Danish entry at this year's film festival at Cannes, is the first feature film to have been made at Laterna Film's new studio – or perhaps one should say using the new studio as an operational base. For »Doctor Glas«, as is increasingly the case with modern films, was largely shot on location. The studio has for this very reason been furnished with completely modern, handy, lightweight equipment such as Arriflex cameras, Nagra sound recording equipment, colour-tran quartz lighting equipment, etc. In the course of Mai Zetterling's work on »Doctor Glas«, it has proved its complete efficacy as an operational base for a modern, flexible team of film-makers.

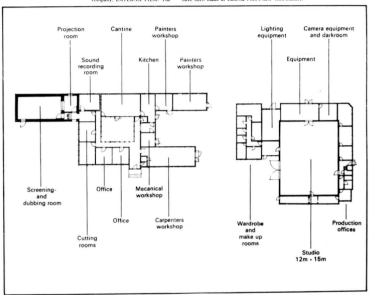

Projection room · Cantine · Painters workshop · Lighting equipment · Camera equipment and darkroom · Sound recording room · Kitchen · Painters workshop · Equipment · Screening- and dubbing room · Office · Mecanical workshop · Office · Carpenters workshop · Wardrobe and make up rooms · Production offices · Cutting rooms · Studio 12m · 15m

Knud Leif Thomsen was born in Copenhagen in 1924. Educated as a painter and pianist (at the Royal Academy of Music), he started working in film at Teknisk Film in 1952. From 1954 onwards he directed shorts and wrote scripts at Nordisk Film, Minerva Film and elsewhere. Then came a period of stydying in Paris, and a spell at an advertising film company. Since 1961 he has directed several features, among them *The Duel* (1962), *The School of Suicide* (1964), *Tine* (1964), *Venom* (*Gift*, 1966), *The Troll and the Pixy* (1967), and *They all do It* (1968).

63

*Lone Hertz and
Per Oscarsson in
DR. GLAS, directed by
Mai Zetterling.*

*Harriet Andersson and
Erik Wedersoe in
PEOPLE MEET AND
SWEET MUSIC FILLS
THE HEART.*

Finland

the current situation

At the end of the Fifties Finnish cinema was artistically and economically on the brink of collapse. A few years ago, however, an exciting era in Finnish production began with new directors, producers, cameramen, and actors. Mikko Niskanen's *Under Your Skin*, which was a big success both in the eyes of the critics and audiences, was the first significant film in this youthful movement. It has now been sold to more than 30 countries, and has launched its production enterprise, FJ-Filmi (headed by Jörn Donner and Arno Carlstedt), on a programme of films for international audiences.

Niskanen's second picture was *Girl of Finland*, based on a popular political play called "Lapua Opera", and it dealt controversially with the Fascist movement in Finland during the Thirties and the attitude of modern youth towards it. FJ-Filmi was further boosted when Jörn Donner founded his own company, participating in productions in the form of foreign trade and artistic and financial support. With Erkko Kivikoski, who had won a Silver Bear at Berlin some years before with a short called *Market Place*, they proceeded to make *Hot Cat*. This is a story of a young schoolboy expelled from school because of his drinking and falling in love with his teacher. It blends social criticism with romantic lyricism in a small and beautiful Finnish town. The film won the highest monetary prize from the State in its year, with *Girl of Finland* as runner-up. Now Jörn Donner has made his début as a director on the Finnish scene, after making four features in Stockholm. *Black on White* is his first colour film, and enjoyed tremendous success in Finland. Next summer two films are being prepared by FJ-Filmi and Jörn Donner Productions — *The Asphalt Lamb*, by Mikko Niskanen, and *Little Red Riding Hood*, by Timo Bergholm.

new and forthcoming films

THE ASPHALT LAMBS (Asfalttilampaat). *dir:* Mikko Niskanen. *phot:* Esko Nevalainen (Eastmancolor). *players:* Kirsti Wallasvaara, Eero Melasniemi. Produced by Arno Carlstedt for FJ-Filmi and Jörn Donner Productions.
LITTLE RED RIDING HOOD (Punahilkka). *dir:* Timo Bergholm. *phot:* Kari Sohlberg (Eastmancolor). *players:* Kristiina Halkola, Petra Fray, Hannu Kahakorpi. Produced by Jaakko Talaskivi for FJ-Filmi and Jörn Donner Productions.
BLACK ON WHITE (Mustaa valkoisella). *dir:* Jörn Donner. *phot:* Esko Nevalainen (Eastmancolor). *players:* Jörn Donner, Liisamaija Laaksonen, Kristiina Halkola, Lasse Mårtenson. Produced by Arno Carlstedt for FJ-Filmi and Jörn Donner Productions.

Sir,

I have the pleasure of informing you that the new Finnish cinema is doing very well. All the four features we have released so far have made enough money in the home market to enable us to continue.

International sales prospects are bright. UNDER YOUR SKIN, directed by Mikko Niskanen, has been sold to most markets. My own BLACK ON WHITE (in color) seems to interest more people than any other film I have directed.

Sex is not absent in the films we are producing; nor is youth. In fact, we have introduced quite a few beautiful Finnish Birds to the audience. We are open to any collaboration, any madness, any sales prospects, any discussions, anything we like and love, i.e. FILMS.

We have decided to outwit the Swedes too.

> Cordially,
> Jörn Donner (Dictated, not read)

JöRN DONNER PRODUCTIONS - Kirkkokatu 2
HELSINKI 17 - Finland   Phone 666054
Cable: DONNPROD

P.S. We are currently producing two more or three more, all in color and live action.

Kristiina Halkola stars in Jörn Donner's BLACK ON WHITE.

GIRL OF FINLAND (Lapualaismorsian). *dir:* Mikko Niskanen. *phot:* Osmo Harkimo. *players:* Kristiina Halkola, Pekka Laiho, Kirsti Wallasvaara, Aulikki Oksanen. Produced by Arno Carlstedt for FJ-Filmi and Jörn Donner Productions. **HOT CAT? (Kuuma kissa?).** *dir:* Erkko Kivikoski. *players:* Maarita Mäkelä, Eero Melasniemi, Kurt Ingvall, Marja-Leena Kouki. Produced by Arno Carlstedt for FJ-Filmi and Jörn Donner Productions.

Jörn Donner was born in Helsinki in 1933, and began writing as author, critic and journalist in 1951. Is well known for such essays in reportage as *Report from Berlin* and *Report from the Danube*, not to mention a study of Ingmar Bergman. He completed 5 short films before turning to features with *A Sunday in September*, made in Sweden and awarded the Premio Opera Prima at Venice in 1963. Then followed *To Love*, *Adventure Starts Here*, and *Rooftree*, all shot under the Swedish banner. But though a Swedish-language Finn, Donner has never considered himself at home in Sweden, and it was no surprise when he returned to Helsinki to stimulate a new film industry there and to fling all his talents into *Black on White*, where he plays the leading role as well as directing.

New Finnish films:
Maarita Mäkelä in
HOT CAT? (top),
and Kristiina Halkola
in GIRL OF
FINLAND (below).

France

introduction   by Peter Cowie

1968 proved to be one of the most calamitous years ever experienced by the French cinema. It began in February with the clumsy dismissal of Henri Langlois, founder and *monstre sacré* of La Cinémathèque Française. He was restored unofficially some $2^1/_2$ months later after a howl of protest from directors, stars, and writers everywhere. It continued in May with the most childish display of nationalism ever seen in the film world when the Cannes Festival was brought to an untimely halt by a group of extremists led by Godard and, surprisingly in view of his usual temperate outlook, Truffaut.

Since the spring, then, the industry has been in chaos. Productions have been postponed or virtually severed in half (like Clouzot's poor *La Prisonnière*). Business at the cinemas themselves sustained a crippling blow when projectionists joined the General Strike and Paris seemed like a city under curfew in wartime. The left-wing directors formed a self-styled "States General" of the French cinema (harking back to the Revolution), and campaigned vigorously against the "colonialist" attitudes of the Centre National du Cinéma. The closure of Cannes brought this national problem rudely into international focus. The rebels wanted the industry to be managed along Communist lines, whereby a national body would dispense financial aid to experimental and avant-garde films and not (as the Centre allegedly does now) just to commercially attractive projects. They called too for a new film school, more closely integrated with the industry and not so ineffective or unpopular as IDHEC. Technicians campaigned for shorter hours and more money.

But the fact is that unless French cinema can make the impact abroad, both on box-offices and critics, that it did some years ago, it can never recover even according to these idealistic schemes.

Statistics for 1967 now seem oddly irrelevant. 120 films produced, compared with 130 in 1966 and 142 in 1965. Only 47 of these were entirely French and cost an average of 2,840,000 francs to complete. One remarkable fact: only 4 of those French films were shot in black-and-white . . .

new and forthcoming films

BAISERS VOLÉS. *dir:* François Truffaut. *players:* Jean-Pierre Léaud, Delphine Seyrig, Claude Jade, Michel Lonsdale. For Les Films du Carrosse/Productions Artistes Associés.

MR. FREEDOM. *dir:* William Klein. *players:* John Abbey, Delphine Seyrig, Philippe Noiret, Samy Frey. For O.P.E.R.A./Les Films du Rond Point.

HO! *dir:* Robert Enrico. *players:* Jean-Paul Belmondo, Joanna Shimkus, Sidney Chaplin. For Les Films Marceau, Filmsonor (Paris)/Film (Rome).

TEL PÈRE, TEL FLIC. *dir:* Serge Korber. *players:* Adamo, Pierre Brasseur.

LA SIRÈNE DU MISSISSIPPI. *dir:* François Truffaut. *players:* Jean-Paul Belmondo, Catherine Deneuve. For Les Films du Carrosse.

LES BICHES. *dir:* Claude Chabrol. *players:* Jean-Louis Trintignant, Jacqueline Sassard, Stéphane Audran. For Films La Boétie.

FLAMMES SUR L'ADRIATIQUE. *dir:* Alexandre Astruc. *players:* Gérard Barry, Claudine Auger. For Films La Boétie.

LA FEMME INFIDÈLE. *dir:* Claude Chabrol. *players:* Stéphane Audran, Maurice Ronet, Michel Duchaussoy.

UN SOIR, UN TRAIN. *dir:* André Delvaux. *players:* Yves Montand, Anouk Aimée. For Parc Film/Fox-Europa/Les Films du Siècle.

Z. *dir:* Costa-Gavras. *players:* Yves Montand, Michel Piccoli, Irene Papas, Jean-Louis Trintignant, Jacques Perrin, Charles Denner. For O.N.I.C.

GOTO, L'ILE D'AMOUR. *dir:* Walerian Borowczyk. *players:* Pierre Brasseur, Ligia Branice, Jean-Pierre Andréani, Guy Saint-Jean. For René Thevenet/Louis Duchesne.

LA CHAMADE. *dir:* Alain Cavalier. *players:* Michel Piccoli, Catherine Deneuve, Roger van Hool. For Films Ariane, Productions Artistes Associés (Paris)/P.E.A. (Rome).

LES OUISTITIS. *dir:* François Reichenbach. *players:* Kim Cochet, J. J. Forgeot, Sylvie Daes.

MARIE POUR MÉMOIRE. *dir:* Philippe Garrel. *players:* Zouzou, Didier Léon, Nicole Laguigner, Thierry Garrel. For Philippe Garrel.

Claude Rich and Olga Georges-Picot in Alain Resnais's new film JE T'AIME, JE T'AIME.

Jeanne Moreau and Charles Denner in LA MARIÉE ÉTAIT EN NOIR.

LA MARIÉE ÉTAIT EN NOIR
(The Bride Wore Black)

Script: François Truffaut and Jean-Louis Richard, from the novel by William Irish; *Direction:* Truffaut; *Photography:* Raoul Coutard (Eastmancolor); *Music:* Bernard Herrmann; *Players:* Jeanne Moreau, Claude Rich, Jean-Claude Brialy, Charles Denner, Michel Bouquet, Michel Lonsdale, Daniel Boulanger, Alexandra Stewart. For Les Films du Carrosse, Productions Artistes Associés (Paris)/Dino De Laurentiis (Rome).

The outrageous, sometimes cruel style of Hitchcock combines with Truffaut's own warmth and sense of humour in *The Bride Wore Black*. One is reminded of *Vertigo* as Jeanne Moreau arrives like an "apparition" at Claude Rich's wedding in Cannes, and by the defenestration that follows. *Torn Curtain* comes to mind as Michel Bouquet writhes protractedly in his death agonies after drinking some poisoned arak. Bernard Herrmann's music too is made up of those throbbing chords that distinguish his scores for Hitchcock. As a polished entertainment the film is unquestionably successful, charting the widow's quest for her victims with sheer affrontery and finesse until the extended encounter with Charles Denner (the painter she kills with an arrow while posing as the goddess Diana). Here the film sags perceptibly, but happily Truffaut recovers his form with the brilliant *dénouement* as Miss Moreau (looking more than ever like Bette Davis) despatches her husband's murderer with a carving knife while she serves her long term in prison. The idiosyncrasies of each character in *The Bride Wore Black* are pinned down adroitly by the script. The widow surfaces in men's lives like a bad conscience, all the more ironical in that the original murder was a stupid mistake — **Peter Cowie.**

71

UNE HISTOIRE IMMORTELLE

Script and Direction: Orson Welles, from the story by Isak Dinesen; *Photography:* Willy Kurant; *Music:* Erik Satie; *Players:* Jeanne Moreau, Orson Welles, Roger Coggio, Norman Ashley. For Albina-Films, Paris. 58 mins.

For his new film, of little more than medium length, Orson Welles has chosen a story by Isak Dinesen (Karen Blixen). It is a variation on the favourite theme of this gifted Danish writer: man as a pawn, manipulated like a puppet by the invisible strings of Fate. An ageing American merchant in Macao, enormously rich, discusses with his secretary the story of a sailor who was invited to the bed of a young woman by her old husband. When the secretary dismisses it as a typical sailor's story, the merchant is furious and decides to make it come true. He hires a young sailor to go to bed with a woman at his sumptuous home, but he cannot command people's feelings, and dawn finds him dead in a chair, surprised by an unexpected turn in his plot.

It is a very slender story, and Welles has not quite succeeded in finding a visual counterpart to Karen Blixen's brilliant style and elaborate composition. He has made an attractive and harmonious little film, using filters and veils to achieve muted colours and a romantic mood, but he is only scratching the surface of the fable. The tempo is slightly ponderous, and even Jeanne Moreau's performance lacks her usual inspiration. Of course Welles himself is impressive as the old merchant, but *Une Histoire Immortelle* is decidedly a minor film in the career of a great director — **Arne Svensson.**

PLAYTIME

Script: Jacques Tati, with the assistance of Denise Giton, Sophie Tatischeff, and J. F. Galland; *Direction:* Tati; *Photography:* Jean Badal, Andréas Winding (Eastmancolor, 70m.m); *Editing:* Gérard Pollicand; *Music:* Francis Lemarque; *Art Direction:* Eugène Roman; *Players:* Jacques Tati, Barbara Dennek, Jacqueline Lecomte, Valerie Camille, Billy Kearns. For Specta Films (Bernard Maurice, René Silvera).

The film begins in an airport hall as a group of American tourists arrive to see Paris. Behind his cameras, Jacques Tati watches these innocents during their 36 hours in the city, with as humorous and affectionate an eye as does Monsieur Hulot on the screen. He sees them become entangled in a continual uproar of jargon, sales talk, music — and inefficiency, a state of affairs all too clearly manifest in the France of 1968. Hulot seems at a loss when confronted with the monstrous buildings and bureaucratic paraphernalia. He is constantly hailed by friends he has not seen for years or who he cannot remember, and his timid attempts at explaining himself are drowned by noise or by the louder conversations of neighbours.

The rhythmical structure of *Playtime* is extraordinary, starting slowly and quietly, gradually accelerating to the climax at the Royal Garden restaurant, and finally descending to the tranquillity of the evening departure from Orly. Sounds carry infinite weight, like the squeak of a chair as Hulot sits down tentatively in the waiting room, or the hammering footsteps of a petty official as he approaches the camera from a distance. Through the whole film peeps Tati's tolerance of human quirks, so that by the end a sense of friendship and gaiety has been instilled into everyone in *Playtime*, perhaps because of Monsieur Hulot's clumsy but sincere intrusion into events — **Peter Cowie.**

Jacques Tati and Barbara Dennek.

73

West Germany

introduction   by Peter F. Gallasch

The cinema situation in Western Germany in 1968 was marked by two developments: the arrival and success of the third wave of young directors and their films, and the first organised appearance of West German underground film. About 80 full length feature films have so far been completed or are in the making, by young film-makers. Their rank and file do not, however, include a group of young Hamburg leftist authors, directors and cameramen who dislike commercial cinema so much that they prefer even not showing their films to the public to coming to terms with the established film industry. Instead they founded a cooperative of their own to arrange screenings in "closed circuit". In Spring 1968 they had their own "festival" at Hamburg, mostly attended by fellow travellers and students of Hamburg University. While these young people will, for the time being, not conquer the West German film market, their "elders" have already succeeded. On the other hand the Hamburg group and their sympathisers point out that the successful young directors *did* succeed, but at the price of selling themselves to a corrupt industry. The Hamburg group started trouble at this year's Oberhausen short film festival by showing a pornographic attack on Bonn's official film promotion law. While all this happened West Germany's established film industry turned out another batch of conventional and mostly uninteresting films.

new and forthcoming films

DIE GOLDENE PILLE. *dir:* Horst Manfred Adloff. *phot:* Michael Marszalek. *players:* Petra Pauly, Inge Marschall, Claudia Butenuth, Horst Naumann.
ENGELCHEN ODER DIE JUNGFRAU VON BAMBERG. *dir:* Marran Gosov. *phot:* Werner Kurz. *players:* Gila von Weitershausen, Uli Koch, Dieter Augustin, Gudrun Vöge, Hans Clarin.
NEGRESCO. *dir:* Klaus Lemke. *phot:* Michael Marszalek. *players:* Ira Fürstenberg, Gérard Blain, Serge Marquand, Christa Linder, Ricky Cooper, Paul Hubschmid.
TAMARA. *dir:* Hansjürgen Pohland. *phot:* Robert van Ackeren, Jürgen Jürges. *players:* Petrus Schloemp, Hansi Linder, Wolfgang Preiss, Barbara Rütting, Hans-Peter Hallwachs.
JET GENERATION. *dir:* Eckhart Schmidt. *phot:* Gernot Roll. *players:* Dginn Moeller, Roger Fritz, Jürgen Draeger, Isiter Jung, Yella Bleyler.
MAKE LOVE NOT WAR. *dir:* Werner Klett. *phot:* Perikles Papadopoulos. *players:* Gibson Kemp, Claudia Bremer, Heinz-Karl Diesing.
DIE ARTISTEN IN DER ZIRKUSKUPPEL: RATLÖS. *dir:* Alexander Kluge.
LEBENZEICHEN. *dir:* Werner Herzog. *players:* Peter Brogle, Wolfgang Reichmann, Athina Zacharopoulou.

MIT EICHENLAUB UND FEIGENBLATT. *dir:* Franz-Josef Spieker. *phot:* Wolfgang Fischer. *players:* Werner Enke, Birke Bruck, Hans Fries, Christian Friedel, Ariana Calix.

PAARUNGEN. *dir:* Michael Verhoeven. *phot:* Henning Kristiansen. *players:* Lili Palmer, Paul Verhoeven, Karl Michael Vogler, Ilona Grübel, Michael von Harbach.

KURZER PROZESS. *dir:* Michael Kehlmann. *phot:* Karl Schröder. *players:* Helmut Qualtinger, Alexander Kerst, Otto Tensig, Kurt Sowinetz.

Titles of other West German films produced during the Year:
Geständnis eines Mädchens, Treibgut der Großstadt, Der Mönch mit der Peitsche, Mister Dynamit — morgen küßt euch der Tod, Feuer frei auf Frankie, Seitenstraßen der Prostitution, Fast ein Held, Heißes Pflaster Köln, Geheimnis Leben, Wenn es Nacht wird auf der Reeperbahn, Das große Glück, Liebesnächte in der Taiga, Die Schlangengrube und das Pendel, Helga, Mittsommernacht, Tränen trocknet der Wind . . ., Spur eines Mädchens, Der Lügner und die Nonne, Eine Handvoll Helden, Herrliche Zeiten im Spessart, Tanja — die Nackte von der Teufelsinsel, 48 Stunden bis Acapulco, Wenn Ludwig ins Manöver zieht, Rheinsberg, Die Heiden von Kummerow und ihre lustigen Streiche, Heubodengeflüster, Heißer Sand auf Sylt, Der Hund von Blackwood Castle, Der nächste Herr — dieselbe Dame, Die Wirtin von der Lahn, Unruhige Töchter, Das Wunder der Liebe, Vulkan der höllischen Triebe, Die Abenteuer des Kardinal Braun, Straßenbekanntschaften auf St. Pauli, Dynamit in grüner Seide, . . . und noch nicht sechzehn, Sünde mit Rabatt, Lux mundi, Wegen Reichstums geschlossen.

DER SANFTE LAUF

Script: Haro Senft and Hans Noever; *Direction:* Senft; *Photography:* Jan Curik; *Editing:* Thurid Söhnlein; *Music:* Erich Ferstl; *Players:* Bruno Ganz, Verena Buss, Wolfgang Büttner, Lia Eibenschütz, Hans Putz, Dany Mann, Jan Kacer. For Haro Senft Filmproduktion. 81 mins.

Bernhard got into trouble in an inn by knocking down a man who pronounced his hatred of the Jews. When leaving prison he tries to come to terms with society although his feelings do not correspond with practical purposes. He falls in love with the daughter of a rich industrialist who promotes Bernhard's carreer because he regards the young man as his coming son-in-law. A short trip to Prague reveals the arrogance of West German VIPs towards Eastern countries, and people. Finally Bernhard gives in and lives up to his easy life. Haro Senft, renowned short film-maker, has made his first full length feature a convincing example of how the group of new German directors are able to suceed if they manage to endure difficulties of organisation, money and so forth. His first film is a model of vivid dialogue and acting, of precise observation of contemporary youths and their way of life and thinking, brilliantly photographed by the Czech cameraman Jan Curik and acted with spontaneity and naturalism.

Der sanfte Lauf is thought-provoking and intelligent, forcing the spectator to draw his own conclusions.

TÄTOWIERUNG

Script: Günter Herburger; *Direction:* Johannes Schaaf; *Photography:* Wolf Wirth; *Players:* Helga Anders, Christof Wackernagel, Rosemarie Fendel, Alexander May. For Rob Houwer. 86 mins. British dist: Cinecenta.

A 16 year old West Berlin boy leaves an orphanage and joins a wealthy family who take him in as their son. He falls in love with the daughter of his fosterfather. Soon he starts to dislike the permanent and pressing care of the family and to stand up against them. At the end of the film he shoots his fosterfather in an act of despair. Günter Herburger, one of the foremost young writers on the West German literary scene, and Johannes Schaaf, a prominent television director, have given us a film that articulates the problems and antagonisms of the generation which a few months later launched their spectacular uprising: a generation of youngsters who hate the establishment and official order, who prefer anarchy to sterile rules of life. Sometimes they just fight out of sheer opposition against what ever confronts them at any given moment. Herburger and Schaaf, however, have achieved something more: they dispel the rosy image of West Berlin as the bulwark against Bolshevism; they show the city as a place for tourists who love the sensation of being able to peep over The Wall and see genuine, living Communists. Wolf Wirth, once a wonderful and promising cameraman, and during the past few years responsible for a great deal of over-glamorous photography in commercial films, has given Herburger and Schaaf's film a fine sense of pictorial awareness and quality.

ZUR SACHE, SCHÄTZCHEN

Script and Direction: May Spils; *Photography:* Klaus König; *Players:* Werner Enke, Uschi Glas, Henry van Lyck, Inge Marschall, Helmut Brasch. For Peter Schamoni. 80 mins.

Two Munich students, Martin and Henry, live the typical life of young hoboes: drinking a lot and doing nothing, pulling Metropolitan Police's legs and nourishing their private philosophy. Martin falls in love with Barbara, daughter of a wealthy family. He hopes that she will save him from his present life which to a certain degree he detests. But things refuse to go the way he wishes. May Spils (26), whose short film *Portrait* gained acclaim at Oberhausen, has made a witty, nonsensical and sophisticated film which has even achieved commercial success, running for weeks and weeks in West German cinemas. Though critics hailed it as a wonderfully light-hearted and funny affair and placed it high among recent young films, the Selection Committee at Cannes did not accept the film for the 1968 Festival, claiming it did not reach the quality level required. May Spils, a highly talented girl, is, however, regarded as a hope for West German film. *Zur Sache, Schätzchen* seems to be the first genuine proof that young film-makers in the Federal Republic do not merely turn out serious and gloomy films, but may also develop strains of humour.

Verena Buss and Bruno Ganz look out over Prague in DER SANFTE LAUF.

Uschi Glas and Werner Enke in ZUR SACHE, SCHATZCHEN, produced by Peter Schamoni and directed by May Spils.

CHRONIK DER ANNA MAGDALENA BACH

Script: Jean-Marie Straub and Danièle Huillet; *Direction:* Straub. *Photography:* Ugo Piccone; *Editing:* Straub; *Players:* Gustav Leonhardt, Christiane Lang. For Franz Seitz/IDI Cinematografica. 90 mins.

This is a film of highhy ascetic quality, made by a young director who has never conceded to commercial pressures, and who has never become a traitor to his own ideals. As in his first full length feature film *Nicht versöhnt*, an adaptation of Böll's novel "Billiard um halb zehn", he has worked without professional actors. Johann Sebastian Bach, his wife and his friends are played by musicians who do not perform; rather merely live themselves before the camera. The film tells the story of a composer who was forced to corrupt himself in order to survive. Long passages of Bach music are played and photographed by an almost unmoving camera; documents are shown; the atmosphere is as calm as that of Ozu's films, though Straub would never like to be named a follower of the renowned Japanese director. In Ozu however, it is the language of fine and beautiful images which play their role in the structure of his films. For Straub, images just exist and often do not even correspond with the philosophical background of what he wants to tell the spectator. His film is at one and the same time a historical recording of real events and a timeless, perennial story of man's suffering. This is not a suitable film for the commercial cinema, but an interesting experiment in how far a director can go in articulating his personal ideas without bending to the visual desires of the public.

East Germany

the current scene   by Stanley Forman

Most of the outstanding developments in GDR cinema in 1968 have been in the documentary field. However, one exciting feature film that does merit international attention is Konrad Wolf's *I Was 19*. Set in Nazi times, it is a semi-autobiographical account of a young teenage German, the son of parents living in political exile in the Soviet Union who returns to Germany with the Red Army. The film is tenderly made, straightforward and unpretentious, and rings profoundly true. A new young actor named Jeakki Schwarz gives a beautifully rounded performance as the hero. *I Was 19* is a film to watch for, dealing as it does with an aspect of the war never previously touched upon. Konrad Wolf has a rare talent, and it is surely timely for him to tackle a theme concerned with present day problems and life in the GDR.

Without doubt the best achievement among documentaries is the mammoth, 4-part *Pilots in Pyjamas*, an account of the visit paid to North Vietnam by Walter Heynowski and Gerhard Scheumann. The films consist of 10 interviews in depth with American pilots shot down over North Vietnam. They are made cleanly and clinically in the style developed by this GDR team in *The Laughing Man* (reviewed in IFG 1968). By some strange alchemy, these 4 full-length films reveal a good deal more about the American condition and the climate that could provoke the murder of Martin Luther King and the Kennedys than any other films I have seen. This group (originally shown as a series on television) constitutes a remarkable achievement that will stand the test of time.

Two films of merit in quite a different genre have been made by Richard Cohn-Vissen and Karl Gass. They are about the Brecht composer *Paul Dessau*, and a singer of Brecht, *Ernst Busch*. Gass's film on Busch is somewhat below his usual high standard, but is interesting for the personal picture it gives of the singer. Cohn-Vossen's *Paul Dessau* is quite brilliant, a charming fusion of Dessau talking about his work and his feelings, Dessau rehearsing his Bach variations with an orchestra, and Dessau (at his happiest) giving a lesson in elementary composition to a class of very young children. At the end of the half hour one really knows the essence of Dessau, and he emerges as one of the liveliest musical brains in Europe today.

Some mention should be made in this brief review to the recent activities of the Thorndikes (of *German Story* and *Russian Miracle* fame). They have been engaged on the GDR'S first 70 mm full length documentary, *The Germans*. It is now nearing completion and should provide a great stimulus to the next Leipzig Documentary Film Festival where it will no doubt have a prominent place.

In short, GDR films are doing very well indeed in the field of what one might term "long shorts" (their popular scientific films and research films are also first-class), but one still awaits the first group of features that will dig deeply and truly into life in the GDR here and now.

79

PLANET FILM DISTRIBUTORS Ltd

**Independent
Producers and Distributors:**

*for United Kingdom
Distribution of:*

"THE 10TH VICTIM"
Marcello Mastroianni   Ursula Andress

"THE PAWNBROKER"
Rod Steiger

"CHIMES AT MIDNIGHT"
Orson Welles

"THE TRAMPLERS"
Joseph Cotten

"NIGHT OF THE BIG HEAT"
Christopher Lee   Peter Cushing (Guest Star)

"DUTCHMAN"

**III, WARDOUR ST.,
LONDON, W.I.**

Great Britain

introduction   by Peter Cowie

Probably over 40 million dollars are being invested annually in "British" films by American companies, and nobody seems to be suffering as a result. On the contrary, this finance has helped to raise the prestige of the British cinema abroad to the level of the early sixties and higher. Polanski, Kubrick, Lester, and even Godard have been at work in London.

Statistics continue to look gloomy, however. The number of cinemas in operation has plunged dangerously compared with Germany, France, Spain, Japan, and the U.S.A. At the end of May 1968 only 1,743 theatres were open, even if more and more of these were being renovated and converted into smaller, more intimate auditoriums to meet the demands of a new generation of filmgoers. In the West End of London alone the Plaza and Paramount at Piccadilly Circus, the Odeons at Marble Arch and Leicester Square, the Leicester Square Theatre, and the ICA Theatre in the Mall were either opened or refurbished during the year under review.

Attendances in 1967 fell too, by more than 900,000 per week. The total amount of "Eady Money", the tax fund which is used to encourage the making of British films, is being reduced, although the new regulations will enable more low-budget films, often the most exciting creatively and also the most lucrative, to be embarked upon.

new and forthcoming films

ALL NEAT IN BLACK STOCKINGS. *dir:* Christopher Morahan. *players:* Victor Henry, Jack Shepherd, Vanessa Forsyth. *prod:* Leon Clore for Anglo-Amalgamated release.
SECRET CEREMONY. *dir:* Joseph Losey. *players:* Elizabeth Taylor, Robert Mitchum, Mia Farrow, Peggy Ashcroft. *prod:* John Heyman and Norman Priggen for Universal release.
THE LION IN WINTER. *dir:* Anthony Harvey. *players:* Peter O'Toole, Katharine Hepburn, Jane Merrow, John Castle. *prod:* Martin Poll for Joseph E. Levine/Embassy release.
INTERLUDE. *dir:* Kevin Billington. *players:* Oskar Werner, Barbara Ferris. *prod:* Domino (David Deutsch) for Columbia release.
THE BED SITTING-ROOM. *dir:* Richard Lester. *players:* Ralph Richardson, Rita Tushingham, Jimmy Edwards. *prod:* Oscar Lewenstein and Richard Lester for United Artists release.
DECLINE AND FALL. *dir:* John Krish. *players:* Colin Blakely, Robert Harris, Leo McKern, Genevieve Page. *prod:* Ivan Foxwell for Fox release.

Triangle Film Productions Ltd

Associated with
**L'EDITION FRANÇAISE
CINEMATOGRAPHIQUE**

Represented in U.S.A. by
Annette Honan, 196 Garth Road
Scarsdale, New York 10583

"MIDNIGHT EPISODE"
"LEONARDO DA VINCI"
"VAN GOGH"
"MOLIÈRE"
"BERNARD SHAW"
"CHOPIN"

"CHINESE THEATRE" (Eastmancolor)
"TEIVA" (Eastmancolor)
"THE SIXTH DAY OF CREATION" (Eastmancolor)
"CORSICA" (Eastmancolor)
"MONT ST. MICHEL" (Eastmancolor)
"SEEDS IN THE WIND"
"SALVADOR DALI" (Eastmancolor)
"HUNGRY EARTH"
"EDITH PIAF"
"IS VENICE SINKING?" (Eastmancolor)

In preparation:
"FOG ON THE RIVER" (Eastmancolor)
"BYRON" & "SHELLEY"

Directors Théodora Olembert   Jan Read   Rodney Phillips
15 Oslo Court, Prince Albert Rd. London N.W. 8 722 5656

THE TOUCHABLES. *dir:* Robert Freeman. *players:* Judy Huxtable, Esther Anderson, Marilyn Richard, Kathy Simmonds. *prod:* John Bryan for 20th. Century-Fox release.

THREE INTO TWO WON'T GO. *dir:* Peter Hall. *players:* Rod Steiger, Claire Bloom, Judy Geeson, Peggy Ashcroft. *prod:* Julian Blaustein for Universal release.

ONE PLUS ONE. *dir:* Jean-Luc Godard. *players:* Anne Wiazemsky, Ian Quarrier, The Rolling Stones. *prod:* Cupid Productions.

NEGATIVES. *dir:* Peter Medak. *players:* Peter McEnery, Diane Cilento, Glenda Jackson, Billy Russell. *prod:* Judd Bernard for Paramount.

SINFUL DAVEY. *dir:* John Huston. *players:* John Hurt, Pamela Franklin, Nigel Davenport. *prod:* William N. Graf for United Artists release.

BOOM. *dir:* Joseph Losey. *players:* Elizabeth Taylor, Richard Burton, Noël Coward, Joanna Shimkus. *prod:* John Heyman and Norman Priggen for Universal release.

OEDIPUS THE KING. *dir:* Philip Saville. *players:* Christopher Plummer, Richard Johnson, Orson Welles, Lilli Palmer. *prod:* Michael Luke for Universal release.

THE BOFORS GUN. *dir:* Jack Gold. *players:* Nicol Williamson, Ian Holm, David Warner. *prod:* Robert A. Goldston and Otto Plaschkes for Universal release.

THE ADVENTURES OF GERARD. *dir:* Jerzy Skolimowski. *player:* Peter McEnery. *prod:* Henry Lester and Gene Gutowski for United Artists release.

THE MILLSTONE. *dir:* Waris Hussein. *players:* Sandy Dennis, Eleanor Bron. *prod:* Palomar.

A NICE GIRL LIKE ME. *dir:* Desmond Davis. *player:* Barbara Ferris. *prod:* Anglo-Embassy/Embassy.

THE BIRTHDAY PARTY. *dir:* William Friedkin. *players:* Robert Shaw, Patrick Magee, Moultrie Kelsall, Helen Fraser. *prod:* Harold Pinter and William Friedkin for Palomar.

THE RECKONING. *dir:* Volker Schlöndorff. *players:* David Warner, Anna Karina. *prod:* Jerry Bick, Elliott Kastner, and Claude Ganz for Columbia release.

THE SEA GULL. *dir:* Sidney Lumet. *players:* Vanessa Redgrave, James Mason, Simone Signoret, David Warner. *prod:* Warner Bros./Seven Arts.

THE KILLING OF SISTER GEORGE. *dir:* Robert Aldrich. *players:* Beryl Reid, Susannah York, Coral Browne. *prod:* The Associates & Aldrich/Palomar.

IF. *dir:* Lindsay Anderson. *players:* Richard Warwick, Malcolm McDowell, Peter Jeffrey. *prod:* Lindsay Anderson and Michael Medwin for Paramount release.

83

Bowman's one-man pod tries to retrieve the corpse of Astronaut Poole in 2001:A SPACE ODYSSEY.

2001
A Space Odyssey

Script: Stanley Kubrick and Arthur C. Clarke, based partly on the short story "The Sentinel" by Clarke; *Direction:* Kubrick; *Photography:* Geoffrey Unsworth (Metrocolor, Super Pana-vision-Cinerama); *Editing:* Ray Lovejoy; *Music:* Richard Strauss, Johann Strauss, Aram Khachaturian, György Ligeti; *Art Direction:* John Hoesli; *Special Effects:* Wally Veevers, Douglas Trumbull, Con Pederson, Tom Howard; *Players:* Keir Dullea, Gary Lockwood, William Sylvester, Daniel Richter, Douglas Rain. For M-G-M. 141 mins.

Arthur C. Clarke and Stanley Kubrick share a disenchanted view of man's prospects on this planet, Clarke in stories like *If I Forget Thee, Earth . . .* and *Expedition to Earth*, and Kubrick in *Paths of Glory* and *Dr. Strangelove*. All the multitudinous and sometimes admittedly prolix ideas in *2001* spring from the premise that a superior intelligence has watched over man since he first grovelled to escape from ape-hood, and will do so even when his spaceships comb the solar system. The development of computers (and HAL9000 obviously rivals his masters) is a crucial link with this omniscient, impassive life force expressed in the film by the gleaming monolith on earth, on the moon, and in the space above Jupiter.

Man, the script suspects, has the potential of a machine while a machine has the potential of man. At times, and especially when he is robbed of his memory banks, HAL9000 seems more vulnerable and more humane than the sluggish, robot-like men who accompany him.

This spell-binding film, a masterpiece of the science-fiction genre, has a visual flair and grace that temper the sinister implications of its theme. On the one hand there is the psychedelic voyage "beyond the infinite" that flings up images belonging to some 21st century Book of Revelations; on the other, the serene flow of traffic between moon and earth, set to the music of "The Blue Danube". By relating so intimately how man will live two generations from now, Kubrick and Clarke extol his ingenuity and his capacity for learning, always warning him that he is puny in the context of the stars — **Peter Cowie.**

THE DANCE OF THE VAMPIRES

Script: Roman Polanski and Gerard Brach; *Direction:* Polanski; *Photography:* Douglas Slocombe (Metrocolor/Panavision); *Editing:* Alastair McIntyre; *Music:* Christopher (Kryzsztof) Komeda; *Art Direction:* Fred Carter; *Players:* Jack MacGowran, Roman Polanski, Sharon Tate, Alfie Bass, Ferdy Mayne, Terry Downes. For Cadre Films-Filmways/M-G-M. 107 mins (in Britain).

Polanski's long-awaited parody of horror films emerges as a visual delight, full of livid greys and greens, weirdly draped halls and corridors, and characters who revel in the atmosphere of Grand Guignol. The director himself is Alfred, the cherry-faced, tremulous, and faithful pupil of Professor Abronsius. During a stay at a Transylvanian inn, Sarah, the publican's daughter whose foam bathing has intrigued Alfred, is dragged through a skylight by a marauder. The Professor and his assistant pursue them by sledge to a nearby castle and there encounter a melancholy Count, flanked by his homosexual werewolf of a son, and a slobbering hunchback who acts as a porter.

Polanski's blend of manic humour and grisly settings is absolutely fitted to his tale. By his own example he imposes a uniform style of breathless, almost lusty acting on his players. The *pièce de résistance* is the midnight Ball of the Dead in the castle, with Alfred, the Professor, and Sarah joining in a mirthless dance in order to escape detection by the Count. Until, of course, they notice that only three figures are reflected in the huge wall mirrors ... *The Dance of the Vampires* succeeds because, like the best parodies, it bears its subject both respect and affection, and for all its slapstick interludes, can be classed with the masterpieces of Dreyer and Murnau in its imaginative conception of horror (never forgetting Pierre Etaix's devastating short, *Insomnie*) — **Peter Cowie.**

CHARLIE BUBBLES

Script: Shelagh Delaney; *Direction:* Albert Finney; *Photography:* Peter Suschitzky (Technicolor); *Editing:* Fergus McDonell; *Music:* Misha Donat; *Art Direction:* Jose Macavin; *Players:* Albert Finney, Colin Blakely, Billie Whitelaw, Liza Minnelli. For Memorial Enterprises/Universal.

The predicament of the newly rich in Britain's affluent society is the central point of *Charlie Bubbles*, a film that with its restraint and subtle comment shows Finney to be as good a director as he is an actor. Finney the actor does not dominate *Charlie Bubbles* as much as one might expect. He is supposed to be a successful writer, and though he radiates no literary talent, he stands for all those whizz kids on the verge of middle age who have only their paper money to give in exchange for services rendered. He is bored with the dishonesty of his existence — the London house with its closed circuit television, the American secretary whose headpiece lies abandoned on the pillow as she stirs him to make love, the football match that through the glass of the directors' box yields only a vague and insubstantial drama. Contrasted effectively with this luxury is the moorland farm where Charlie's ex-wife (Billie Whitelaw) lives with their son, and where Charlie sees the boy being spoilt just as he has been spoilt by success. His final ascent into the undemanding skies by balloon stretches the allegorical framework of the script too far, but the achievement of *Charlie Bubbles* lies in the earlier scenes, in its discreet treatment of a flashy and apparently unimportant life, in its communication of sexual indolence and bought privacy — **Peter Cowie.**

Albert Finney and Billie Whitelaw in CHARLIE BUBBLES.

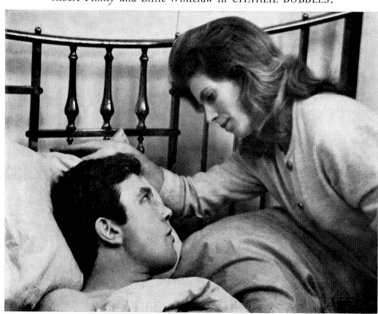

Scotland

Film production in Scotland is steadily extending in range. Recognising that feature film-making is necessary to make an impact on international audiences, Films of Scotland (3 Randolph Crescent, Edinburgh 3) took the initiative in having a film commissioned by the Children's Film Foundation, through a Scottish unit, International Film Associates (Scotland) Ltd. The success of this film, *Flash the Sheepdog*, which was awarded the young pioneer's vote at the Moscow Film Festival, has led to a further commissioning. Another C.F.F. picture, *The Big Catch*, scripted by the young Scottish writer Charles Gormley, was directed by Laurence Henson, produced by him and Edward McConnell, who also photographed the film. This is a story of one-up-man-ship between two boys, the one town, the other country bred, and is told against the rugged seafaring villages of Wester Ross and their Aegean-like Summer Isles.

IFA are also producing, for Films of Scotland, a new impressionistic film for the Harris Tweed Association, a film to inter-weave the manufacture of this uniquely hand-loomed cloth with the lives of the Hebridean islanders. Shot in Techniscope, the film will rely on sound and musical associations to carry its story. IFA have in addition completed an architectural film profile on Britain's most famous modern architect, Charles Rennie Mackintosh. **Mackintosh** has a music score by Frank Spedding, in total sympathy with the architect's own emergence from the Art Nouveau of *fin de siècle* Glasgow to the strength of his later pioneering work. Shot by Edward McConnell and Oscar Marzaroli, *Mackintosh* was written and directed by Murray Grigor for Films of Scotland and the Scottish Arts Council.

Other IFA films include one for the new town of Livingston, near Edinburgh, and a sponsored 16 mm account of the international refractory manufacturer, John G. Stein & Co. Ltd. Both have been produced for Films of Scotland.

The story of Inverness as told in *Highland Capital*, produced by Campbell Harper Films (8 Hill Street, Edinburgh) for Films of Scotland and the Inverness and Loch Ness Tourist Association, is the story of a meeting place down through the ages. The outline treatment by Neil Gunn is well evoked in the opening sequence along Loch Ness, photographed by the young cameraman, Mark Littlewood.

Aberdeen, as another holiday centre, is covered in a new film produced by Templar Film Studios (7 Lynedoch Street, Glasgow C.3) for Films of Scotland and the Aberdeen City Corporation. Templars have also been engaged in projects that include *Book Production* for Collins and *Euclid in Scotland*.

Robin Crichton, of Edinburgh Film Productions (Marfield, Penicuik, Midlothian) continues to enlarge his film-making activities and is devoting his attention to the development of what amounts to Scotland's first film studio. Plans for a mobile projection theatre (twin tracks) will provide a useful facility for visiting production companies. Crichton lays great importance on this, hoping that it will stimulate European film and television effort in Scotland. He has already assisted in the Scottish contribution for an international folk-lore series produced by Horstfilm, Germany.

Cumbernauld as a community is the theme for Crichton's most ambitious documentary to date, to be produced in association with Films of Scotland. Concentrating on the people that inhabit Britain's most successful "new town", the film will not be hindered by the striking architecture that saddles Cumbernauld hill.

Architecture, following the film *Mackintosh* produced for the 1968 Edinburgh Festival Centenary Exhibition, continues to be a theme for Educational Films of Scotland (16-17 Woodside Terrace, Glasgow C.3.). *Sir William Bruce* (1630-1710) produced by Douglas Gray (Park Films, 3 Park Terrace, Glasgow C.3.), brings the subject up to the time of the well known Adam family. And *Alexander "Greek" Thomson*, (1817-1875) Glasgow's Classical Victorian architect, is the subject for a film profile by William Thompson. The same architect features in *Battle of the Styles* (Park Films): here his classical architecture is finally defeated by the growing prevalence for English Gothic in late Victorian Glasgow.

Other subjects include *The Highland Buzzard* by C. E. Palmar and *Hugh Mac-Diarmid at Work* (Park Films).

From CHARLES RENNIE MACKINTOSH, a 30 minute Eastmancolor appreciation of this important architect. Produced by I.F.A. (Scotland) Ltd. for Films of Scotland, and directed by Murray Grigor.

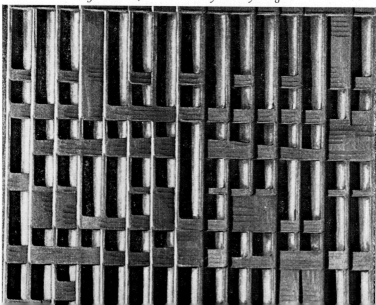

From BIG CATCH, a one-hour Eastmancolor feature produced by I.F.A. (Scotland) Ltd., for the Children's Film Foundation, and directed by Laurence Henson.

INTERNATIONAL FILM ASSOCIATES (SCOTLAND) LIMITED
1 Park Terrace Glasgow C3   **DOUglas 3620**

The Edinburgh Film Productions crew in action

EDINBURGH FILM PRODUCTIONS

Production and Facilities

**By Penicuik, Midlothian, Scotland
Telephone Penicuik 154 or 864**

Hungary

introduction by Peter Cowie

Attendances at Hungarian cinemas have nearly trebled since 1950, and now, with some 50,000 high school pupils studying film aesthetics, the figures should move still further upwards. There have been three major flowerings of the postwar Hungarian film. The neo-realist pictures like *Somewhere in Europe* and *The Soil under your Feet* in the late forties; the classic productions of Zoltán Fábri in the mid-fifties (like *Professor Hannibal* and *Merry-Go-Round*); and the enthusiastic activity of the late sixties, which has reflected the struggle for social progress and national independence of the last decade. Gaál, Kósa, Herskó, Jancsó, Kovács, Bacsó, Sándor, and Szabó constitute a formidable "school" of directors. All of them are fighting against the alienation of the individual in contemporary life.

Furthermore, the production system of the Hungarian cinema has been reformed this year. As Róbert Bán has written, after a script has been completed (with the eventual director also involved), it will be submitted to the film department of the Hungarian Ministry of Education. The script is then either approved or (where there are extreme moral or political objections) rejected within two weeks. If the idea is authorised, then the production group will be given 2 million forints from the state budget. This, in practice, means between 40% and 60% of the film's costs. The rest of the budget can be met by Hungarofilm, the foreign trading company, or by MOKEP, which distributes the films domestically. Obviously, the system is still in its teething stages, but it should bring Hungary into line with countries like Sweden, Denmark, and Yugoslavia where similar arrangements have proved successful and stimulating to production.

forthcoming films

THE PAUL STREET BOYS *(A Pál utcai fiuk)*. *dir:* Zoltán Fábri. *script:* Zoltán Fábri and Endre Bohem, based on the novel by Ferenc Molnár. *phot:* György Illés. *players:* Anthony Kemp, William Burleigh, John Moulder-Brown, Julian Holdaway. For Bohem Associates (Hollywood) and Mafilm Studio I (Budapest).
SHOT IN THE HEAD *(Fejlövés)*. *dir:* Péter Bacsó. *script:* Péter Zimre and Péter Bacsó. *phot:* János Zsombolyai. *players:* Kati Kovács, József Méhler, Károly Horváth.
YOU'VE BEEN A PROPHET, MY DEAR *(Próféta voltál, szivem)*. *dir:* Pál Zolnay. *script:* Ferenc Szécsényi and Pál Zolnay. *phot:* Ferenc Szécsényi. *players:* Ivan Darvas, Kati Berek, Tünde Szabó, Teri Torday.
THE STARS OF EGER *(Egri csillagok)*. *dir:* Zoltán Várkonyi. *script:* István

Nemeskürty, from the novel by Géza Gárdonyi. *phot:* István Hildebrand. *players:* Vera Venczel, István Kovács, Imre Sinkovits, Tibor Bitskey.
ESZTERKE. *dir:* Róbert Bán. *script:* Péter Müller, based on an idea by Tamás Bárány. *phot:* Miklós Herczenik. *players:* Judit Halász, Mariann Moór, László Tahi Tóth, Ferenc Kállai, László Márkus.
BEFORE GOD AND MAN *(Isten és ember elótt).* *dir:* Károly Makk. *script:* Lajos Galambos. *phot:* János Tóth. *players:* Slobodanka Markovic, Zoran Becic. Irén Psota, János Görbe, Jácint Juhász, Lajos Balázsovits.

AGENTS for all Hungarofilm productions are kept well informed of studio plans and activities. In England, applications should be made to: Ian R. Warren, London and Overseas Film Services Ltd., 3 Vere Street, London W.1. In **France**, to: Zoltan Mohos, Intercontinental Film, 79 Champs-Elysées, Paris VIII. In **West Germany**, to: Alexander S. Scotti, Interfilm, Kapellenstrasse 34, Wiesbaden.

Ferenc Kósa was born in Nyíregyháza in 1937. He graduated from the Budapest Academy for Dramatic and Film Art in 1963. Since then, he has worked as assistant at the Hungarian Film Studios. He completed three shorts *(Etude about a Working Day, Light,* and *Notes on the History of a Lake)*, before embarking on his first feature, *Ten Thousand Suns* (1967), which won the Prize for Best Direction at Cannes, and, although tending to be slow and self-conscious at times, revealed him as a director with an acute understanding of his country's recent history and an eye for composition in depth on the wide screen.

István Gaál was born in Salgótarján in 1933. He worked for a while as an electro-technician, and did not graduate at the Academy for Dramatic and Film Art until 1959. But immediately afterwards he went to Centro Sperimentale in Rome for 4 terms, and this may account for his fluid, almost Latin style of direction. Since 1958 he has shot several shorts, newsreels, and documentaries. His three feature films are *Current* (1964), which has enthused a whole generation of film-goers in Hungary, *The Green Years,* and *Baptism,* which deals with the antagonism between two school friends when they have grown up and find themselves morally, politically and emotionally opposed to each other.

Zoltán Latinovits and Eva Ruttkay in István Gaál's new film, BAPTISM.

CSILLAGOSOK, KATONÁK
(The Red and the White)

Script: Georgi Mdivani, Gyula Hernádi, Miklós Jancsó; *Direction:* Jancsó; *Photography:* Tamás Somló; *Editing:* Zoltán Farkas; *Art Direction:* N.I.Thobotariev; *Players:* Tatyana Konyukova, Krystyna Mikolaiewska, Mikhaïl Kozakov, Viktor Avdiushko. For Mafilm Studio No. IV (Budapest) / Mosfilm (Moscow). 92 mins.

It has been said that if Miklós Jancsó were to make a film about the Nazi concentration camps, it would be the first time that the real humiliation of that period had been grasped by the cinema. In *The Red and the White,* set in Russia during the bleak civil war of 1918, men and women are stripped naked and stand meekly, almost complaisantly, beneath the eyes of their guards. A group of Reds is exterminated in a decrepit, walled town. Some nurses from a field hospital are forced to dance with each other in a woodland glade. These mesmeric scenes are Jancsó's method of describing humiliation, which for him is as contagious and corrupting a disease as any mankind has discovered. He chooses a war setting because in war the slender barriers of civilised behaviour are swept aside and sadists flourish. In *The Red and the White* he keeps deliberately aloof from his characters, watching them like a hawk, just as the unidentified monoplanes wheel in arcs above the fugitives in *My Way Home.* He packs a tremendous degree of detail into each shot, accentuating the implacability of his theme by using very marked black and white tones in the photography. Like all his films, *The Red and the White* is concerned with the business of survival. This gives it a powerful, gripping tension, and a respect for personal honour. It would surely have won the Palme d'Or at Cannes 1968 had the competition been concluded — **Peter Cowie.**

Two new films by Miklós Jancsó; THE RED AND THE WHITE (above), and SILENCE AND CRY (below).

FALAK
(Walls)

Script and Direction: András Kovács; *Photography:* György Illés; *Music:* Mikis Theodorakis and Ismael; *Players:* Miklós Gábor, Zoltán Latinovits, Philippe March, Zsuzsa Bánki, Mári Szemes, Bernadette Lafont, Andrea Drahot: Judit Tóth. For Mafilm Studio No. I.

András Kovács is a deeply committed director who focuses his entire attention on the state of Hungary today: the predicament of its rootless intellectuals and of those in positions of responsibility. *Cold Days* dealt with men who had suffered from the stress of war. Kovács's latest film, *Walls*, revolves round a dilemma of contemporary political conscience. Benkó, the engineer whose return to Budapest from an overseas trip will decide the future of his friend and subordinate, Ambrus, is a 40 year-old with experience of the various phases of Hungary's postwar development. In Paris he talks through the night with an old friend, an *émigré* since the 1956 Uprising, about his right to intervene in the case awaiting him in Budapest. To be a passive observer, or an active member of Communist society — this is the question posed by the film.

While the interest of Jancsó's work lies chiefly in its imagery, in *Walls* the dialogue holds all the subtleties and weight of meaning. Kovács admits that the meagre action (the waiting for the plane, the journey across Paris) is a pretext for the film and its conversations. The unique strength of *Walls* is its marriage of public and private problems. Each of its many characters typifies a branch of opinion and morality in modern Hungary — **Peter Cowie.**

Zoltán Latinovits and Andrea Drahota in Kovács's WALLS.

A shot from CLOWNS ON THE WALLS, directed by Pál Sándor.

BAHÓC A FALON
(Clowns on the Walls)

Script: Zsuzsa Tóth and Pál Sándor; *Direction:* Sándor; *Photography:* János Zsombolyai; *Music:* Zdenkó Tamássy; *Players:* Gábor Ferenczi, Balázs Tardi, Miklós Szurdi, Vera Venczel. For Mafilm Studio No. III. 74 mins.

Clowns on the Walls smacks of a fresh and uninhibited approach to young life in Hungary. Kiki, the likeable adolescent hero, shelters from a storm on the shores of Lake Balaton. But he is trapped in a tiny room when the owners of the cottage arrive unexpectedly. His two friends squeeze out through a small hole in the roof; Kiki stays behind, and, to pass the time, he falls to inventing incidents about his youth. They mingle with his genuine memories until fact and fantasy are indistinguishable. These brief visions, delightfully funny and moving in themselves, comprise a mosaic of Hungarian attitudes today. (One notes, too, how the older generation is heard but not seen, separated from Kiki by the wall on which he doodles.) Kiki feels himself to be free of the legacies of the past as he parades through the streets of Budapest with his "gang". When, in one of his wish-dreams, the farm where he stayed as a boy collapses on top of him, it seems as if his childhood was being symbolically buried. Pál Sándor has previously devoted his talent to shorts. He is still under 30, and, with his cast of non-professionals, he has now made a striking début as a feature film director — **Peter Cowie.**

STORY OF HUMAN GREATNESS AND HUMAN WEAKNESS

ankhen

"THE EYES" EASTMANCOLOR

STARRING
DHARMINDER · MALA SINHA

WRITTEN, PRODUCED
& DIRECTED BY
RAMANAND SAGAR · MUSIC **RAVI** · LYRICS **SAHIR**

Overseas rights with JYOT FILMS (London), 45 Penywern Road, London S.W.5.
Cables: JAYFILMS, London S.W.5.

India

introduction   by Chidananda Das Gupta

India is one of the largest film producing countries in the world with an average annual output in the last three years of more than 300 features backed up by 61 studios, 39 laboratories, 1000 producers and 1200 distributors. The first half of the 20th century saw the decline of the traditional forms of folk entertainment and the phenomenal rise of the cinema in an industrially backward country. Yet the daily cinema-going does not cover more than 5 million out of the population of 500 million, and the number of cinemas, at 6000, is less than in Japan. A total capital investment of some £ 60 million sterling results in annual box-office collections of a like amount. About 150 features are imported annually, mostly from the USA and the UK by virtue of bilateral agreements restricting the repatriation of profits. Showings of films from other countries are largely confined to the 100 or so film societies spread out through the country.

India's Constitution recognises 16 languages (including English) and film production falls inevitably into two categories — the national (in Hindustani) and the regional in various languages. While Bombay and Madras are the centres of the all-India film, Calcutta is the most important producer of regional films, making 25 to 30 features a year, some of which enjoy a *succès d'estime* in India and abroad. The pattern of production is independent and not studio-based except partly in Madras. The star-system, inherited from the days of studio production, persists. Indian stars command very high fees and work in several films at a time.

The first film exhibition in India was given in Bombay in 1896 by the Lumière brothers. In 1899, the first short film was made; the first feature came in 1913, and the first talkie in 1931. The first international film festival, held in 1952, gave a neo-realist impetus to some sections of Indian cinema, and resulted in Bimal Roy's *Do Bigha Zamin* in 1953. In 1955 came *Pather Panchali* which launched Satyajit Ray on a brilliant career and brought others in Bengal, in his wake, into an Indian avant-garde led by him. Among these are Ritwick Ghatak and Mrinal Sen, some of whose work has been noticed at international film festivals.

Other qualitative growth factors were brought in by the central government who, after conducting a comprehensive inquiry in 1951, established one of the best-equipped film schools in the world at Poona, a system of awards, occasional international festivals, a central censorship for all the 16 states, a film finance corporation, and a national film archive.

new and forthcoming films

MATIRA MANISHA. *dir:* Mrinal Sen.

BALIKA BODHU. *dir:* Tarun Majumdar. *players:* Partha Chatterjee, Mousum Chatterjee. *A nostalgic film about child-marriage in the old days (Bengali).*

CHHUTI. *dir:* Arundhati Debi. *players:* Mrinal Mukhopadhaya, Nandini Maleya.

INDIA 1967. *dir:* S. Sukhdev. *An hour-long documentary, highly praised in India.*

GOOPI GAIN O BAGHI BAIN. *dir:* Satyajit Ray. *A fantasy based on a well-known story by Ray's grandfather.*

THE GURU. *dir:* James Ivory. *players:* Rita Tushingham, Michael York, Utpal Dutt, Madhur Jaffery, Aparna Sen. For 20th. Century-Fox.

THE EYES. *dir:* Ramanand Sagar.

CHIDIAKHANA *(The Zoo).* *dir:* Satyajit Ray. *players:* Uttam Kumar etc. *A detective thriller that has been poorly received in India, save for one superb sequence where a song from an old film gives a clue to the identity of the murderer. Originally, the film was to have been made by some of Ray's assistants under his supervision; but towards the end he decided to sign as director.*

A. R. Varma (right) is one of the leading producers of short films in India. He is a diploma holder in film, radio, and television, and a popular figure and prominent member of the Indian Documentary Producers Association. He has been responsible for several films for the television market such as *Dances of India*, *Festival Songs*, *Payal ki Jhankar*, etc.

Ramanand Sagar was born in 1917, and is now recognised as one of India's most famous film personalities, equally well known as writer, director, and producer. In the past 12 years he has written 7 films; 6 of them have been Silver Jubilee hits. He is a proficient scholar of Urdu, Hindi, Persian, and English, and his new film *The Eyes* opened in India this autumn. His films are characteristically Indian, but they also appeal to world audiences, witness his earlier success, *Arzoo*.

Still (left) from *Pinjara*, produced by Akar Films of Bombay and directed by Kantilal Rathod. This is just one of a number of short films by Akar on India's lowly craftsmen, the carders, the shoemakers, etc. It was made in black-and-white on 16 mm. For his central character in *Pinjara*, Rathod went round Bombay and found a bearded old carder, Rasulla Khudabaksh, who responded wonderfully and remained natural and unaffected in front of the cameras. Notable is a dream sequence portraying the carder's ambition of being dressed as a Nawab smoking a hukka. Akar Films are widely known in the West for their excellent animated work.

At right: from Ramanand Sagar's production, THE EYES.

Israel

the general situation

Despite a limited population, some 80 feature films have been completed in Israel since 1960. Two new pictures are based on stories by Sholom Aleichem; one is an adaptation of a classic piece of Jewish dramaturgy, *The Dybbuk;* six were shot against the background of the 1948 War of Liberation and the 1967 Six Day War; and four are realistic accounts of life in Israel, whether the setting be the Palestine of the thirties or the night life of modern Tel-Aviv. Films projected for 1968-69 deal with a wide variety of subjects, including the story of Massada; the Dead Sea Scrolls; a documentary history of the Jewish people; the life story of Orde Wingate; espionage in Palestine under the Ottoman Empire; and several thrillers, romances, and films based on legend.

Plans are under way for the building of Israel's first colour laboratory, for the establishment of a company to provide serveces to film production, for the import of more modern equipment, and for the design and construction of sets and stages for particular types of films, such as Westerns.

Television has been introduced in Israel during 1968, and, while this could prove a rival to cinema initially, producers are confident that the increase in skilled technicians and experienced artists will have a favourable influence on the industry in the long term.

There are 32 members of the Israel Film Producers Association, and inquiries should be addressed to the Israel Export Institute, 9 Ahad Haam Street, Tel-Aviv.

Menahem Golan was born 37 years ago in Tiberias, and has studied at the Old Vic, and the University of New York. He was assistant to Roger Corman, and, on his return to Israel, had a huge success with *El Dorado*, a film which he produced and directed himself, and which starred the then unknown Hayim Topol. Shortly afterwards he formed his own company Noah Films, and has produced more than ten features as several documentaries and shorts. His major triumph to date has been *Salah* (9 international awards and an Oscar nomination). His *Tevye and his 7 Daughters* was the official Israeli entry at Cannes this year. He is now at work on *The Optimist*, a comedy adventure by the writer of Corman's *The Wild Angels*, and *The Bet*.

103

new and forthcoming films

TEVYE AND HIS 7 DAUGHTERS. *dir:* Menahem Golan. *phot:* Nissim Leon (colour). *mus:* Dov Seltser. *players:* Shmuel Rodensky, Peter Van Eyck, Robert Hoffman, Tikva Mor, Judith Solle. *prod:* Arthur Brauner and Menahem Golan.

THE MIRACLE. *dir:* Leo Filler. *phot:* Marko Yakobi (Eastmancolor). *mus:* Yohanan Zaray. *players:* Gad Yagil, Hadas Hadari, Yaakov Nitzan, Shachar Kol. *prod:* Menahem Golan.

IRIS. *dir:* David Greenberg. *phot:* David Gurfinkel. *players:* Mandy Rice-Davis, Gideon Shemer, Sammy Kraus. *prod:* David Greenberg.

THE DAYS BEFORE TOMORROW. *dir:* Ellida Geyra. *phot:* Adam Greenberg, Amnon Solomon. *players:* Rina Ganor, Israel (Poly) Poliakov, Dasi Hadari, Arie Elias. *prod:* Zvi Geyra.

Opposite page: TEVYE AND HIS 7 DAUGHTERS. A Ukrainian village was built in Galilee under the supervision of the film's art director, Koli Sender. TEVYE is produced and directed by Menahem Golan. Shmuel Rodensky (far left), and Tikva Mor are the leading stars.

At right: THE MIRACLE, a musical with Leo Filler that won a Silver Lion in Venice. Producer: Menahem Golan.

THE PRODIGAL SON. *dir:* Joseph Shalhin, Alfred Steinhardt. *phot:* Marco Yakobi. *players:* Shaul Shalkin, Itzhak Shiloh, Ninette Dinar, Dasi Hadari. *prod:* Israel Motion Picture Studios Ltd.

THREE LOVE STORIES. *dir:* Yaakov Wardy. *phot:* Emil Knebell, H. Yachin, Amnon Solomon. *players:* Ninette Dinar, Yael Aviv, Elias Kulia, Teddy Tsarfati. *prod:* Geva Films.

FORTUNA. *dir:* Menahem Golan. *phot:* Itzhak Herbst. *players:* Pierre Brasseur, Ahuva Goren, Saro Urzi, Yossi Bannai, Mike Marshall.

SALAH. *dir:* Ephraim Kishon. *phot:* Floyd Crosby. *players:* Haim Topol, Gila Almagor, Arik Einstein, Geula Noni. *prod:* Menahem Golan.

Italy

introduction   by Lucio Settimio Caruso

According to the statistics, it has been a steady year in the Italian cinema. At the start of 1968 there were 10,350 cinemas, with a total of 5,450,000 seats. In 1967, attendances stood at 690 millions, only 2.8% less than the previous year, while 516 foreign films were bought for distribution, Italy produced 275 films, 4 more than in 1966, of which 151 were wholly national and 124 made in co-operation with other countries. There has been a distinct trend towards colour film-making, and a movement away from the wide-screen. The new film law, the development of the State bodies for production and distribution, a higher level of television program-mes, did not make the differences that had been hoped, but they have undoubtedly stimulated the cinema.

On the artistic side, it has been a mediocre year, with no masterpieces to speak of, but an increase in the number of politically and ideologically committed pic-tures. The Italian "engaged" cinema is one inspired either by Marxism or by Christianity, those two forces that used to be violently opposed to each other and which now, in the context of the cinema at least, seem to be reconciled and attack each other only in dialogue.

What matters in the Italian film world, as in many others, is the box-office, and even at the International Cinema Conference at Assisi (which I direct each year) many film directors fell in with this. "It is much better to say something to many — than to try and say much more to empty seats," they said. This is essentially because the production branch in Italy is dominated by the distribution branch, which in turn is owned for the most part by huge foreign companies with American capital behind them. Even the State cinema bodies here are in jeopardy because of this stranglehold.

The television situation is rather interesting. It has and it grants, compared to the cinema, a greater freedom of ideas and moreover it does not compete with the cinema, because it entrusts the production of its own films to film companies and film directors. These pictures are often edited in two different versions, one for the cinemas, another for the small screen. Among these film-telefilm directors are Roberto Rossellini, with his *La lottà dell'umanità per la sopravvivenza (Humanity's Struggle for Survival);* Franco Rossi, with his *Odissea* played by Irene Papas and Bekim Fehmiu; Alfredo Giannetti, who directed *La Famiglia Benvenuti*, with Enrico M. Salerno and L. Emmer; Liliana Cavani, a young woman director who earned a name with her provocative and modern version of *Francesco d'Assisi* in 1966 and has now made *Galileo Galilei* as a co-production between Italy and Bulgaria; Ales-sandro Blasetti, with *Benvenuto Cellini;* and finally Luigi Filippo D'Amico, who is engaged on a series on the world of Pirandello as novelist.

*From EDIPO RE,
directed by Pier Paolo
Pasolini.*

EDIPO RE
(Oedipus Rex)

Script and Direction: Pier Paolo Pasolini, from
the tragedy by Sophocles; *Photography:* Giuseppe Ruzzolini; *Editing:* Nino Baragli; *Art Direction:* Luigi Scaccianoce; *Players:* Franco Citti,
Silvana Mangano, Alida Valli, Julian Beck,
Carmelo Bene. For Arco Film (Alfredo Bini).

This is neither a theatrical performance of Sophocles's play, nor a pretext for a
different kind of message. The tragedy is a sort of symbolic key to the director's
own life, and it is thus more faithful to the spirit than to the letter of the play. The
film starts with a baby's being born in an Italian middle-class household about
1920; his mother is a fine lady, his father an army officer (in fact, Pasolini was born
in 1922, his mother was a teacher and his father too an army officer). Suddenly the
father sees the child as almost a rival who diverts his wife's love from him, and he
feels a kind of subconscious hatred towards him that expresses itself in the Freudian
gesture of holding the baby's ankles in his hands. Here Sophocles's influence is
apparent, for the poetry of grief prevails over violence and erotism, and the need
for expiation prevails over the despair of being obliged by fate to assume the blame
for faults uncommitted. This film is very poetical, and perhaps even more so than
The Gospel according to St. Matthew. One can note two personalities in Pasolini's
work: one that is influenced by rationalism and appears as a Marxist, a Freudian,
a middle-class, or a revolutionay man; and the other relying on artistic inspiration,
as can be found in his books like *L'Usignolo della Chiesa Cattolica* or in films like
Accattone. In *Edipo Re* the acting of Alida Valli and Silvana Mangano is exceptionally good — **Lucio Settimio Caruso.**

LA CINA E' VICINA
(China is Near)

Script: Marco Bellocchio and Elda Tattoli; *Direction:* Bellocchio; *Photography:* Tonino Delli Colli; *Music:* Ennio Moricone; *Players:* Glauco Mari, Elda Tattoli, Paolo Graziosi, Daniela Surina, Pierluigi Aprà. For Vides (Franco Cristaldi).

This second film by Bellocchio is part success, part failure. A success because it shows Bellocchio to be a versatile and evolving director. A failure because it lacks the excitement and incisiveness of *I Pugni in Tasca*. *La Cina è vicina* takes place in a North Italian province, and focuses on three decadent descendants of a noble family: Vittorio, learned, complicated, opportunist, chameleon-like in his politics; Elena, a moralist in administering the family estate and in her outward behaviour, but vicious and cynical in private life; and Camillo, a boy of 16 who supports the Chinese cultural revolution on account more of adolescent sentimentalism than of a genuine political conscience.

At first sight the film seems to be a satire on political commitment, on the family, on religion, on society. But in fact it is more a protest against easy compromise than an attack on commitment; more a protest against unfaithful bigotry than an attack on religion; more a condemnation of politics and working-class corruption than a polemic against the working classes themselves or family politics.

Why this particular title? Bellocchio comments, "China is very far for those who think she is near, and very near for those who think she is far away." — **Lucio Settimio Caruso.**

Terence Stamp in the brilliant Fellini episode in HISTOIRES EXTRAORDINAIRES, based on stories by Edgar Allan Poe.

Claudia Cardinale and Franco Nero in THE OWL'S DAY.

IL GIORNO DELLA CIVETTA
(The Owl's Day)

Script: Damiano Damiani and Ugo Pirro from a novel by Leonardo Sciascia; *Direction:* Damiani; *Photography:* Tonino Delli Colli; *Music:* Giovanni Fusco; *Players:* Claudia Cardinale, Franco Nero, Lee J. Cobb, Gaetano Cimarosa, Serge Reggiani. For Panda Cinematografica.

This is the most courageous and accomplished film of a talented director. Damiani takes only the kernel of his story and atmosphere from the novel by Sciascia, and turns his film into a violent attack on the Mafia, harshly unmasking its power tactics, its political protectionism, its efforts to turn religion and state authority to its own end.

While Petri's *A ciascuno il suo* dealt with the Mafia question in the style of a psychological thriller, Damiani's film is a denunciation that can be compared to a modern political Western, representing a struggle fought in the name of justice. The protagonists are an army captain and an aged but very brave Mafia chief. The captain tries to pin several offences on the chief, and succeeds in having him arrested. But the Mafia free their leader, and the captain is punished in the end.

The bright sunshine of Sicily in summer dominates the imagery: dazzling even by night, and stifling, like the aura of killing, lying, and blackmail. The film is a brilliant *andante mosso*, by virtue of the skilful subtleties of the interrogation dialogues; and the pessimistic atmosphere is used by Damiani as a means of arousing his public's indignation. Unfortunately gangsterism linked with power and respectability is not merely a Sicilian phenomenon, and so this film does not refer just to a parochial situation. One wishes, in fact, that Damiani had been even more uncompromising and obstinate here — **Lucio Settimio Caruso.**

new and forthcoming films

GRAZIE ZIA *(Thank You, Aunt). dir:* S. Samperi. *phot:* Aldo Scavarda. *players:* Lou Castel, Lisa Gastoni, Gabriele Ferzetti. For Doria Film.

ESCALATION. *dir:* Roberto Faenza. *phot:* Luigi Kuveiller. *players:* Claudine Auger, Lino Capolicchio, Gabriele Ferzetti. For Cemo Film.

BANDITI A MILANO *(Bandits in Milan). dir:* Carlo Lizzani. *phot:* Giuseppe Ruzzolini. *players:* Gian Maria Volontè, Don Backy, Tomas Milian. For Dino De Laurentiis.

I SOVVERSIVI *(The Subversionists). dir:* Paolo and Emilio Taviani. *phot:* Narzisi, Giuseppe Ruzzolini. *players:* Giorgio Arlorio, Giulio Brogi, Pier Paolo Capponi. For Ager Film.

IL GIARDINO DELLA DELIZIE *(The Garden of Delights). dir:* Silvano Agosti. *phot:* Aldo Scavarda. *players:* Lea Massari, Maurice Ronet. For Doria Film.

TEOREMA *(Theorem). dir:* Pier Paolo Pasolini. *players:* Silvana Mangano, Massimo Girotti, Terence Stamp, Anne Wiazemsky. For Aetos Film/Euro International.

GALILEO GALILEI. *dir:* Liliana Cavani. *players:* Cyril Cusack, Gigi Ballista, Giulio Brogi. For Leo Pescarolo (television production).

SEQUESTRO DI PERSONA *(Unlawful Confinement). dir:* Gianfranco Mingozzi. *players:* Pierluigi Aprà, Charlotte Rampling.

IL SOSIA *(Partner). dir:* Bernardo Bertolucci. *players:* Tina Aumont, Stefania Sandrelli, Pierre Clementi. For Italnoleggio/Red Film.

SERAFINO. *dir:* Pietro Germi. *players:* Adriano Celentano, Saro Urzi, O. Piccolo. For RPA/Rizzoli.

UN TRANQUILLO POSTO DI CAMPAGNA *(A Quiet Country Spot). dir:* Elio Petri. *players:* Vanessa Redgrave, Franco Nero, Georges Geret. For Pea Cinematografica.

QUEMADA *dir:* Gillo Pontecorvo. *player:* Marlon Brando. For Pea Cinematografica.

METTI, UNA SERA A CENA. *dir:* Giuseppe Patroni Griffi.

Japan

introduction   by Donald Richie

During 1967 the Japanese cinema industry released 410 feature films (excluding documentaries and television productions), 241 of which were made by the five major companies (Toho, Nikkatsu, Toei, Daiei, and Shochiku) and 169 independent films — the majority of which were "eroductions", but which also included the new films by Hani and Oshima. This, compared with the 1966 total of 436, indicates that the Japanese industry is continuing to undergo what the Americans used to call "rationalisation", meaning a gradual loss of audience and a consequent new search for production patterns.

Some of the new patterns have become apparent. Three years ago the ratio between colour and black-and-white films (among the five-company films, at any rate) was about even. Now black-and-white films are less than one quarter of the total. Eight years ago about one third of the films were period *Jidai-geki;* now they number only one tenth. At the same time there has been another drop in available cinemas. In 1965 there were 4,649 houses; in 1966, 4,119; this year even fewer.

This does not necessarily mean that many less people are seeing Japanese films, however. The new audience is a selective one and if it tends to neglect ordinary Japanese cinema, it will flock to films such as *A Man Vanishes* and Hani's *The Inferno of First Love*, as well as unusual star-combinations (Mifune and Ishihara in *Kurobe no Taiyo)* and such war film block-busters as Toho's *Isoroku Yamamoto.*

It also tends to patronise foreign films. Last year the U.S.A. led yet again, due to its own distribution circuits, with 117 released films; followed by Italy, 52; France, 32; and Britain, 26. The money-makers were *Grand Prix*, *You Only Live Twice*, *The Bible*, and yet another revival of *Gone With The Wind.* Japan's new leisure class has obviously discovered the delights of the occasional (big) movie, and local companies will surely have to accommodate this new audience.

new and forthcoming films

TORA, TORA, TORA. *dir:* Akira Kurosawa and Richard Fleischer. For Kurosawa Productions/20th. Century-Fox. *A reconstruction of the Pearl Harbor attack. Shooting begins November 1968.*
WAR OF THE SEXES. *dir:* Kaneto Shindo. For Shochiku. *A sex comedy.*
KILL! *dir:* Kibachi Okamoto. For Toho. *A period film starring Tatsuya Nakadai.*
THE YOUTH OF JAPAN. *dir:* Masaki Kobayashi. For Toho. *A melodrama about a war veteran.*
THE BURNED MAP. *dir:* Hiroshi Teshigahara. For Daiei. *A gang melodrama starring Shintaro Katsu.*

111

Cat people: the mother and her daughter in KURONEKO, directed by Kaneto Shindo and the official Japanese entry at Cannes 1968.

THE SECOND SEX. *dir:* Yasuzo Masumura. *About a girl athlete accused of being a man.*

PEONIES AND LANTERNS: A GHOST STORY. *dir:* Satsuo Yamamoto. *A well-made ghost story in the pattern of UGETSU MONOGATARI.*

HELL SCREEN. *dir:* Shiro Toyoda. For Toho. *A screen version of the Akutagawa story.*

DOUBLE SUICIDE AT AMIJIMA. *dir:* Masahiro Shinoda. *Composer Toru Takemitsu's version of the famous Bunraku puppet-play. An independent production.*

FLAMES OF DEVOTION. *dir:* Kurahosa.

KURONEKO. *dir:* Kaneto Shindo. *players:* Kichiemon Nakamura, Nobuko Otowa, Kiwako Taichi. For Toho. *A stunning if somewhat academic exercise in vampirism.*

KOSHIKEI
(Death by Hanging)

Script: Tsutomu Tamura, Mamoru Sasaki, Michinori Fukao, Nagisa Oshima; *Direction:* Oshima; *Photography:* Yasuhiro Yoshioka; *Editing:* Sueko Shiraishi; *music:* Hikaru Hayashi. *Art Direction:* Shigemasa Toda; *Players:* Kei Sato, Fumio Watanabe, Toshiro Ishido, Masao Adachi. For Sozo-Sha. 117 mins.

A short while ago a young Korean student murdered and raped two Japanese girls. Director Oshima has returned to the case and questioned not the guilt of the student but the justification of capital punishment and the whole problem of discrimination against the Koreans in Japan. He does not do so directly, however. Instead, he has chosen a Brechtian form. The young Korean, though hanged, refuses to die and so the police officers must act out his crime in order to convince him of his guilt. In so doing one of the officers inadvertently murders a girl. The ironies of the picture multiply — law is impossible without crime, for example — and the film ends with the unassailable logic of the young Korean's observation upon being warmly assured that it is indeed very bad to kill, that "then it is bad to kill me." The second half of *Koshikei* is somewhat loose and more than a little indulgent, but the general structure and the first half are remarkably incisive — **Donald Richie.**

NINGEN JOHATSU
(A Man Vanishes)

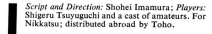

Script and Direction: Shohei Imamura; *Players:* Shigeru Tsuyuguchi and a cast of amateurs. For Nikkatsu; distributed abroad by Toho.

Several years ago a young man named Masao Oshima simply vanished. His fiancée has been looking for him ever since. A Tokyo television station carried the story and director Imamura decided it would make a film. The result is a controlled exercise in *cinéma-vérité* during which everyone who knew the man is interviewed, and the intrepid fiancée (played by herself) slowly begins to be attracted to the man (the only actor) playing the principal investigator. Since much of the film was made without the participants knowing, several "invasion of privacy" suits ensued, including one from the fiancée who did not realise that her scenes with the actor were being filmed. The result is fascinating, particularly in one brilliant sequence when, after a long conversation in what both we and the principals have taken to be a small restaurant, Imamura suddenly gives a command, the walls are lifted away, the ceiling raised, and we find ourselves on a sound stage surrounded by lights, cameras, microphones etc. The film is also, however, mendacious. People's emotions are played upon pitilessly and only in a country as libel-lawless as Japan could this picture have been made. It has not been shown outside the country mainly due to subtitling difficulties, but it is one of the most brilliant films from this always *(Insect Woman, The Pornographer)* brilliant director — **Donald Richie.**

HATSUKOI JIGOKUHEN (The Inferno of First Love)

Script: Susumu Hani and Shuji Terayama; *Direction:* Hani; *Photography:* Yuji Okumura; *Music:* from Toru Takemitsu and Akio Yashiro; *Players:* Akio Takahashi, Kuniko Ishii, Koji Mitsui, Kazuko Fukuda, Minoru Yuasa. For Art Theater Guild.

This very moving film — perhaps the best Japanese film of the year — is about a boy and a girl, both seventeen, who meet in Tokyo and fall in love. Both are completely innocent and though she works as a nude model and the man he calls his father takes a more than fatherly interest in him, their innocence remains untouched until the end. Treating his film as a modern fairy tale, Hani has put his children in some hair-raisingly kinky situations, including a full-scale all-girl s-m show in Shinjuku, and cuts freely back and forth to show remembered glimpses of childhood. It is not, however, that innocence is somehow good and experience somehow bad. It is, rather, that innocence, like all else, passes, and this spectacle is touching. Innocence, after all, is real; and experience is a series of illusions. One may disagree with the end, there is no reason why a fairy tale should not end happily, but everything else is logical, powerful, and shown with rare economy. Hani has deliberately created a film so adult, so perverse, so scandalous and shocking that it permits one to catch genuine reflections of a world of purity and childlike innocence — **Donald Richie.**

Kuniko Ishii and Akio Takahishi, both amateurs, in Hani's THE INFERNO OF FIRST LOVE (Hatsukoi Jigokuhen).

The police act out the criminal's childhood in Nagisa Oshima's DEATH BY HANGING.

Netherlands

introduction   by Peter Cowie

The Dutch cinema must solve the problem of its feature film industry before long. If, as recent box-office returns suggest, the Dutch audiences simply will not accept domestic productions, then the young directors like Weisz, van der Heyde, Ditvoorst, and Daalder, may well be forced overseas to find an outlet for their talents. Ten new-look features were premiered between January 1966 and March 1968. Nearly all of them have been catastrophic failures on the commercial front.

On the other hand, there is also evidence to suggest that if these "young Turks" can be given the guidance of an enlightened and solid production machine, they might very well win recognition from the public. It is encouraging to know that as from January 1969 the 16% entertainments tax on cinema performances will be abolished in the Netherlands. The Production Fund of the Nederlandsche Bioscoop-Bond amounts to over 1,125,000 guilders, but until this figure is drastically increased, it is difficult to see how more than three or four features can be produced annually in the country.

Dancers performing in Hattum Hoving's brilliant new experiment with colour film, entitled MIXUMMERDAYDREAM and available through Cinecentrum of Hilversum.

In 1967, some 383 features were imported from abroad (118 from the U.S.A., 65 from France, 65 from Italy, 64 from Britain, etc.). The number of cinemas in the Netherlands amounted to 468, as opposed to 490 in 1966. Only four features were produced by Dutch companies with the aid of the Production Fund.

The Netherlands government remains the principal sponsor of short films. On July 1, 1968, 79 subjects were in production, some of these foreign language versions of existing films. These shorts are enormously popular outside the Netherlands. *Sky over Holland*, John Ferno's prize-winning documentary in 70 mm, has been released by Warner Bros./Seven Arts in the U.S.A. and Canada as a "second feature" (and not as a short film), with a guaranteed minimum of about 100 prints.

In Switzerland, distributors have begun launching Dutch shorts linked to feature films on a similar subject (art, geography, etc.). Shaw International Theatres, of San Jose, California, have launched three films by Herman van der Horst *(Amsterdam, Pan,* and *Surinam)*, and one film by Charles Huguenot van der Linden *(Big City Blues)*, in a single programme entitled *Search for Peace*. The non-theatrical market (16 mm commercial) for Dutch films is also expanding more and more, especially in the U.S.A.

short films

Shorts recently produced in the Netherlands (other than those reviewed in this section) include: *Een dag Zuiderzee* (Jan Wiegel), *Van uur 0 tot 24* (Pim Korver), *Een bewoonbaar land* (Jan Wiegel), *De Hoge Veluwe* (Nico Crama), *Het Nationale*

Marline Fritzius and John Thiel in WITHIN BOUNDS (Het Compromis), directed for Parkfilm by Philo Bregstein.

The young and prominent Dutch filmcompany

CINEPRODUCTIE

51 Vondelstraat Amsterdam Phone 187943

Made an important contribution to new Dutch film with a.o.

THE REALITY OF KAREL APPEL director Jan Vrijman,
Golden Bear Berlin 1962

SOUS LE CIEL , SUR LA TERRE director Jan Vrijman,
Arnhem Festival 1965

A SUNDAY ON THE ISLAND OF THE GRANDE JATTE director Frans Weisz,
Dutch State Prize 1965, Silver Bear Berlin 1965

VIEILLE RUE ET SCENE PITTORESQUE director Henk Meulman,
Benelux Festival Award 1966

THE FAITHHEALER director Jan Vrijman,
Oberhausen Award 1967

ILLUSION IS A GANGSTERGIRL director Frans Weisz,
Berlin Filmfestival 1967

THE ENEMIES director Hugo Claus, 1968

IN THE BEGINNING, AT LAST director Frans Weisz, 1968

Forthcoming **A MUSICAL COMEDY** 1969

Cineproductie is an official co-producer for the Netherlands

Park (Nico Crama), *De Krant* (Theo van Haren Noman), *Toets-Touch-Touche* (Tom Tholen), *Bagger* (Tom Tholen), *Holland Terra Fertilis* (Ronny Erends), *Sabotage* (Nouchka van Brakel), *Trein Anoniem* (Paul Schneider), *Lichaam en Ziel* (Renée Daalder), *Caleidoscope* (Jan Wiertsema), *Ice Cream Soda* (Kees Meyering), *Een Wand* (Wim van der Velde), *Schiphol, Amsterdam International Airport* (Gerard J. Raucamp), *Mixummerdaydream* (Hattum Hoving), and *Retour Madrid* (Bert Haanstra). *Toets-Touch-Touche* won a Silver Bear in Berlin 1968.

TOCCATA

Script, Direction, Photography, Editing: Herman van der Horst; *Music:* Johann Sebastian Bach; *Players:* Feike Asma, Dolph de Lange. For Ministry of Culture. 30 mins.

Herman van der Horst's latest film, which has taken nearly two years to complete, is a somewhat attenuated but fascinating blend of sound and image. A little boy searches for his cat in the Old Church, Amsterdam, while an organist practises Bach on his 18th century instrument, struggling at first against a background of workmen hammering, jets screaming overhead, and a cleaner hoovering the floor. The situation is a pretext for van der Horst to explore the potential of film rhythm, which is most stirring in the final few minutes, as the organist flings heart and soul into Bach's Toccata in F, the physical exertion of manipulating the baroque organ counterpointed by his shouts and exclamations to his assistants, and by the climbing beauty of the music itself — **Peter Cowie.**

The organist at the climax of Herman van der Horst's TOCCATA.

ROBduMEE

PARKFILM n/v

92 SARPHATIPARK / AMSTERDAM ZUID / PHONE 020 71 83 98

produced in 1967/68

THE WHIPPING CREAM HERO

a funnyhipcruelmodern comedy

script Heere Heeresma
directed by Erik Terpstra
with Ramses Shaffy / Wies Andersen /
Hetty Verhoogt

THE COMPROMISE

written and directed by Philo Bregstein
camera Gerard VandenBerg
with Marline Fritzius / Gerben Hellinga /
John Thiel / and the members
of The Living Theatre

(in co-production with Sofidoc/Brussels)

MONSIEUR HAWARDEN

based on a 19th century diary

script Jan Blokker
directed by Harry Kümel
camera Eduard van der Enden
with Ellen Vogel / Hilde Uitterlinden /
Xander Fischer / Senne Rouffaer
a.m.o.

PARKFILM distributed for the Netherlands

QUI ETES-VOUS POLLY MAGGOO? (Klein/France)   JOHNNY COOL (William Asher/USA)
DUTCHMAN (Anthony Harvey/USA)   GARDEN OF DELIGHT (Silvano Agosti/Italy)
IT HAPPENED HERE (Brownlow-Mollo/England)   ECHOES OF SILENCE (Peter Goldman/USA)
WALKOVER (Jerzy Skolimowski/Poland)   FISTS IN THE POCKET (Marco Bellocchio/Italy)

John Ferno, with his son and cameraman Douwes, receives the Grand Prix at Cannes 1967 for SKY OVER HOLLAND from Virna Lisi.

Bert Haanstra adds yet another award to his collection of over fifty from all parts of of the world. (Foto v. d. Reijken).

5 scenes from Harry Kümel's MONSIEUR HAWARDEN, starring Ellen Vogel, Hilde Uitterlinden, and Xander Fischer, for Parkfilm n.v., Amsterdam.

MONSIEUR HAWARDEN

Script: Jan Blokker from the novel by Filip de Pillecijn; *Direction:* Harry Kümel; *Photography:* Eddy van der Enden; *Music:* Pierre Bartholomée; *Art Direction and Costumes:* Stefania Unwin and Tom Payot; *Players:* Ellen Vogel, Hilde Uitterlinden, Xander Fischer, Senne Rouffaer, Dora van der Groen. For Rob du Mée /Parkfilm (Amsterdam) and Sofidoc (Brussels).

With one extraordinary film Harry Kümel takes his place among the best directors in Europe. *Monsieur Hawarden* is a 19th century tragedy in a modern idiom, dedicated to von Sternberg, but reminding one by its cool, disciplined intensity more of Bergman or Wajda. Meriora Gillibrand fled from Vienna at the age of 19 after stabbing her lover's rival to death. She wanders through Europe for years, disguised as a man, until she is forced to come to terms with her real identity. We see her arriving at a country estate accompanied by her young maid, Victorine. Here she observes, in the rivalry of two men over the girl, a parallel to her own disfigured past. Although Ellen Vogel has masculine features, she behaves with such grace and reticence that her sex is never in doubt. Her ceaseless struggle to preserve control over her personality is brilliantly reflected in Kümel's style, in the pattern of images that are grave and elegant in composition but disturbed in their order and rhythm. There is in fact scarcely an orthodox shot in this film; nor is there a pretentious one. The effect of black clothes against white walls and skies, the death of Victorine and her last shuddering stare at her mistress, or the search by torchlight in the forest, are felicities that emphasise Kümel's crisp and imaginative approach to cinema — **Peter Cowie.**

Wim Verstappen is 31 years old, and together with his inseparable companion, Pim de la Parra, has been one of the "storm troopers" of the new Dutch cinema, determined to make low-budget pictures outside the system and to achieve commercial success. He made something of an international reputation among critics with *Joszef Katús*, a full-length feature completed for apparently a mere £1,000, and screened during the Critics' Week at Cannes, in 1967. It also won a key prize at the Pesaro Festival in the same year. Verstappen followed this with *Confessions of Loving Couples*, starring Kittie Courbois and Shireen Strooker. He also directed a film for German television in 1967, and has many plans ahead.

In the course of the activities promoting cultural co-operation between the member states of the Council of Europe in the field of the film, the need was felt for a vocabulary giving the specialised film terminology most used in the member countries. This has resulted in a film vocabulary containing about 900 film terms in French, English, Dutch, Italian, German, Spanish and Danish. It is the first film publication of this scope to be published under the auspices of an intergovernmental organisation.

The film vocabulary is intended as a handy aid for practical use by all who are concerned with educational and cultural films. It makes no claims to be exhaustive, and is not meant to compete with more elaborate publications which have already appeared in this field. The technical studio terms and specialised expressions included are in fairly general use in the member countries.

Despite the fact that compilation of the film vocabulary required considerable effort and consultation, it has proved to be a success: the 6th edition has just come off the press.

Mr. S. I. van Nooten, Director of Films Division of the Netherlands Government Information Service, compiled and arranged the final text with the aid of many international bodies.

Copies of the Film Vocabulary may be ordered with an International Money Order for 10 Dutch Guilders. Orders should be addressed to:

NETHERLANDS GOVERNMENT INFORMATION SERVICE, 43 NOORDEINDE, THE HAGUE, NETHERLANDS.

Del Negro and Robbe de Hert in THE ENEMIES (De Vijanden). Photograph courtesy Jan Vrijman Cineproductie.

DE VIJANDEN
(The Enemies)

Script and Direction: Hugo Claus; *Photography:* Herman Wuyts; *Editing:* Jan Bosdriesz; *Music:* Misja Mengelberg; *Players:* Del Negro, Fons Rademakers, Robbe de Hert, Ida Bons, Raymonde Serverius. For Jan Vrijman Cineproductie (Amsterdam)/Visie pvba (Antwerp). 85 mins.

Co-productions (shot in English language) may well be the salvation of the young Dutch cinema — at least as long as the public in the Netherlands remain indifferent to all but foreign films. *The Enemies*, directed by the novelist Hugo Claus, uses a war setting, which some have found responsible for the film's "dated" look. But Claus is interested more in characterisation than in the war as such. *The Enemies* shows how a fragile but worthwhile relationship gradually forms between a highly-strung American G.I., a Belgian youth, and a German soldier they capture at a lonely farm house during the Ardennes campaign. "It's an attempt," says Claus, "to adapt the technique of the comic-strip to the cinema. The characters are deliberately given banal lines of dialogue, like the bubble-talk in comics." Certainly the most impressive aspect of *The Enemies* is its accumulation of unrelated incidents, as confusing as war really is, and linked together by dissolves rather than cuts, creating a kind of telescoped time. This is one of the few recent Dutch productions not weighed down by personal preoccupations. It's a film that could be accepted and understood, like the B features of Irving Lerner, in any country — **Peter Cowie.**

short films

van pelt.

AUSTRIA
Niederländische
Handelskammer
für Österreich
Mr L M Swennen
IV, Schwarzenbergplatz 10
A-1041 Vienna

USA
Contemporary Films
Textfilm Division/
McGraw-Hill Book Company
Mr L R Dratfield
330 West 42nd Street
New York N Y 10036

CANADA
Canadian Film Institute
Mr Roy Little
1762, Carling Avenue
Ottawa 3

GREAT BRITAIN
Contemporary Films Ltd
Mr Charles Cooper
14,Soho Square
London W1

USA
Film Authors
Mr F D Kahlenberg
1270, Sixth Avenue
New York 20

PORTUGAL
SPAC
Mr F Correia de Mattos
Avenida da Liberdade, 245
Lisbon (2)

WEST GERMANY
Ifagé Filmproduktion GmbH
Mr H Wisser
Unter den Eichen
62 Wiesbaden

DENMARK
A/S Nordisk Films Kompagni
Mr O Børgesen
Valby
Copenhagen

NETHERLANDS
Ervédé
Noordeinde 43
The Hague

from holland

Edina Ronay, with Ben Carruthers (top), and at far right; also Liesbeth List (left) in TO GRAB THE RING, directed by Nikolai van der Heyde.

TO GRAB THE RING

Script: Nikolai van der Heyde and George Moorse; *Direction:* van der Heyde; *Photography:* Gerard Vandenberg; *Editing:* Ko Koedijk; *Music:* Frans Mijts; *Players;* Ben Carruthers, Al Mancini, Vladeck Sheybal, Edina Ronay, Françoise Brion, Liesbeth List. For John Rosinga's Telefund. 101 mins.

There is a distinctly French sophistication in the work of Nikolai van der Heyde, and *To Grab the Ring*, although a miserable failure at the box-office, still has enough good sequences to suggest that this 31 year old director may be the most promising of his generation, given the right scenario and the right producer. The dialogue is almost entirely in English, but it suffers from poor post-synchronisation. Otherwise this is a technically immaculate film, brilliantly and intimately photographed by Gerard Vandenberg. It is the drama of an American in his early thirties, Alfred Lowell (Ben Carruthers), who is tempted back to Europe by a petty gangster and tries to retrieve the threads of an affair he enjoyed five years earlier with a French woman (Françoise Brion). Lowell has a facility for seducing pretty girls *en route*, but he is deeply unhappy. "I'm not as wise as I could be," he says after a bout of love-making. "I resent the kids having fun." Thus the film is sustained by his fear of growing old, of losing his foothold in his generation. The action leaps swiftly and, it must be admitted, disjointedly from London to Berlin, Amsterdam, and Paris — **Peter Cowie.**

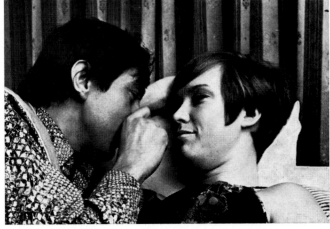

Ramses Shaffy and Hetty Verhoogt in DE VERLOEDERING VAN DE SWIEPS (The Whipping Cream Hero), directed by Erik Terpstra for Rob du Mée/Parkfilm, Amsterdam.

131

The formidable team of **Gerard J. Raucamp, Ted de Wit,** and director **Ronny Erends**
(above, l to r) are the leading lights of Carillon Films, a Dutch-based company, founded in 1949, with an international outlook on sponsored films. A staff of over 30
work full-time on films that can improve business communications and that can provide entertainment for sophisticated audiences throughout the industrial and diplomatic worlds. Some of their most famous productions: *Holland Today*, *Holland Off
Guard, European Rhapsody, Holland Terra Fertilis,* and now a majestic aerial view of
the Netherlands, . . . *and they named it Holland.* "It is only by working together
in harness, as a team, that you can keep up to date," comments Raucamp, who
has also launched Topspot, a production company thriving on the manufacture of
TV commercials for a growing domestic network.

Carillon Films N.V. HOLLAND

Twenty years of world-wide experience

in communication

Gerard J. Raucamp
Ted de Wit

45, Koninginnelaan, Rijswijk (Z.H.), Holland.
Phone 070 / 98 67 65

TRADE ORGANISATIONS

Nederlandsche Bioscoop Bond
Jan Luykenstraat 2
Amsterdam. Tel: 020-79.92.61

(Business Federation comprising most exhibitors, distributors and producers)

Nederlandse Beroepsvereniging
van Filmers
Weteringschans 95
Amsterdam. Tel: 020-23.79.31

(Professional Film-makers Organisation)

GOVERNMENT DEPARTMENTS

Ministerie van Cultuur, Recreatie en
Maatschappelijk Werk
Steenvoordelaan 370
Rijswijk Z.H. Tel: 070-90.76.00

(Ministry of Cultural Affairs, Recreation and Social Welfare)

Rijksvoorlichtingsdienst
Noordeinde 43
The Hague. Tel: 070-18.38.30

(Netherlands Government Information Service)

Renée Daalder was born in 1944 on the island of Texel. In the early sixties he studied at the Film Academy in Amsterdam, and in 1964 shot his first short, *Wat een approach*, on 16mm. In 1965 there followed *1, 2, 3 rhapsodie*, another short, and then *Body and Soul (Pt I)*, a tragi-comedy about a body-builder who worries about his body outgrowing him. *Pt II* (1967) ran for 30 minutes and starred Andrea Domburg and John Smit. This won the Critics' Prize at Cinemanifestatie, Utrecht, in 1968. He has prepared scripts for two feature films, *The Colony*, and *De Blanke Slavin*.

New Zealand

The New Zealand Government, one of the first in the world to make consistent use of motion pictures, began producing films in 1916. The main purpose was to publicise the country's scenery and to promote trade. For some time they were produced by private contractors. In 1936 the Tourist and Publicity Department bought the studios of one of these contractors, a self-contained plant at Miramar, Wellington, equipped with cameras, a laboratory and editing facilities. These studios formed the nucleus of the National Film Unit set up by the Government in 1941 primarily to help with wartime publicity.

The New Zealand National Film Unit is now known chiefly for its high technical standards and for beautiful photography. Because its main function is to publicise New Zealand, it seldom makes full-length features, but concentrates on the short subject. In this field the unit has become expert. Originality, combined with variation and presentation, is rewarded each year at International festivals. Over 80 awards have been collected in recent years and the unit receives more invitations to film festivals than it can accept.

Overseas film-makers have been active in New Zealand. Last year the Fukuhara Film Company of Tokyo filmed *Mysterious White Land* which features skiing against a backdrop of spectacular scenery at New Zealand's famous ski grounds in the South Island. Also, Greenpark Productions, London, made *The Taking Mood* last year. Written and produced by Derek Williams, it used New Zealand actors and was filmed by the National Film Unit.

some recent films

Spindrift (*dir* Michael G. Ryan, *ph* Lynton Diggle, Brian Cross, and Kell Fowler *in colour*, 9 mins) is an attractive reflection of the pace and mood of yacht-racing in the waters around Auckland, while *This Auckland* (*dir* Hugh MacDonald, *ph* Lynton Diggle *in colour*, $14^1/_2$ mins) takes a close look at that city's people at work and at energetic play, at its geography, and at its industry. The music score helps this jaunty documentary along no end. For children, there is *The Great Fish of Maui*, animated and modelled in his unique style by Fred O'Neill to create an air of magic as the old-time Maoris haul the North Island of New Zealand out of the sea. This runs for 8 minutes, and another programme filler worth booking is *Birth of a Rainbow*, about the trout hatcheries in New Zealand. 16mm prints of these and other major productions are available from New Zealand diplomatic missions throughout the world.

THE TAKING MOOD, made on location in New Zealand by Greenpark Productions of London.

Poland

the current situation   by Ryszard Koniczek

There was little change in the vital statistics of the Polish industry during 1967, except that fewer full-length features were produced. On the other hand, more 30 minute films were produced for television. Here are the figures; in 1967, 184 foreign films were released, 8 of them in non-commercial cinemas. The U.S.S.R. led with 37 films, followed by the U.S.A. with 29, France with 26, Czechoslovakia with 16, Yugoslavia and Hungary with 11 each, and Britain with 10. Foreign films are selected by professional and not commercial criteria. The choice is made by a Film Repertory Board composed of critics, producers, educationalists and cultural workers. *War and Peace* attracted nearly 3 million spectators. There were 3,694 cinemas in operation at the end of the year, with 694,100 seats. This works out at

FILM POLSKI

EXPORTERS AND IMPORTERS OF FILMS

OFFERS

feature, documentary, animated experimental and educational films, 35 and 16mm., available for cinemas, TV and non-commercial distribution.

PROVIDES

services for foreign producers for making films of any kind in Poland, and places studios, technical equipment and experienced shooting units, directors, cameramen, production managers, etc. at their disposal.

ACTS

as intermediary between Polish actors, directors and cameramen and foreign producers who wish to engage them.

SUPPLIES

on demand publicity material, catalogues and stills.

FILM POLSKI

Warszawa, Mazowiecka 6/8, Poland
Cables: Imexfilm, Telex: Ixfilm wa 81640,
Phone: 26-04-41, 26-23-70, 27-57-85

only 21.6 seats per 1,000 inhabitants, and television and poor technical presentation are blamed by the authorities for this low figure. The total number of spectators decreased in fact by 1% in comparison to the previous year.

Three studios produce feature films: in Warsaw, Lodz, and Wroclaw. They also make TV films. The largest and most modern, with 4 stages each measuring 900 square metres, is at Lodz. Warsaw also has a separate studio for documentary films and newsreels. There are three major cartoon studios, "Miniatury" in Warsaw, "Se-Ma-For" in Lodz, and Bielsko-Biala in Silesia. 20 new features were released from Polish studios in 1967, 7 less than in 1966.

films released in 1967

THE SCOURGE *(Bicz Bozy)*. *script* and *dir:* Maria Kaniewska. *phot:* Adolf Forbert. *mus:* Wojciech Kilar. *players:* Pola Raksa, Stanislaw Mikulski, Barbara Drapinska.

THE BOXER *(Bokser)*. *script:* Bohdan Tomaszewski and Jerzy Suszko. *dir:* Julian Dziedzina. *phot:* Mikolaj Sprudin. *players:* Daniel Olbrychski, Leszek Drogosz, Tadeusz Kalinowski, Malgorzata Wlodarska.

FORWARD! *(Cala Naprzód)*. *script:* Ewa Szuminska and Stanislaw Lenartowicz. *dir:* Stanislaw Lenartowicz. *phot:* Tadeusz Wiezan and Jerzy Stawicki. *mus:* Wojciech Kilar. *players:* Zbigniew Cybulski, Zdzislaw Maklakiewicz, Teresa Tuszynska, Krzysztof Litwin.

SKINNY AND OTHERS *(Chudy i Inni)*. *script:* Wieslaw Dymny. *dir:* Henryk Kluba. *phot:* Wieslaw Zdort. *mus:* Wojciech Kilar. *players:* Wieslaw Golas, Franciszek Pieczka, Mieczyslaw Stoor, Ryszard Pietruski.

THE NUTCRACKER *(Dziadek do Orzechòw)*. *script:* Halina Bielinska and Maria Kruger, from the novel by E.T.A. Hoffmann. *dir:* Halina Bielinska. *phot:* Wladyslaw Forbert. *mus:* Zbigniew Turski. *players:* Wienczyslaw Glinski, Barbara Wrzesinska, Leon Niemczyk, Elzbieta Zagubien, Janusz Pomaski.

WHERE IS THE THIRD KING? *(Gdzie jest trzeci Król)*. *script:* Joe Alex. *dir:* Ryszard Ber. *phot:* Jacek Korcelli. *mus:* Adam Walacinski. *players:* Andrzej Lapicki, Alicja Wyszynska, Wienczyslaw Glinski, Kalina Jedrusik.

JOWITA. *script:* Tadeusz Konwicki, from the novel *Disneyland* by Stanislaw Dygat. *dir:* Janusz Morgenstern. *phot:* Jan Laskowski. *mus:* Jerzy Matuszkiewicz. *players:* Daniel Olbrychski, Barbara Kwiatkowska, Zbigniew Cybulski, Kalina Jedrusik.

LET'S LOVE SIRENS *(Kochajmy Syrenki)*. *script:* Jacek Federowicz. *dir:* Jan Rutkiewicz. *phot:* Waclaw Dybowski. *mus:* Adam Walacinski. *players:* Bohdan Lazuka, Jacek Federowicz, Alicja Sedzinska.

CONTRIBUTION *(Kontrybucja)*. *script:* Roman Bratny. *dir:* Jan Lomnicki. *phot:* Boguslaw Lambach. *mus:* Andrzej Kurylewicz. *players:* Wojciech Zasadzinski, Krystyna Mikolajewska, Jan Englert.

MARRIAGE OF CONVENIENCE *(Malzenstwo z Rozsadku)*. *script:* Kryzsztof Gruszczynski. *dir:* Stanislaw Bareja. *phot:* Franciszek Kadziolka. *mus:* Jerzy Matuszkiewicz. *players:* Elzbieta Czyzewska, Daniel Olbrychski, Bohdan Lazuka.
BIG BEAT *(Mocne uderzenie)*. *dir:* Jerzy Passendorfer. *phot:* Kazimierz Konrad. *mus:* Andrzej Zielinski. *players:* Magda Zawadzka, Jerzy Turek, Irena Szczurowska, Wienczyslaw Glinski.
THE MURDERER LEAVES CLUES *(Morderca zostawia Slad)*. *script* and *dir:* Aleksander Scibor-Rylski. *phot:* Kurt Weber. *mus:* Wojciech Kilar. *players:* Tadeusz Schmidt, Zbigniew Cybulski, Krystyna Mikolajewska.
RETURN TO EARTH *(Powrót na Ziemie)*. *script:* Kryzsztof Gruszczynski. *dir:* Stanislaw Jedryka. *phot:* Stanislaw Loth. *mus:* Wojciech Kilar. *players:* Ewa Krzyzewska, Stanislaw Mikulski, Barbara Bargielowska.
WE ARE ALL FRIENDS *(Sami Swoi)*. *script:* Andrzej Mularczyk. *dir:* Sylwester Checinski. *phot:* Stefan Matyjaszkiewicz. *mus:* Wojciech Kilar. *players:* Waclaw Kowalski, Wladyslaw Hancza, Ilona Kusmierska.
THE STABLE ON SALWATOR *(Stajnia na Salwatorze)*. *script:* Jan Józef Szczepanski. *dir:* Pawel Komorowski. *phot:* Wieslaw Zdort. *mus:* Wojciech Kilar. *players:* Janusz Gajos, Tadeusz Lomnicki, Ryszarda Hanin, Joanna Szczerbic.
THE WITCHES' WALL *(Sciana Czarownic)*. *script:* Andrzej Bonarski and Jerzy Suszko. *dir:* Pawel Komorowski. *phot:* Krzysztof Winiewicz. *mus:* Jerzy Matuszkiewicz. *players:* Zbigniew Dobrzynski, Jerzy Jogalla, Marta Lipinska, Iga Cembrzynska.
WESTERPLATTE. *script:* Jan Józef Szczepanski. *dir:* Stanislaw Rózewicz. *phot:* Jerzy Wójcik. *mus:* Wojciech Kilar. *players:* Zygmunt Hubner, Arkadiusz Bazak, Józef Nowak.
CRAZY NIGHT *(Zwariowana noc)*. *script:* Zdzislaw Skowronski, from the novel by Natalia Rolleczek. *dir:* Zbigniew Kuzminski. *phot:* Wieslaw Rutowicz. *mus:* Adama Walacinski. *players:* Maria Gella, Krystyna Chmielewska, Krystyna Sienkiewicz.
THE TENANT *(Sublokator)*. *script* and *dir:* Janusz Majewski. *phot:* Kurt Weber. *mus:* Andrzej Kurylewicz. *players:* Barbara Ludwizanka, Katarzyna Laniewska, Magda Zawadzka, Jan Machulski.
PARIS-WARSAW WITHOUT VISA *(Paryz-Warszawa bez Wizy)*. *script:* Kazimierz Kozniewski, based on short stories by Kazimierz Slawinski. *dir:* Hieronim Przybyl. *phot:* Stanislaw Loth. *mus:* Waldemar Kazanecki. *players:* Mieczyslaw Kalenik, Pola Raksa, Mieczyslaw Czechowicz.

notes on more recent productions

Three directors made their début in 1968: Witold Leszczynski, with *The Life of Matthew*, Jerzy Ziarnik, with *Trip into the Unknown*, and Jerzy Antczak, with the two-part historical epic *Countess Cosel*. A contemporary drama, *Julia, Anna, and Genevieve*, by Anna Sokolowska, has been received favourably by the critics, and the new film by Wojciech Has, *The Doll*, is ready for release. Wajda has dedicated the script of his *Everything is for Sale* to the late Zbigniew Cybulski.

4 shots from Andrzej Wajda's new film, EVERYTHING IS FOR SALE, starring Beata Tyszkiewicz and Elzbieta Czyzeska.

In *Westerplatte* one can find that rationalistic approach to the last war, so memorably outlined by the work of Andrzej Munk, in which heroism is vindicated within the scope of objective circumstances. *Westerplatte* tells of the remarkable defence of a stretch of the Polish coast by a handful of soldiers against German attacks from sea, land, and air. Throughout the Occupation this was the brightest symbol of sacrifice, patriotism, and heroism. Rózewicz follows the story closely, for it contains a good deal of truth, but he also shows the limits of struggle and resistance. The capitulation of soldiers from Westerplatte means, according to Rózewicz, preserving the forces for a different kind of resistance against the Nazi occupation.

The Life of Matthew, partly completed with the aid of the Lodz Film School, is a far cry from the average Polish movie. Slightly Scandinavian in atmosphere (for it was based on a novel by the Norwegian writer Tarjei Vesaas), it deals with the common problems of humanity. The undisputed visual beauty of this film and its hieratic rhythm has made a big impression, and reveals Leszczynski as a sensitive director who is using the cinema to discuss philosophical points of view.

Irena Karel and Marek Perepeczko (left) and Daniel Olbrychski in MR. WOLODYSOWSKI, directed by Jerzy Hoffman.

Maja Wodecka in DANCING IN HITLER'S HEADQUARTERS, directed by Jan Batory, and produced by the "Syrena" Film Unit, Film Polski.

Lucyna Winnicka (left), and Wieslaw Golas (right), in PLAY, directed by Jerzy Kawalerowicz.

Portugal

the current situation   by Vasco Granja

Nothing important has happened in the Portuguese cinema during the past year.
There are two basic reasons for this: the small number of cinemas in operation
(336 for the whole country); and the increasing influence of television (in 1958
there were 17,569 licences delivered by the state, and this number increased to
269,005 in 1967).

A new, young director, António de Macedo, has made a promising film *Domingo
à Tarde (Sunday in the Afternoon)*, but his second feature, *Sete Balas Para Selma*
(a satire about spy pictures) had no dramatic turning point to provide a real background for what was basically an adventure thriller. There are other promising
young directors like Fernando Lopes, Faria de Almeida, and Alfredo Tropa, but
they are compelled to work on commercial films, waiting to realise their own pet
projects. Paulo Rocha is another young film-maker with a bright future. He completed two highly evocative dramas in which the Portuguese locales appeared con-
vincingly: *Os Verdes Anos (The Green Years)*, and *Mudar de Vida (A Change in
Life)*.

Film societies in Portugal are fast disappearing in the face of tremendous
difficulties. Ten years ago there were 30 societies; now there are a mere 15. It is just
not possible to show films outside their normal commercial release, although
foreign embassies have helped the situation with their 16mm libraries. In 1967 some
355 films were imported, nearly half (155) coming from the U.S.A. There are
24 distributors, and 27 first-run cinemas (19 in Lisbon and 8 in Oporto). 7 features
were made domestically in 1967, which is about the average number of the past few
years.

recent films

SETE BALAS PARA SELMA *(Seven Bullets for Selma)*, *dir:* António de Macedo.
players: Florbella Queirós, Sinde Filipe, Baptista Fernandus. For Imperial Filmes.

A CRUZ DE FERRO *(The Iron Cross)*. *dir:* Jorge Brum do Canto. *players:* Jorge
Brum do Canto, Cremilda Gil, Octávio de Matos, Maria Domingas. For Tobis
Portuguesa.

142

Spain

the current situation   by William Dyckes

After a steady five-year climb, Spanish film production finally leveled off, finishing up with only 125 pictures in 1967 compared with 164 the year before. In large part this was due to a tightening up by the government, which was determined to cut out the cheaper, low-quality films. Italy, as always, led the co-production parade with 43 shared pictures; Argentina was the runner-up with 6. A promising 21 all-foreign productions worked in Spain during the year, again mostly Italian. And with the devaluation of the peseta making Spain a bargain once more, this trend seems likely to continue.

Television has apparently begun to have an effect on audiences, although attendance, at an average of 13.1 times a year per inhabitant, continues to be among the highest in Europe. A total of 337 films were premiered in Spain during 1967, of which 51 were national and another 51 Spanish co-productions. The U.S.A. led the import list with 98 and Britain was second with 38. In general, film import licences were up and the number of distributors increased.

The biggest news in distribution was the unexpected success of the new *art et essai* cinemas. Cidensa, a subsidiary of Mercurio Films, has tied up most of the market and expects to have more than 20 theatres throughout Spain by 1969, an incredible number given the Spaniard's lack of patience with other languages. Six art cinemas opened in Madrid alone within the first few months.

1968 was a tougher year for the young film-makers, who had begun to pick up speed the previous year. This seems largely due to the tightening of money and censorship after the devaluation. The most important casualty was the disappearance of the *Dirección General* of Cinema, now included under the heading of Popular Entertainment and Culture for reasons of economy, and the consequent loss of José Maria García Escudero, the man who was responsible for most of the recent advances and programmes to help the young film-makers. The death of Cesareo Gonzalez, one of the country's few large-scale producers, will also have a negative effect.

new and recent films

EL PRECIO DE UN HOMBRE (The Price of a Man). *dir:* Eugenio Martín, *players:* Richard Wyler, Tomás Milian. For Tecisa and Discóbolo Film.

HOMENAJE PARA ADRIANA (Homage to Adriana). *dir:* Miguel Picazo. *players:* Aurora Bautista. For Nova Cinematografica.

143

MAÑANA SERA OTRO DIA (Tomorrow is Another Day). *dir:* Jaime Camino. *players:* Sonia Bruno, Juan Luis Galiardo. For Tibidabo Films.

NOCTURNO 29 (Nocturno 29). *dir:* Pedro Portabella. *players:* Lucia Bosè and Gabrielle Ferzetti. For Films 59.

NO SOMOS DE PIEDRA (We're Not Made of Stone). *dir:* Manuel Summers. *players:* Alfredo Landa, Ingrid Garbo. For Kalender Films International and Eco Films.

STRESS ES TRES (Stress is Three). *dir:* Carlos Saura. *players:* Geraldine Chaplin, Fernando Cebrián, Juan Luís Galiardo. For Elias Querejeta.

UN DIABLO BAJO EL ALMOHADA (A Devil Under the Pillow). *dir:* José María Forqué. *players:* Ingrid Thulin, Maurice Ronet, Gabriele Ferzetti. For P. C. Orfeo, S.A.

Geraldine Chaplin in Carlos Saura's PEPPERMINT FRAPPÉ, winner of the best direction prize at Berlin 1968.

Sweden

introduction   by Peter Cowie

A week's "Mostra" of films at the Sorrento festival this September was the climax of one of the healthiest years in the Swedish cinema industry. In the five years since Svenska Filminstitutet was established, feature film production has doubled, export revenue has increased by more than 300%, yearly Swedish box-office receipts have moved up from 27 million dollars to 38 million dollars. Bo Widerberg's *Elvira Madigan* earned enormous rentals in America and would surely have won an Oscar had the Swedish Film Academy not nominated Troell's *Here is Your Life* instead. By so doing, the Academy put principles ahead of opportunism — and fell between two stools, for the Troell picture, though more important than *Elvira Madigan*, was unknown in America.

Despite the comparative commercial failure of *Ole dole doff*, Troell is now engaged on the biggest production ever undertaken by Svensk Filmindustri, a two-part adaptation of Vilhelm Moberg's sequence of novels about the Swedish emigration to America in the 1850s. Both films, *The Emigrants* and *Unto a Good Land*, will be shot partly in Canada and the U.S.A., from a script by Troell and Bengt Forslund, his producer and mentor.

Another ambitious project is a co-production with the U.S.S.R., directed by Mikhaïl Bogin, on the trade between Sweden and the Soviet Union in the twenties when an international boycott was in practice. The film is financed jointly by Gorky Film, Moscow, and Svensk Filmindustri.

On the economic front, a far-sighted decision has been taken, empowering Svenska Filminstitutet to guarantee loans of up to 25% of a domestic film's budget. To create this Guarantee Fund (which will come into operation in July 1969), the Institute will reduce its general support to Swedish films in relation to their box-office receipts and the sums that have gone to producers of films that have won quality awards but not broken even.

The top monetary awards of the Institute in 1967 went to *Persona* (555,000 Kr.), *Here is Your Life* (475,000 Kr.), and *Elvira Madigan* (280,000 Kr.). Special awards (Guldbaggar) went to Bibi Andersson, Per Oscarsson, Jan Troell, and Krister Wickman; while the magazine *Chaplin* gave its prizes to Kjell Grede, Göran Lindgren, Lena Nyman and Vilgot Sjöman, and to Christer Frunck's VI-Film, one of the few independent importers of quality films in Scandinavia. Frunck, who helped to launch Stig Björkman's feature, *I Love, You Love*, is a former Head of Information at the Film Institute, and over the past three years he has purchased titles like *Le Signe du Lion*, *Paris nous appartient*, *Vidas Secas*, *Oz Fuzis*, and several Chris Marker documentaries.

COMING  EVENTS

Ingmar Bergman's
SKAMMEN
The Shame

Cast: Liv Ullmann, Max von Sydow, Gunnar Björnstrand, Sigge Fürst
Photography: Sven Nykvist
World première September 1968
Production: AB SVENSK FILMINDUSTRI
World distribution (outside Scandinavia): UNITED ARTISTS

Bo Widerberg's
THE ÅDAL RIOTS

Based on the strike disorders in northern Sweden in 1931.
A colour film in red and black —
the symbolic colours of the Ådal drama.

Shooting scheduled for the summer of 1968
Production: AB SVENSK FILMINDUSTRI

Jan Troell's UTVANDRARNA
och
INVANDRARNA
The Emigrants and Unto a Good Land

Film dramatisation of the first two of Vilhelm Moberg's sequence of four novels
on the Swedish emigration to America in the 1850s. Screenplay: Bengt Fors-
lund, Jan Troell.
Cast: Liv Ullmann, Max von Sydow and others.
Photography: Jan Troell
Shooting to begin in January 1969.
Première scheduled for Christmas 1970.
Production: AB SVENSK FILMINDUSTRI

AB SVENSK FILMINDUSTRI, Kungsgatan 36, 111 35 STOCKHOLM, Sweden
Telephone: 22 14 00 Cables: FILMINDUSTRI

In the period July 1967 to June 1968, 22 Swedish feature films were released, and some 303 foreign features were released for distribution. There are now 1,655 cinemas operating in the country.

recent and forthcoming films

ÅDALEN (The Ådal Riots). *dir:* Bo Widerberg. *2 tone colour.* For Svensk Filmindustri. *Based on the strike disorders in Northern Sweden in 1931.*

BADARNA (The Bathers). *dir:* Yngve Gamlin. *phot:* Jan Lindeström. *players:* Ingrid Thulin, Gunilla Olsson, Halvar Björk, Björn Gustafson. For Sandrews.

BOKHANDLAREN SOM SLUTADE BADA (The Bookseller who Stopped Bathing). *dir:* Jarl Kulle. *players:* Allan Edwall, Jarl Kulle, Margareta Krook. For Sandrews.

DOM KALLAR OSS MODS (They Call Us Misfits). *dir. and phot:* Stefan Jarl and Jan Lindqvist. *players:* Kenta Gustafsson, Stoffe Svensson. For Svenska Filminstitutet.

FLICKORNA (The Girls). *dir:* Mai Zetterling. *phot:* Rune Ericson. *players:* Bibi Andersson, Harriet Andersson, Gunnel Lindblom, Gunnar Björnstrand. For Sandrews.

HOT SNOW. *dir:* Torbjörn Axelman. For Nordisk Tonefilm.

KORRIDOREN (The Corridor). *dir:* Jan Halldoff. *players:* Per Ragnar, Agneta Ekmanner, Ake Lindström, Inga Landgré. For Svensk Filmindustri.

Max von Sydow and Liv Ullmann in Ingmar Bergman's THE SHAME (Skammen), produced by Svensk Filmindustri, Stockholm.

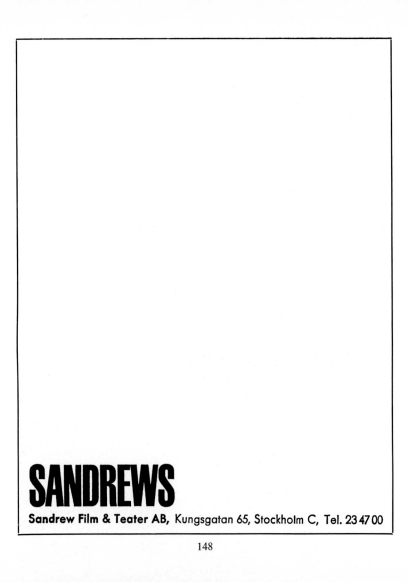

SANDREWS

Sandrew Film & Teater AB, Kungsgatan 65, Stockholm C, Tel. 23 47 00

MADE IN SWEDEN. *dir:* Johan Bergenstråhle. *players:* Per Myrberg, Lena Granhagen. For Svensk Filmindustri.

OOMPH! *dir:* Stig Björkman. *players:* Lou Castel, Evabritt Strandberg.

RITORNA (The Rites). *dir:* Ingmar Bergman. *phot:* Sven Nykvist. *players:* Ingrid Thulin, Anders Ek, Gunnar Björnstrand, Erik Hell. For Sveriges TV.

SKAMMEN (The Shame). *dir:* Ingmar Bergman. *phot:* Sven Nykvist. *players:* Liv Ullmann, Max von Sydow, Gunnar Björnstrand, Sigge Fürst. For Svensk Filmindustri.

SOM NATT OG DAG (Like Night and Day). *dir:* Jonas Cornell. *players:* Agneta Ekmanner, Gösta Ekman, Keve Hjelm. For Sandrews.

STOCKHOLMSSOMMAR (Summer in Stockholm). *dir:* Tor-Ivan Odulf. *players:* Lena Madsen, Anders Petersen. For Sandrews/Tor-Ivan Odulf/Svenska Filminstitutet.

SVARTA PALMKRONOR (The Black Palm Trees). *dir:* Lars-Magnus Lindgren. *phot:* Gunnar Fischer (colour). *players:* Max von Sydow, Bibi Andersson, Thommy Berggren, Toralf Maurstad. For Sandrews.

UTVANDRARNA and INVANDRARNA (The Emigrants and Unto A Good Land). *dir. and phot:* Jan Troell. *players:* Liv Ullmann, Max von Sydow, Eddie Axberg. For Svensk Filmindustri.

VILLERVALLE I SÖDERHAVET (Villervalle in the South Seas). *dir:* Torgny Anderberg. *phot:* Bengt Dalmde, Bengt Börjesson (colour). *players:* Roland Grönros, Olof Thunberg, Gittan Wemström. For Nordisk Tonefilm.

VINDINGEVALS (Vindinge Waltz). *dir:* Ake Falck. *phot:* Mac Ahlberg (colour). *players:* Gio Petré, Keve Hjelm, Diana Kjaer, Erik Hell, Cay Bond. For Minerva Film.

Kenta Gustafsson and Stoffe Svensson in THEY CALL US MISFITS, produced by Svenska Filminstitutet and directed by Jan Lindqvist and Stefan Jarl.

HUGO OCH JOSEFIN
(Hugo and Josefin)

Script: Kjell Grede and Maria Gripe, from the latter's books; *Direction:* Grede; *Photography:* Lasse Björne (colour); *Editing:* Lars Hagström; *Music:* Torbjörn Lundqvist; *Players:* Frederik Becklén, Marie Ohman, Inga Landgré, Helena Brodin, Bellan Roos, Beppe Wolgers. For Sandrews. 82 mins.

A children's film for adults might be the best description of *Hugo and Josefin*, the first feature by Kjell Grede, husband of Bibi Andersson and heretofore a writer and painter. Josefin is a stout-hearted, independent little girl, seven years old. She becomes fast friends with Hugo, whose father is apparently a conscientious objector serving a term in prison. Their adventures, their conversations, their discoveries: these form the fabric of the film. This is a children's vision of things and yet we, the adults, can interpret the facts that Hugo and Josefin can only absorb with curiosity. We can appreciate the kindly tact and concern with which the old gardener treats his two young charges. It is difficult too, not to respond to the unself-conscious acting of Marie Öhman and Frederik Becklén, and to the atmosphere of the Swedish countryside in summer, evoked so warmly by Lasse Björne's colour photography. "Before it opened," says Grede, "I showed the film to two children. One said afterwards that it was fun because it was like a Sunday morning when one lies in bed and experiences a lot of things and one does not know whether or not one is awake or in a dream" — **Peter Cowie.**

Sven Bertil Taube and Essy Persson in *SUMMER OF THE LION (Lejonssommar)*, directed with zest and humour for Nordisk Tonefilm by Torbjörn Axelman, whose first comedy, *OJ OJ OJ*, we welcomed so enthusiastically in IFG 1967.

Another eloquent shot from SUMMER OF THE LION.

Jarl Kulle under his own direction in the new Sandrews production THE BOOKSELLER WHO STOPPED BATHING (Bokhandlaren som slutade bada).

Bibi Andersson, Harriet Andersson, and Gunnel Lindblom play the leading roles in Mai Zetterling's THE GIRLS (Flickorna), produced by Sandrews of Stockholm.

VARGTIMMEN
(The Hour of the Wolf)

Script and Direction: Ingmar Bergman; *Photography:* Sven Nykvist; *Editing:* Ulla Ryghe; *Music:* Lars Johan Werle, Bach, Mozart; *Art Direction:* Marik Vos-Lundh; *Players:* Liv Ullmann, Max von Sydow, Erland Josephson, Gertrud Fridh, Ingrid Thulin, Gudrun Brost. For Svensk Filmindustri. 90 mins.

Like Strindberg, Bergman persists in distilling his inner emotions through his art, masochistically shedding those obsessions that spring from a stern and confined childhood. Johan Borg as the painter is revealed to be a far more complicated and devious personality than his outward shyness suggests. He is a prey to demons, personified in the Baron von Merkens and the sinister occupants of his castle. A lassoo of positive hatred and viciousness seems to close tighter and tighter round Johan until at last he is trapped by his predatory hosts in a swamp where the trickling water could as well be blood. The film is terrifying because it has the hallucinatory texture of a dream — a dream materialised, as it were, by the director. But the structure of the script — flashbacks illustrating Johan's diary — is just not strong enough to withstand the pressures that Bergman's weird imagination exerts upon it. The characters are described in rather trite terms; and Erland Josephson, as the Baron, is a medieval concept of Death dressed too meticulously in modern clothing. So one refers to *The Hour of the Wolf* not for a unified expression of Bergman's

Per Myrberg and Lena Granhagen in MADE IN SWEDEN, directed by Johan Bergenstrahle for Svensk Filmindustri, Stockholm.

themes but for some unnerving sequences that command admiration for their sheer visual sorcery and communion of anguish: the after-dinner interlude with the toy theatre and *Die Zauberflöte;* or the struggle with the boy among the rocks, while Lars Johan Werle's music whirrs, buzzes, and shrieks in the background — **Peter Cowie.**

JAG ÄR NYFIKEN
(I Am Curious)

Idea and Direction: Vilgot Sjöman; *Photography:* Peter Wester; *Editing:* Wic Kjellin; *Music:* Bengt Ernryd; *Players:* Lena Nyman, Börje Ahlstedt, Peter Lindgren, Gunnel Broström. For Sandrews. Yellow Edition 121 mins. Blue Edition 107 mins.

The two parts of *I Am Curious* comprise an intensely cruel and witty salvo against the complacency of Swedish society. The ubiquitous Lena Nyman tries on Sjöman's behalf to rouse the apparently dead animal that is social democracy in Sweden today. But all her research, all her diligent and impudent inquiries, finally convince this lively blonde that she cannot cling to her ideal of non-violence, and that it is, above all, inapplicable to private life. Whereas the *Yellow* part is dominated by a welter of sexual happenings, the *Blue* edition takes Sjöman's *cinéma-vérité* explorations to more persuasive and less flippant ends. His dialectic grows increasingly disenchanted. He claims that Sweden boasts about sociological advances that are in truth very amateurish. He touches on the penal system and the division between Church and State. Over three hours, then, of opinions and jokes, a political broadsheet rather than a work of art. Bergman has called it a masterpiece, but while the experimental nature of *I Am Curious* is never in doubt, the blend of sex and socialism is still uneasy and — in a foreigner's eyes — parochial — **Peter Cowie.**

Agneta Ekmanner and Per Ragnar in Jan Halldoff's new film, THE CORRIDOR (Korridoren), produced by Bengt Forslund for Svensk Filmindustri, Stockholm.

Lena Nyman in I AM CURIOUS, Blue Edition.

*Diana Kjaer
in the title role of
FANNY HILL
IN SWEDEN,
produced by
Minerva Film AB,
Stockholm.*

Borrow short films
about Sweden from our
distributors abroad:

Great Britain
Sound-Services Ltd.
Kingston Road
Merton Park
LONDON SW 19

USA
Modern Talking Picture
Service Inc.
1212 Ave. of the Americas
NEW YORK, N.Y.
10036

Australia
National Library of
Australia
Film Division
113 London Circuit
CANBERRA CITY,
A.C.T.

New Zealand
National Film Library
Clifton Terrace
WELLINGTON C. 1

France
Céfilm
31, av. Pierre 1 er de
Serbie
PARIS 16e

Belgium
Sofedi-Films
147, av. de l'Hippodrôme
BRUSSELS

Netherlands
RVD
Noordeinde 43
THE HAGUE

Technical Film Centre
152 Stadhouderslaan
THE HAGUE

Italy
DIFI
Via G.L. Lagrange 9
00197 ROME

Germany
Landesfilmdienst
Rheinallee 59
532 BAD GODESBERG

KFW Filmothek
7407 ROTTENBURG/
Neckar

Austria
Wirtschaftsförderungs-
institut
Hoher Markt 3
VIENNA 1

Switzerland
Schmalfilm-Zentrale
Erlachstrasse 21
3000 BERN 9

Denmark
Statens Filmcentral
Vestergade 27
COPENHAGEN K

We have a great variety of 16 mm short films on different aspects of Swedish life and culture in English (or American), French, German, Spanish, Portuguese, Italian, Dutch, Finnish, Japanese and a few other languages. Most of them in colour. Also available through Swedish embassies abroad.

For a **40-page Film Catalogue and futher information (also about sale of films) please contact**

THE SWEDISH INSTITUTE
Film Section
Box 3306
S-103 66 STOCKHOLM, Sweden

JAG ALSKAR, DU ALSKAR

(I Love, You Love)

Script: Stig Björkman, Jonas Cornell; *Direction:* Björkman; *Photography:* Andreas Bellis, Roland Lundin; *Editing:* Ingemar Ejve; *Music:* Hansson & Karlsson; *Players:* Evabritt Strandberg, Sven Wollter, Agneta Ekmanner, Dexter Gordon, Olle Björling. For Sten & Helena Co-Op, Svenska Filminstitutet. 92 mins.

Images and lines of dialogue, unfunny on their own, are fused by Stig Björkman to create a bright and appreciable hilarity in *I Love, You Love*. The film whisks along between its pauses of shared intimacy in the life of a couple. Sten and Helena are expecting a baby at the wrong end of their affair. They both feel rather amateurish about the business of parenthood. Sten's frustration before the happy event prompts him to sleep with another girl; Helena's emotional weariness after the birth leads to the end of the relationship. There are no acrimonious quarrels; the bitter taunts remain unspoken. Björkman's relaxed style finds perfect expression through Evabritt Strandberg, previously noted in Widerberg's *Love 65*. She has the same introspective, sensual knack of staring as Monica Vitti, and manages to be beautiful even when pregnant. Without uttering a word, she seems to out-argue the girl in the canteen who harangues her for having children. The only weakness of the film is that some of its best scenes, like those with Agneta Ekmanner, or the parody-within-a-parody of gangster films involving Harriet Andersson and Gösta Ekman, are essentially marginal to the theme. But as a début, *I Love, You Love* is excellent, marrying sex and verbal wit as effectively as *Hugs and Kisses* did last year — **Peter Cowie.**

Evabritt Strandberg.

157

OLE DOLE DOFF
(Eeny Meeny Miny Moe)

Script: Bengt Forslund, Jan Troell, Clas Engström, from the latter's novel "The Island Sinks"; *Direction, Photography, Editing:* Jan Troell; *Music:* none; *Players:* Per Oscarsson, Kerstin Tidelius, Ann-Marie Gyllenspetz, Harriet Forssell, Bengt Ekerot. For Svensk Filmindustri. 110 mins.

The modern Swedish cinema burst on the international scene nearly 25 years ago with *Frenzy*. The film was set in a boys' school. Now Jan Troell, whose *Here is Your Life* established him as a major director, has returned to the theme. But this time it is the schoolmaster who feels himself persecuted and inadequate. The script of *Ole dole doff* is unusually intelligent, shifting from its early tone of sympathy with the master to an objectivity that shows both teacher and children to be victims of their own illusions, unable to cross the no-man's land that lies between them. The film was shot in Troell's old school in Malmö, but it also finds its visual drama in the environment of the city and in nature. Oscarsson is seen discreetly as the outcast from a happy community, the gull disliked by the other birds, as the glimpse of Sucksdorff's *Trut!* at the school film society emphaises. He is misled by his own zeal; undermined by a cold and childless marriage; and finally ineffectual because he sides instinctively with the class against himself. Only once, in a beautifully written scene with Ann-Marie Gyllenspetz in the forest, does he achieve peace and a degree of self-knowledge. Troell has photographed and edited the film himself, contrasting moments of happiness and glamour with the harsh routine of the school, where the cacophony of shrill voices and slamming desks frays the patience of the teachers — **Peter Cowie.**

Per Oscarsson as the schoolteacher in OLE DOLE DOFF.

158

Bibi Andersson and Max von Sydow in THE BLACK PALM TREES (Svarta palmkronor), directed by Lars Magnus Lindgren for Sandrews of Stockholm.

Diana Kjaer and Mats Olin in VINDINGE WALTZ, produced by Minerva Film AB, Stockholm.

Switzerland

the current situation

by Felix Bucher

The greatest surprise that inaugurated the 1967-68 season in Swiss cinema was for many the quality of the final exercises produced by pupils at the first Film Training Course. Under the tuition of Krut Früh, Prof. Stanislas Wohl, and Hans-Rudolf Strobel, future directors, scriptwriters, cameramen, and producers were able to learn the basic rules and had to shoot a communal film at the end of it all. Eleven films and a short documentary about the work during the course: no masterpieces, certainly, but proof of several talented young students who are addicted to the cinema.

Below: from Helmut Förnbacher's SOMMERSPROSSEN, produced by Atlantic-Film (Zürich).

In Soloturn, however, where for two or three days each year one has the opportunity of seeing nearly the entire range of Swiss film production, the long awaited breakthrough was not yet apparent. Many amateurs came to present their work, most of it underexposed, blurred, clumsily edited and overlong, and these were the very people who criticised the work of the Zürich film course (mentioned above) because they felt that organised schooling would inhibit freedom of expression.

It did become clear in Soloturn, nevertheless, that the French-speaking cantons were rather more advanced than their German-speaking neighbours. In Lausanne, Geneva, and other towns, there is obviously a good deal of thought and ideas being given to film-making. There are many projects that should turn out well, and, furthermore, directors in French-speaking Switzerland are greatly helped by television. In the German cantons, apprentice film-makers are not encouraged to make shorts that could be shown later on television. The number of plays and documentaries produced for the small screen in Zürich is surprisingly low, both qualitatively and quantitatively.

Steps are being taken, though, apart from financial aid from the Confederation in the form of money prizes, to start a Swiss film centre which would stimulate and supervise the production of shorts, documentaries, and feature films. The idea of such an institute, which would be subsidised from the private sector of the industry as well as by the State, is to banish the malaise that has handicapped national film-making for so long.

Two new features will be completed during 1968, a comedy called *Eugen* by the former cameraman Rolf Lyssy (who photographed *Ursula* last year), and the Swiss-angled Bonnie and Clyde ballad *Sommersprossen*, directed by the actor Helmut Förnbacher. *Sommersprossen* is one of those films which could not have been made without the active help of the brothers Peter and Martin Hellstern, owners of **Atlantic-Film** (production), and **Rialto-Film** (distribution). Atlantic-Film guaranteed Förnbacher an international co-production. Similar cases of financial participation by the Hellsterns in international productions include *Eine Ehe*, directed by Strobel and Tichawsky, and the Yugoslav animated films *Tolerance* (awarded the Gandhi Prize), *The Suitcase*, *The Flower*, *The Things*, *Major and Minor Manoeuvres*, and *1 plus 1 = 3*. The successful educational film *Helga* was a personal production of the Hellstern brothers, while co-productions have been arranged for similar pictures such as *Eva, die verstandene Frau* and *Du* (by Professors Giese and Hochheimer).

Furthermore the Hellsterns are proud to announce that after *West and Soda* they have also acquired for world distribution Bruno Bozzetto's second full-length cartoon, *VIP, My Brother Superman*. Their Swiss distribution of new German films has also been extended, to include *Tätowierung* and *Schonzeit für Füchse*, *Negresco* (directed by Klaus Lemke), *Zur Sache, Schätzchen* (see our West German section for review), and *Engelchen*, by Maran Gosov, with several more titles in the offing.

Fairly important advances have been made in the field of distribution. A few enterprising firms, such as **Columbus Films** in Zürich and **Ideal** in Geneva, have been increasingly concerned with the small studio film. Columbus is extending its programme of quality pictures, and Ideal is collaborating more and more closely with German television so that communal premières can be arranged.

ANGÈLE

Script and Direction: Yves Yersin; *Photography:* Renato Berta and Pierre Delessert; *Music:* Alfred Thuillard and Roland Sassi; *Players:* Angèle Grammont, Lucie Avenay, André Manuel, Henriette Friederich. For Milos Film, Lausanne.

This deserved success was the only Swiss entry in the important Semaine de la Critique at Cannes in 1968. Yersin's work, which could be termed a medium-length documentary, is part of a 4-episode film entitled *Quatre d'entre elles* (although it can be safely said that the other 3 parts do not reach the high standard set by *Angèle*). This is really a report of an elderly lady who has perforce to settle down in an old folks' hospice near Lausanne and who, spurred by her *joie de vivre* and her desire for communication, escapes from the home. The ending is indecisive. We see her wandering through the streets of the town . . . The events in this old lady's life are re-created with perfect sensitivity by Yersin, and Madame Grammont herself lives the role with an intense look and a wonderful presence. The social criticism implicit in the film arises less from the images than from this remarkable woman's monologue, spoken off-screen spontaneously as she sees again the humiliation and the isolation of the hospice — **Felix Bucher.**

A scene from THE SUIT-CASE, directed by Zlatko Grgic and Branko Ranitovic for Viba-Film and Atlantic Film.

Turkey

the current situation by Atillâ Dorsay

Turkey has been making films since 1914. After a long period during which the Turkish cinema was under the complete domination of the theatre, a new generation, beginning in the Forties, created a true film language. At the present time, cinema still remains the most popular and least expensive form of entertainment. This is the main reason why the annual cinema production is now over 200 films per year. Nearly 400 foreign films are imported and there are about 1,000 cinemas in the entire country, a number which is certainly not sufficient for a country whose population is over 30,000,000. Istanbul has always been the centre of the cinema industry and the "Yesilçam Street" is Turkey's Hollywood. During the last ten years, Turkey has been participating in international film festivals and the "Golden Bear" prize, received at the Berlin Film Festival in 1964 for Metin Erksan's *Susuz Yaz (The Dry Summer)* has marked a turning point in the Turkish cinema. At the moment, Turkish film directors are trying to take their part in the most international and the most communicative of all arts. Lütfü Ö. Akad, Metin Erksan, Memduh Ün, Atif Yilmaz, Halit Refiğ, and Turgut Demirağ are some of the most significant directors in the Turkish cinema today.

recent and forthcoming films

THE REVENGE OF THE GIANTS. *dir:* Fevzi Tuna. *phot:* Ali Yaver. *script:* Fevzi Tuna. *players:* Fikret Hakan, Erkut Taçkin, Zeynep Aksu, Erol Tas. For And Film, Turgut N. Demirağ.
THE STORY OF A MOUNTAIN. *dir:* Turgut N. Demirağ. *phot:* Gani Turanli. *script:* Turgut N. Demirağ. *players:* Türkân Soray, Murat Soydan, Kuzey Vargin, Erol Tezeren. For And Film, Turgut N. Demirağ.
ABBASE THE SULTANA. *dir:* Turgut N. Demirağ. *phot:* Cahit Engin. *script:* Sevda Sezer. *players:* Türkân Soray, Murat Soydan. For And Film, Turgut N. Demirağ.

A.I.K - FILM

c/o S. Ürkmez	Rindögatan 19,
Hasircibasi Sokak 34/5	3 Tr.
Kadiköy Istanbul	115-36 Stockholm No.
TURKEY	SWEDEN

Production—Co-production—distribution of feature and TV films in Turkey and Sweden.

165

―AND FILM―

Turgut N. Demirag
Agacami arkasi - Eren Han, Beyoglu
Istanbul, Turkey

Production - Distribution - Co-production

AHMED THE SHEIK. *dir.*: Ertem Egilmez. *script:* Bülent Oran. *phot:* Kenan Kurt (Eastmancolor). *players:* Sara Stephan, Fikret Hakan. For Ayten Kuyululu and Irfan Unal, A.I.K. Film. *Based on the same story that inspired the Rudolph Valentino vehicle, with the emphasis on the social aspect of the legend. Ahmed is the young, idealistic leader of an oriental and uneducated tribe.*

THE WORLD IS SMALL. *dir:* Fevzi Tuna. *script:* Ayten Kuyululu and Ismet Soydan. *phot:* Gani Turanli. *players:* Fikret Hakan, Ilhan Kuyululu. For Ayten Kuyululu, A.I.K. Film. *This is a semi-documentary feature film about the Turkish workers who have migrated to Western Europe – their social, economical, and emotional experiences. The film asks why they are leaving their own country, and what they are looking for. And it shows how they are torn between Turkey and Europe.*

MY WOMAN. *dir:* Lütfü ö. Akad. *script:* Safa Onal. *phot:* Ali Ugur. *players:* Türkân Soray, Izzet Günay, Ayfer Feray. For Seref Gür, Seref Film, released through Erman Film.

THE KILLER. *dir. and script:* Lütfü ö. Akad. *phot:* Ali Ugur. *players:* Yilmaz Güney, Hülya Darcan, Hayatî Hamzaoglu. For Seref Gür, Seref Film, released through Erman Film.

SEYIT HAN. *dir. and script:* Yilmaz Güney. *phot:* Gani Turanli. *players:* Yilmaz Güney, Nebahat Çehre, Hayatî Hamzaoglu. For Güney Film, released through Erman Film.

A WOMAN NEVER FORGETS. *dir.* Orhan Aksoy. *script:* Hamdi Degirmenci and Orhan Aksoy. *phot:* Ilhan Arakon (Eastmancolor). *players:* Hülya Koçyigit, Ediz Hun, Selma Güneri, Ahmet Mekin. For Erman Film.

ERMAN FILM

Hurrem Erman

**Alyon sokak, Erman Han,
Beyoglu-Istanbul, Turkey**

Distribution — Production

THE REVENGE OF
THE GIANTS.
*Erkut Taçkin and
Zeynep Aksu.
Distributed by
And Film, Istanbul.*

*A scene from
SEYIT HAN, with
Nebahat Çehre,
distributed by Erman
Film, Istanbul.*

M.G.M. presents
A JOHN FRANKENHEIMER-EDWARD LEWIS PRODUCTION

"THE FIXER"

*a man
who is guilty
of being innocent!*

**starring ALAN BATES
DIRK BOGARDE, HUGH GRIFFITH,
ELIZABETH HARTMAN, IAN HOLM,
DAVID WARNER, CAROL WHITE**

screenplay by Dalton Trumbo
produced by Edward Lewis
directed by   John Frankenheimer

U.S.A.

the current situation   **by Margot S. Kernan**

Commercial production in the United States is undergoing some interesting changes. Despite cries of "runaway production" from the Hollywood unions, more and more major American motion pictures are being made abroad with international casts and technicians, leaving the Hollywood studios increasingly occupied with television production. Changing business patterns have produced mergers, such as Transamerica Corporation with United Artists, and Gulf and Western with Paramount. Taking their cue from McLuhan perhaps, publishing firms have started buying into film companies. TIME, Inc. now owns 315,000 shares of M-G-M, and is represented on the M-G-M board of directors. Contemporary Films and its 35mm affiliate, Pathé Contemporary, are now divisions of McGraw-Hill publishing company.

Most noteworthy, perhaps, is the recent sharp rise in the appreciation of film as an art form in the United States. This can be attributed to several sources: the increasing financial support of independent film production from the major foundations, the increase in film teaching courses, and the formation in 1967 of the American Film Institute, which has established a generous programme of support for independent directors, student film-makers, and scholars.

The Institute, headed by George Stevens, Jr., is a non-government organisation, mainly funded by grants from the Ford Foundation, the Motion Picture Association of America, and the National Council on the Arts and Humanities. Institute grants to independent and student film-makers are given quarterly. The first independents to receive financial support were: Nell Cox, David Abramson, Storm De Hirsch *(Goodbye in the Mirror)*, Thomas McDonough (who co-directed *12-12-42)*, Robert Russett, Paul Sharits, and Jimmy Murakami *(The Top)*. First Student awards were given to Mark Fine, James Mannas, and Edwin Lynch of New York University, Thom Andersen and James Bryan of UCLA, and Howard Smith of Northwestern.

Besides independent production, the Institute is also supporting film education and history projects ($10,000 to UCLA for a taped "oral history" of the motion picture in America) and is making a major effort to build a definitive American archive. "Lost" films, especially those made in America between 1912 and 1942, are being tracked down by Institute archivist Richard Kahlenberg and will be preserved in the Library of Congress under the curatorship of Dr. John Kuiper, head of the Motion Picture section there.

Foundation assistance to individual film-makers comes also from Guggenheim and Ford. Recent winners of Guggenheim Fellowships for film include James Blue *(Les Oliviers de la Justice)*, Robert Downey (whose *Chafed Elbows* was reviewed in

169

"WE MAKE THE BIG ONES BIGGER"

Every picture handled with $T.L.C.$ *(tender loving care)*

A MAN AND A WOMAN

BATTLE OF ALGIERS

BELLE de JOUR

---

and coming:

CLAUDE BERRI'S "MAZEL TOV OR THE WEDDING"

ALLIED ARTISTS

230 West 41st St., New York, N. Y. 10036

"Makes the BIG ones BIGGER"

170

IFG 1968), Jordan Belson *(Allures)*, Bruce Baillie *(To Parsifal)*, and Robert Hughes (writer and producer of the Academy Award winning documentary, *Robert Frost, A Lover's Quarrel with the World*).

In 1968, the Ford Foundation donated $40,000 to the Film Culture Non-Profit Corporation — to assist the Filmmakers Cinémathèque theatre in New York and to support the work of directors Shirley Clarke, Jonas Mekas, Ed Emshwiller, P. Adams Sitney, Kenneth Anger, Stan Brakhage, and Andy Warhol.

The issues of the Vietnam war and civil rights are being examined by American film-makers with increasing candour. One outstanding example is William C. Jersey's documentary, *A Time for Burning*, an impressive direct cinema record of a minister's attempt to integrate his Omaha church. Another is Robert Kramer's feature film, *The Edge*, a riveting study of a would-be presidential assassin and his milieu, reminiscent of Rivette's *Paris nous appartient*. Kramer, Robert Machover (who photographed *The Edge*), and Peter Gessner *(The Time of the Locust)* are all associated with the "Newsreel" group in New York, an organisation established to produce "politically and socially committed" news films from the New Left.

The National Student Association hopes to expand its American Student Film Festival to an International festival, tentatively scheduled for the spring of 1969 in New York. Cultural Affairs Director Arthur Wiener seeks also to assemble a collection of important student films from here and abroad for international distribution.

Gross box-office receipts from U.S. motion picture theatres amounted to an estimated $960,000,000 in 1967, according to the U.S. Department of Commerce. Confirmed tabulations may push that figure twenty million dollars or so higher.

recent and forthcoming films

THE STALKING MOON. *dir:* Robert Mulligan. *players:* Gregory Peck, Eva Marie Saint, Robert Forster, Noland Clay, Joaquin Martinez, Charles Tyner. Produced by Alan Pakula for National General.

THE SUBJECT WAS ROSES. *dir:* Ulu Grosbard. *players:* Patricia Neal, Jack Albertson, Martin Sheen. Produced by Edgar Lansbury for M-G-M.

PAPER LION. *dir:* Alex March. *players:* Alan Alda, Lauren Hutton, George Plimpton, Sugar Ray Robinson. Produced by Stuart Millar for United Artists.

MINGUS. *dir:* Thomas Reichman. *phot:* Lee Osborne, Mike Wadley. *Music and Poetry* by Charles Mingus. Produced by Thomas Reichman. Released by Film-Makers Distribution Center, New York.

SKIDOO. *dir:* Otto Preminger. *players:* Carol Channing, Jackie Gleason, John Phillip Law, Mickey Rooney, Paul Ford, Doro Merande, Frankie Avalon, Cesar Romero, Frank Gorshin. Produced by Otto Preminger for Paramount.

THE SWIMMER. *dir:* Frank Perry. *script:* Eleanor Perry, from a story by John Cheever. *players:* Burt Lancaster, Janice Rule, Janet Landgard. Produced by Frank Perry and Roger Lewis for Columbia.

THE RAIN PEOPLE. *dir:* Francis Coppola. *players:* Shirley Knight, James Caan,

Rip Torn. Produced by Ron Colby and Bart Patton for Warner Bros.-Seven Arts.

THE CONFESSIONS OF NAT TURNER. *dir:* Norman Jewison. *script:* Louis Peterson from the William Styron novel. Produced by David L. Wolper for 20th Century-Fox.

FUNNY GIRL. *dir:* William Wyler. *players:* Barbra Streisand, Omar Sharif, Kay Medford, Anne Francis, Walter Pidgeon. Produced by Ray Stark for Columbia.

HARRY. *dir:* Michael Roemer. *phot:* Robert Young. Produced by Michael Roemer and Robert Young for Dawn Film Company.

THE FIXER. *dir:* John Frankenheimer. *players:* Alan Bates, Dirk Bogarde, Jack Gilford, Elizabeth Hartman, Georgia Brown, David Warner, Ian Holm, Carol White. Produced by Edward Lewis for M-G-M.

THE LATENT HETEROSEXUAL. *dir:* Anthony Harvey. *script:* Paddy Chayevsky, from his own play. *With* Zero Mostel. For Embassy Pictures.

THE WILD BUNCH. *dir:* Sam Peckinpah. *players:* William Holden, Robert Ryan. For Warner Brothers-Seven Arts.

THE LEARNING TREE. *dir:* Gordon Parks. For Warner Brothers-Seven Arts.

CASTLE KEEP. *dir.* Sydney Pollack. *players:* Peter Falk, Burt Lancaster, Richard Crenna, Jean-Pierre Aumont, Tony Bill, Caterina Boratto, All Freeman, jnr., Patrick O'Neal, Astrid Heeren. Produced by Martin Ransohoff and John Calley for Columbia.

FOR LOVE OF IVY. *dir:* Daniel Mann. *players:* Sidney Poitier, Abby Lincoln, Beau Bridges, Nan Martin, Leon Bibb, Laurie Peters, Lonnie Sattin, Dots Johnson, Carroll O' Connor. Produced by Edgar J. Scherick and Jay Weston for American Broadcasting Company.

NO MORE EXCUSES. *dir:* Robert Downey. *script:* Robert Downey. *Players:* Lawrence Wolf, Prentice Wilhite, Linda Diesem, Amy Eckles, Robert Downey. Produced by Phantasma Films and Distributed by Rogosin Films, New York.

HELLO DOLLY. *dir.* Gene Kelly. *players:* Barbra Streisand, Walter Matthau, Michael Crawford, Louis Armstrong, Marianne McAndrew, Danny Lockin. Produced by Ernest Lehman and Roger Edens for 20th Century-Fox.

TOPAZ. *dir:* Alfred Hitchcock. Produced for Universal.

COOGAN'S BLUFF. *dir:* Don Siegel. *players:* Clint Eastwood, Lee J. Cobb, Susan Clark, Don Stroud, Tisha Sterling. Produced by Universal.

THE NIGHT OF THE FOLLOWING DAY. *dir:* Hubert Cornfield. *players:* Marlon Brando, Richard Boone, Rita Moreno, Pamela Franklin. Produced by Elliott Kastner and Jerry Gershwin for Universal.

The forces of darkness: John Cassavetes and Mia Farrow in ROSEMARY'S BABY.

ROSEMARY'S BABY

Script and Direction: Roman Polanski, from the novel by Ira Levin; *Photography:* William Fraker (Technicolor); *Editing:* Sam O'Steen, Bob Wyman; *Music:* Christopher (Kryzsztof) Komeda; *Art Direction:* Richard Sylbert; *Players:* Mia Farrow, John Cassavetes, Ruth Gordon, Sidney Blackmer, Maurice Evans, Ralph Bellamy. For William Castle through Paramount. 134 mins.

Polanski's first American movie again reveals his fascination with the symbolic qualities of architecture, and the affinity for inner space that distinguished many of his other successful films. One remembers how the cameras explored the decaying South Kensington flat in *Repulsion*, the craggy corridors of Lindisfarne in *Cul-de-Sac*, and the subterranean iron scrollwork lavatory in *When Angels Fall*. One of the charms of *Rosemary's Baby* is the way Polanski makes the Dakota-esque apartment house on New York's upper West Side into a dramatic litmus for characters and plot. Phallic iron lilies in the courtyard are juxtaposed with echoing basement spaces, gloomy *art nouveau* rooms are remodelled into fashionable camp

173

décor, and satanic rites take place amid the gimcrack plastic accessories of "gracious living."

Polanski's adaptation of the Ira Levin novel shows a keen eye for American patterns. His casting is very observant — the evil ones are neo-Gothic horrors: hair rollers, gilt-tone wedgies, and "Jokes for the John." The nice people also look and act like believable USA types. The performances are all quite interesting, except perhaps for Ruth Gordon and Patsy Kelly, who are allowed to overact to excess. But perhaps this is intended; for it reveals a rather charming 19th century aristocratic belief that evil is, after all, merely an extreme form of vulgarity.

Rosemary's Baby is highly entertaining. It is the kind of horror movie where audiences shriek at an unexpected face, and cry out advice to screen characters at harrowing moments. The fact that we are in on the plot right from the beginning makes it less harrowing and complex than it might have been if we had been given any reason to doubt Rosemary's sanity. And it is to be hoped that Polanski's real gifts as a director do not become permanently mired in the conventional Hollywood horror movie cycle — **Margot S. Kernan**.

BONNIE AND CLYDE

Script: David Newman and Robert Benton; *Direction:* Arthur Penn; *Photography:* Burnett Guffey (colour); *Editing:* Dede Allen; *Art Direction:* Dean Tavoularis; *Players:* Faye Dunaway, Warren Beatty, Estelle Parsons, Gene Hackman, Michael J. Pollard, Denver Pyle. For Warner Brothers. 111 mins.

When do we first begin to feel a nudging sympathy for Bonnie and Clyde? For some perhaps it is the moment of the family meeting in the tarpaper and matchwood auto court when the two brothers leave Bonnie and Blanche simpering nervously at each other while they retreat into an inarticulate male ritual of witless pummelings and whoopee. The Barrows represent the familiar characters of the rural American family, gone slightly and irrevocably off kilter. It is the Barrows' homespun familiarity, not their perversity, that makes the movie so disturbing for American viewers. *Bonnie and Clyde* also shows us the last vestiges of the American pastoral world. The Barrows skim over fields and pastures, picking up Model A Fords like windfall fruit, while the banjo music of Flatt & Scruggs evokes the comic-folksy clichés of a frontier past. Huck Finn's "territory ahead" has become a corrupted landscape, and finally, violent retribution emerges from the trees: Et In Arcadia Ego.

Like Billy the Kid and Jesse James, the Barrows were psychopaths romanticised by a sensation-hungry public. The vaster violence of Vietnam becomes all the more ominous compared with the simple camaraderie of Clyde and Buck.

Bonnie and Clyde is one of the most important, and unsettling, movies to come from America in many years. The original screenplay, by David Newman and Robert Benton, brilliantly captures the monotone idiom of rural America. The performances of Warren Beatty, Faye Dunaway, Gene Hackman and Estelle Parsons fit Arthur Penn's semi-realistic style, and the superb art direction by Dean Tavoularis evokes the NRA Roosevelt era in minute nostalgic detail — **Margot S. Kernan.**

Katharine Ross and Dustin Hoffman ride off into the sunset on the Santa Barbara City Bus Line in THE GRADUATE.

THE GRADUATE

Script: Calder Willingham and Buck Henry from the novel by Charles Webb; *Direction:* Mike Nichols; *Photography:* Robert Surtees; *Editing:* Sam O'Steen; *Music:* Paul Simon, sung by Simon and Garfunkel; *Art Direction:* Richard Sylbert; *Players:* Anne Bancroft, Dustin Hoffman, Katharine Ross, William Daniels, Murray Hamilton, Elizabeth Wilson. For Embassy.

The Graduate has had a huge popular success in the United States, bringing an Academy Award and financial largesse to producer-director Mike Nichols. The film comes so close to being a trenchant American comedy it seems a pity that it ultimately suffers from a blunting of satirical emphasis. The witty opening sequence, which shows the mournful returning graduate being processed through the kinetic splendours of the Los Angeles airport, gives a promise of fine things ahead. Benjamin Braddock, played very deftly by the gifted and appealing Dustin Hoffman, is a kind of classic fool — and if director Nicho .: had consistently followed this idea of using a mimetic clown to portray an honour graduate of a leading American university, the possibilities might have been more richly comic. But in mid-film the style changes, and the subsequent adventures of Benjamin in love border embarrassingly on soap opera.

Hoffman himself has spoken about how the film was changed to show Benjamin's transformation from *nebbish* to man of action. Somehow the original ideas seem wittier, and one regrets the discarded scenes — such as Benjamin's fantasy about the nightmare family dinner party with a nude Mrs. Robinson eating shrimp cocktail in a forced perspective dining room, or the scene of Benjamin on the Berkeley campus, trying to reach Elaine through a crowd of dancing, circling African students. The musical score by Simon and Garfunkel, which provides rather obvious deep thoughts sung to lush musical settings, also blunts the satiric edge. Would the film have been more incisive if Bob Dylan or *The Doors* had accompanied Benjamin's wanderings? — **Margot S. Kernan.**

FUNNYMAN

Script: John Korty and Peter Bonerz; *Direction and Photography:* Korty; *Editing:* David Schickele; *Music:* Peter Schickele; *Players:* Peter Bonerz, Sandra Archer, Carol Androsky, Larry Hankin, Gerald Hiken, Nancy Fish, Barbara Hiken, Marshall Efron. For Korty Films, Inc.

John Korty has been called the most "European" of American independent filmmakers. The description may seem inaccurate for one as involved in the American scene as Korty is — but there is some truth in it. Few American directors are making films like *Funnyman* and his earlier feature, *The Crazy Quilt*. In their precise feeling for milieu and loving observation of everyday human beings, they remind us of some of the new Czech comedies, or the genre films of Pagnol and Becker.

Funnyman is the story of Perry, a San Francisco coffee-house actor who becomes impatient with the talent that makes him a success at instant satire and at inventing mad slogans for TV commercials. To find himself, he retreats to a solitary life on the Marin County Coast. After a humorous succession of sexual encounters, he meets an appealing Japanese-American family and a beautiful girl who lures him back to the city, for she loves the funnyman better than the serious thinker.

The film, shot in 35mm colour, is largely improvised, using San Francisco actors drawn mainly from "The Committee" satirical theatre. They are all appealing, but Carol Androsky, Larry Hankin, Ethel Sokolow, Nancy Fish, and Marshall Efron are especially so. Peter Bonerz, who co-scripted the film with Korty, makes Perry both truly funny and believable, in spite of the fact that the script tends to let the actors and director down — Perry's voice-over monologues often tell us too much about what we have already observed. The film deserves wider circulation than it has received so far, for few films offer such an unstereotyped view of American life. Korty's eye is keen, and his feeling for people is unaffected and spontaneous. And the witty animated TV commercial sequences, designed by Korty, deserve the special applause they earned at the film's New York Film Festival première — **Margot S. Kernan.**

Peter Bonerz as the coffeehouse comedian who wants to be taken seriously in John Korty's FUNNYMAN.

Charles Mingus, American jazz musician-composer, is the hero of Tom Reichman's new feature-length documentary, released through Film-Makers Distribution Center, New York.

U.S.S.R.

introduction   by V. Baskakov

There is an enormous variety of films being produced in the U.S.S.R. at the moment. Admissions during 1967 amounted to 4.4 billions, an increase of 189 million people on the previous year. Historical films again predominate in this season's productions, such as Tumanov's *Nikolai Bauman*, Arnshtam's *Sofiya Perovskaya*, and Karasik's *The Sixth of July*. All of them have been made at Mosfilm Studios. The following pictures have only recently been completed: *Thunderstorm over . . .*, a Lenfilm production directed by Nemchenko and Chaplin about the military leader, Frunze; *There Served Two Comrades*, directed by Karelov, a film about the Battle of Perekop, one of the most striking episodes in the Civil War; and *Horsemen of the Revolution*, directed by Yarmatov, about the establishment of the Soviets in Uzbekistan.

Other famous directors involved in filming this year include Grigori Kozintsev (*King Lear*), and Sergei Yutkevich (*A Plot for a Short Story*, on the life of Chekhov). Co-production arrangements have prospered. One can cite the Soviet-Mongolian film, *Outcome;* the new Jancsó picture, *The Red and the White*, made in collaboration with Mafilm, Budapest; *First Messenger*, a Soviet-Bulgarian co-production; *People on the Nile*, about the Aswan Dam, a co-production with Egypt; and *Fritjof Nansen*, a study of the explorer made in conjunction with Norwegian cinema authorities.

During the last year, the 50th anniversary of the Soviet state, some 250 festivals, weeks, seasons, and premières were held in 65 countries. This year the U.S.S.R. will take part in no less than 40 international festivals. It is also planned to hold over 20 film festivals, weeks and premières of Soviet pictures in socialist countries, and over 30 in western countries. Last year, 322 cinemas containing 144,000 seats were constructed, and another 350 cinemas are to be built in 1968-1969. New film studios have been opened in Aizerbaigan, Latvia, Lithuania, Tajikistan. More colour, wide-screen, and 70mm productions are being made too.

new and forthcoming films

THE BROTHERS KARAMAZOV. *dir:* Ivan Pyriev. *players:* Kirill Lavrov, Mikhaïl Ulianov, Lionella Skirda. *Based on the novel by Dostoievsky.*
SWORD AND SHIELD. *dir:* Vladimir Basov. *phot:* Timofei Lebeshev. *players:* Stanislav Lyubshin, Valentina Titova. *A film trilogy about the life and work of a Soviet intelligence man in Nazi Germany.*

ONCE MORE ABOUT LOVE. *dir:* George Natanson. *players:* Tatiana Doronina, Alexander Lazarev. *A contemporary love drama.*

SWAN LAKE. *dir:* Appolinary Doudko and Konstantin Sergeyev. *phot:* Anatoly Nazarov. *dancers:* Elena Evteyeva, John Markovsky. *A new screen version of the Tchaikovsky ballet.*

YOUR CONTEMPORARY. *dir:* Yuli Raizman. *phot:* Nikolai Ardashnikov. *players:* Igor Vladimirov, Nikolai Plotnikov. *A moral and psychological problem film concerning different generations.*

THE GOLDEN CALF. *dir:* Mikhaïl Shveitser. *players:* Sergei Yrsky, Leonid Kuravliov, Zinovi Gerdt, Evgeni Yevstigneyev. *Based on the famous satirical novel by Ilf and Petrov.*

THREE POPLARS IN PLIUSHIKHA STREET. *dir:* Tatiana Lioznova. *phot:* Piotr Kataev. *players:* Tatiana Doronina, Oleg Efremov. *A lyrical story about an impossible love.*

THE SIXTH OF JULY. *dir:* Yuli Karasik. *phot:* Mikhaïl Syslov. *players:* Yuri Kayurov, Vassili Lanovoi. *The counter-revolutionary attempt to make a coup-d'état in Moscow in 1918.*

ALONG RUSSIAN PATHS. *dir:* Feodor Filippov. *phot:* Era Savelyeva. *players:* Alexei Loktev, Lyudmila Chursina, Natasha Velichko. *Based on short stories by Maxim Gorky.*

VENDEMIARE
(When Leaves Fall)

Script: A. Tchitchinadze; *Direction:* Otar Iosseliani; *Photography:* A. Maisouradze. *Music:* N. Iosseliani; *Players:* Ramaz Gueorgoliani, Marina Kartzivaeze, Gueorguy Kharabadze. For Grouzia Film. 90 mins.

The first significant picture from the remote Soviet Republic of Georgia is a disarmingly enjoyable trifle, made with affection and a genuine feeling of youthful shyness. The hero is a boy working in a wine plant. He quickly becomes involved in his job, and causes trouble when he claims that a vat of wine is simply not ready for bottling. Simultaneously he is falling in love with a mocking girl who shows visitors round the 18th century cellars. But amorous rivalry in this area is sharply conducted, and at the film's end Niko has received a rather brusque sentimental education, although he has had the satisfaction of boycotting the best bar in town when he and his comrades are served with the premature wine.

Director Otar Iosseliani runs a mischievous and yet unsophisticated eye over the situation, thrusting wryly at the separatist tendencies of the community (some visiting "Russian" tourists are deliberately offered unfit wine to sample), and at its reluctance to accept new-fangled mechanisation in the factory. Certain scenes betray a primitive technique, but one constantly has the sense of life bustling on beyond the range of the camera; and there are several shots near the beginning that sum up a memory of youth as poignantly and as beguilingly as *The Childhood of Maxim Gorky* or *Il Posto* — **Peter Cowie.**

ANNA KARENINA

THE BROTHERS KARAMAZOV

Nikolai Olyalin in THE LIBERATION OF EUROPE

Tatyana Doronina and Oleg Efremov in THREE POPLARS IN PLIUSCHIKHA STREET

Anatoly Papanov in Heifitz's IN THE TOWN OF S.

V GORODYE S
(In the Town of S)

Script and Direction: Josif Heifitz; *Photography:* Ghenrih Marandjan; *Music:* Nadejda Simonian; *Art Direction:* Boris Manevich, Ilya Kaplan; *Players:* Andrei Popov, Anatoly Papanov, Nonna Terentieva, Lidia Stykan, For Lenfilm.

Josef Heifitz, whose *Lady With a Little Dog* was a masterfully cinematic rendition of Chekhov's work, does not achieve the same impact with this more recent attempt. His film presents the author himself, a doctor struggling to find the time to write between discharging his other duties which take him to a remote area of famine. He encounters a figure who inspires him to write the story *Ionych*, to be another illustration of the empty, closed lives of the people. This is then cut into the depiction of Chekhov at work to form the bulk of the film.

Ionych is the young doctor, clumsy and gauche, who worships the coquettish, ambitious Katya, a girl from a wealthy background that includes cultural evenings of dreadful novels specially composed and read for the occasion by Katya's mother as well as feeble practical jokes among the men like exploding cigars. Katya flippantly dismisses her awkward, bumbling suitor who devotes his life to achieving wealth and position. When she at last learns to appreciate the ideals he expressed in his youth and to accept her own limitations, he has sunk into a stupor from which he cannot be aroused.

Heifitz's sense of period is as strong as ever, though the settings are less striking than the Yalta of *Little Dog;* but his success is ultimately limited by the dullness of the people he and Chekhov describe. What was so intensely moving about the lovers of the earlier film was their sensitivity and intelligence, their joint awareness of the better life they could have together if only they could break out from the stifling conventions of their society. Neither Katya nor Ionych are such strong characters and, while Chekhov could hope by showing them to persuade his contemporaries to improve their own lives, there is not the same immediate relevance today. One is also inclined to suspect that Heifitz hasn't quite enough material for a feature, and that this is one reason why Chekhov himself appears. In this role, Andrei Popov creates an authoritative, believable figure, while the rest of the cast perform ably in less striking parts — **Allen Eyles.**

NIEJNOSTI
(Tenderness)

Script: Odelsha Agishev; *Direction:* Elier Ishmuhamedov; *Photography:* Dalshad Fathullin; *Editing:* K. Geldueva; *Music:* Bogdan Trotsiuk; *Players:* M. Sternikova, R. Nakhapetov, R. Agzamov, M. Makhmudova. For Uzbekfilm Studios. 75 mins.

At last the work of the young generation in the U.S.S.R. is starting to trickle through to the West. *Tenderness* was made on location in Tashkent by a 23-year old *cinéaste,* and it is divided into three sections, each named after a leading character. Sangzhar is attracted by a dimpled, sylph-like blonde as he travels idly down stream on a rubber tyre with his friends, and the remaining two sections show how their lives are tangled with those of another girl and boy. But the atmosphere of the film is so evocative as to make the plot of secondary importance. There is a real communication of effervescent *joie-de-vivre* (Sangzhar playing in the local orchestra, for example), contrasted with the sweet, lazy melancholia of summer afternoons, induced by Lena's reminiscences of her other great love. The music strengthens the mood of leisure and wistfulness, while the intelligent camerawork brings the Uzbekistan area of the Soviet Union vibrantly to life — **Peter Cowie.**

Still from THE WILD SHADOWS, directed by Kokan Rakonjac.

Still from WOLF FROM PROKLETIJE, one of the many films produced each year in Macedonia.

184

Yugoslavia

introduction   by Peter Cowie

An all-time record target of 40 feature films may well be achieved this year in Yugoslav studios. Certainly the atmosphere in all six republics has never been so optimistic. Unlike Sweden, Poland, or even Hungary, the international breakthrough has not been led by one major director. The annual festival at Pula seems to reveal new talent all the time, and at festivals abroad too, Yugoslav pictures have been well received, claiming 21 major awards recently. At Oberhausen, the Yugoslav selection was proclaimed the best overall, and the young documentary director Zelimir Zilnik shared the Grand Prix for *The Unemployed*, while Zlatko Bourek's cartoon, *Captain Arbanas Marko*, was awarded a main prize. Petrovic's *Happy Gypsies* was nominated for an Oscar in 1968, and opened at five cinemas simultaneously in Paris.

Away from the festival circuits, Yugoslav films have made a considerable impact abroad. In Stockholm, Svensk Filmindustri organised a week of Yugoslav cinema last April. Eight features and nineteen shorts were screened, while several press conferences with the directors involved were transmitted on Swedish television.

Co-productions are becoming a more regular part of the Yugoslav film scene. *The Curse of a Faithful Wife* was made with American participation, and *Tonnerre sur l'Adriatique*, directed by Alexandre Astruc, was partly financed by France. *The Battle of the Neretva*, a vast enterprise with dozens of stars, is a Yugoslav-Italian-German production.

recent and forthcoming films

EXPEDITION *(Pohod)*. *dir:* Djordje Kadijevic. *phot:* Aleksandar Petkovic. *players:* Slobodan Perovic, Janez Vrhovec, Severin Bijelic. For Avala Film (Belgrade).
POOR MARIA *(Sirota Marija)*. *dir:* Dragoljub Lazic. *phot:* Milorad Kakšic-Fandjo. *players:* Milena Dravic, Ljubiša Samardzic, Mija Aleksic. For Avala Film (Belgrade).
DON'T MENTION THE CAUSE OF DEATH *(Uzrok smrti ne pominjati)*. *dir:* Jovan Zivanovic. *phot:* Jermin Vojcik. *players:* Bekim Fehmiu, Bata Zivojinovic, Pavle Vujisic, Oleg Vidov. For Avala Film (Belgrade).
NOON *(Podne)*. *dir:* Puriša Djordjevic. *phot:* Mihajlo Popovic. *players:* Ljubiša Samardžic, Neda Arneric, Mija Aleksic, Ljuba Tadic. For Avala Film (Belgrade).
THE BLOODY MACEDONIAN WEDDING *(Makedonska krvava svadba)*. *dir:*

Trajče Popov. *phot:* Kiro Bilbilovski. *players:* Risto Siškov, Vera Cukic, Zafir Hadžimanov, Pavle Vujisic. For Vardar Film (Skopje).
VAIN DREAMS *(Pusti snovi).* *dir:* Soja Jovanovic. *phot:* Nenad Jovičič *(colour).* *players:* Mija Aleksic, Mira Banjac, Nuša Marovic. For UFRS (Belgrade).
WOLF FROM PROKLETIJE *(Vuk sa Prokletija).* *dir:* Miomir Stamenkovic. *phot:* Branko Ivatovic. *players:* Ljuba Tadic, Josif Tatic, Branko Pleša, Melihat Ajeti. For Kosmet Film (Pristina), and UFRS (Belgrade).
OUT OF STEP *(U raskoraku).* *dir:* Milenko Strbac. *phot:* Milivoje Milivojevic. *players:* Gizela Vukovic, Ljuba Tadic, Jovan Janicijevic, Bata Stojkovic. For UFRS (Belgrade).
DOCTOR HOMER'S BROTHER *(Brat Doktora Homera).* *dir:* Zika Mitrovic. *phot:* Branko Ivatovic. *players:* Bata Zivojinovic, Voja Miric, Jovan Milicevic. For UFRS (Belgrade).
THE WILD SHADOWS *(Divlje senke).* *dir:* Kokan Rakonjac. *phot:* Aleksandar Petkovic. *players:* Ljuba Tadic, Jelena Zigon, Severin Bijelic, Milan Srdoč. For UFRS (Belgrade).
THE INVISIBLE BATTALION *(Nevidljivi Bataljon).* *dir:* Jane Kavčic. *phot:* France Kerar. *players:* Miha Baloh, Milan Srdoč, Jasmin Skodlar, Mitja Primec, Miha Creganc. For Viba Film (Ljubljana).
PLAYING AT SOLDIERS *(Mali vojnici).* *dir:* Bato Cengic. *phot:* Aleksandar Vesligaj. *players:* Stole Arandelovic, Marika Tocinovska, Zaim Muzaferija, Sead Cakal. For Bosna Film (Sarajevo).
THE BIRCH TREE. *dir:* Ante Barbaja. *phot:* Tomislav Pinter. *players:* Manca Košir, Bata Zivojinovic, Fabijan Sovagovic. For Jadran Film (Zagreb).
I HAVE TWO MUMMIES AND TWO DADDIES *(Imam dvije Mame i dva Tate).* *dir:* Kreso Golik. *phot:* Ivica Rajkovic. *players:* Relja Basic, Mia Oremovic, Fabijan Sovagovic, Vera Cukic. For Jadran Film (Zagreb).
GRAVITATION *(Gravitacija).* *dir:* Branko Ivanda. *phot:* Ivica Rajkovic. *players:* Rade Serbedzija, Snezana Niksic, Jagoda Kaloper, Zaim Muzaferija. For Jadran Film (Zagreb).
THREE HOURS FOR LOVE *(Tri Sata za Lubav).* *dir:* Fadil Hadzic. *phot:* Frano Vodopivec. *players:* Stanislava Pesic, Dragan Nikolic, Tatiana Salaj, Predrag Tasovac. For Jadran Film (Zagreb).
THE SUN FROM ANOTHER SKY *(Sunce tudeg Neba).* *dir:* Milan Kosovac. *phot:* Miroljub Dikosavljevic. *players:* Slobodan Dimitrijevic, Mira Stupica, Pavle Vujisic, Milan Srdoc, Snezana Niksic. For Bosna Film (Sarajevo).

Aleksic is the star of INNOCENCE UNPROTECTED.

NEVINOST BEZ ZASTITE
(Innocence Unprotected)

Based on the 1942 film of the same name by Dragoljub Aleksic; *Compilation and Annotations:* Dusan Makavejev; *Photography:* Branko Perak, Stevan Miskovic; *Editing:* Ivanka Vukasovic; *Music:* Voiislav Kostic; *Players:* Dragoljub Aleksic, Ana Milosavljevic, Vera Jovanovic Bratoljub Gligorijevic. For Avala Film, Belgrade. 72 mins.

Makavejev promises more and more to be the Braque of European cinema. This latest *jeu d'esprit* is a collage of the early forties, when Yugoslavia was under Nazi occupation. In 1942, a professional strong man named Aleksic intermingled documentary footage of his own acrobatic feats with stretches of wide-eyed melodrama in a Serbian film called *Innocence Unprotected.* This pre-Godardian recipe clearly fascinates Makavejev, who has added further layers of meaning to the old film with up-to-date interviews with Aleksic and his cameraman as well as a selection of wartime newsreels. The result, says the director, is "a peculiar cinematic time machine", yielding a portrait-in-depth of Aleksic who even 25 years later appears in real life to be every bit as vain and courageous as he was in the film. Makavejev's own bubbling personality peeps through the scrapbook at every point, and ensures that while we may hiss at the hammy acting or ridicule the grotesque situations, we remain aware of one man's deeply-felt affection and respect for a folk hero of his youth — **Peter Cowie.**

KADA BUDEM
MRTAV I BEO
(When I'm Dead and White)

Script: Gordan Mihic and Zivojin Pavlovic; *Direction:* Pavlovic; *Photography* Milorad Jaksic-Fando; *Players:* Dragan Nikolic, Ruzica Sokic, Neda Spasojevic, Severin Bijelic, Dara Calenic. For FRZ, Belgrade. 75 mins.

Like Aldo in Antonioni's *Il Grido*, the lean and hungry hero of Pavlovic's new film stumbles towards his fate through a drab, grey landscape. People in Pavlovic's world are evasive and permeated with shame. They are human refuse, like the prisoners in Dostoievsky's *House of the Dead*, and *When I'm Dead and White* suggests that only their urgent life force keeps them afloat in a mean and vicious society. Janko's view of life never extends beyond his immediate needs. When he loses his job as a farm worker he steals without a qualm, almost instinctively. He enjoys a short-lived success as a singer, travelling through small Serbian towns with a tawdry blonde at his side, pleasing remote army garrisons and groups of industrial workers. His rodent cunning enables him to fling his women callously aside, leaving them to forage for survival as best they can.

Pavlovic tells all this swiftly and without rancour, exposing a sordid milieu with blunt, unglamorous images. He finds amusing moments (especially at a public singing audition in Belgrade) before he proceeds to Janko's gruesome death, propped up in an outhouse after being shot by the farm manager. There is no cheap attempt to solicit sympathy for him in the last lingering close-up; Pavlovic is merely stating that Janko is part of the human condition, part of our very selves — **Peter Cowie.**

Still: WHEN I'M DEAD AND WHITE.

Above: Milena Dravic in the large-scale production of THE BATTLE ON THE RIVER NERETVA.

jugoslavija film

Paris
JUGOSLAVIJA FILM, Mr. Vladimir Teresak,
6 Rue Cerisoles, Paris 8e. Tel. BALzac 19-28.

Munich
JUGOSLAVIJA FILM, Mr. Bozidar Torbica,
Munich 2, Neuhauser Strasse 3/V, Tel. 22-58-73

New York
Interprogress Trading Co.,
501, Fifth Avenue, New York 17. Tel. Yukon 6-9165

Import - Export of Motion Pictures
Belgrade, Knez Mihajlova No. 19 - Post Box 243
Cables: Yugofilm, Belgrade.
Telephone: 623-071, 623-964, 624-960

Ante Babaja was born in 1927 at Imotski, but went to school in Zagreb and later studied economy there. He has been in the film industry since 1950, when he was at first assistant director to Jacques Becker among others. He won a top award at Pula in 1955 for his short, *A Day on the River*, and since then he has made a number of documentaries and short feature films, including *The Mirror, Misunderstanding, Elbow (as such), Justice, Can You Hear Me?*, and *The Body*. His two full-length features have been *The Emperor's New Clothes* (a variation on Andersen's theme), and *The Birch Tree*, which was successfully entered at Mar del Plata this year.

Zvonimir Berkovic was born in 1928, and studied in Zagreb. He was by turns violinist, music critic, film and theatre reviewer, and stage director. He worked as a screenwriter before directing for the cinema, and won major prizes at Belgrade and Cannes in 1963 for his documentary, *The Flat*. His feature, *Rondo*, made a considerable impression at the Critics' Section at Cannes, and also at the London Film Festival. "I remain a frustrated musician entirely obsessed by the desire to use the film medium in order to obtain the perfection of musical compositional forms," he admits.

Aleksandar Petrovic is 38, and he has worked in the cinema industry since he was 18. He was at first a critic and then concentrated on documentaries. His début as a feature film director came with *When Love Has Gone* in 1961, which marks a turning point in the development of the Yugoslav cinema by virtue of its psychological, poetic, and intimate approach to human problems. Then followed another subtle analysis of contemporary life, *The Days*, and *Three*, a triptych of war stories that was nominated for an Oscar after winning the main prize at Karlovy Vary in 1966. Petrovic really arrived on the international scene, however, with *Happy Gypsies*, which shared a Grand Prix at Cannes and was, like its predecessor, nominated for an Academy Award.

The children in Cengic's honest and decisive statement about the aftermath of war,
PLAYING AT SOLDIERS.

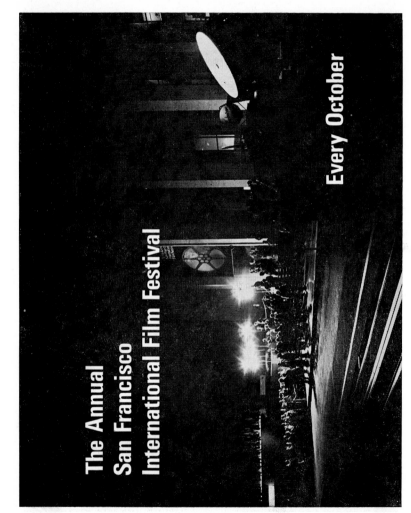

The Annual
San Francisco
International Film Festival

Every October

Festivals

Note: we append herewith brief notes on the most significant festivals at press-time. Readers wanting to learn more about these and the scores of other events during the year should subscribe to Derek Hill's *Festival Diary*, available at £3 annually from 122 Wardour Street, London W.1.

Adelaide & Auckland   August 1969

The Eleventh Adelaide Film Festival works in conjunction with Auckland, New Zealand. Features of this joint festival make it unique in the Southern Hemisphere: cash awards ($U.S.), special Asian section, annual tributes to a selected director and chosen country, organiser of Australian World Television Festival. As a joint two-country festival it can offer unique trade and cultural outlets: both cities are linked to prestigious Government-supported Festivals of Arts and the festival's Business Section makes every effort to secure commercial distribution of films entered. Audiences at Adelaide's 1968 Festival totalled 20,000 with a 2,000 limit on each film. *Inquiries to:* Eric Williams, Director. 79-80 South Terrace, Adelaide, South Australia.

Annecy   June 1969

This is the only competitive festival of animation officially recognised by the International Federation of Film Producers, and the meeting in June 1967 confirmed its status among specialist events. Nearly every animator of note, from Japan to the United States, makes the trip to this attractive resort in south-east France, and as well as new films there are retrospectives of various periods and directors. It is an indispensable forum for the exchange of news and opinions. *Inquiries to:* A.F.D.C., 21 rue de la Tour d'Auvergne, Paris 9, France.

Belgrade   March 1969

Any critic, producer, or distributor who visits this spring festival in Yugoslavia can see *all* the *short* films produced in the country during the past year, in a convivial atmosphere. In the evening there are competition screenings, and in the afternoons there are Information programmes. Some 120 shorts are produced annually in the six republics, on a wide variety of themes. Festival organisation is excellent. *Inquiries to:* Petar Volk, Jugoslavija Film, Knez Mihailova 19, Belgrade.

The Europa Center, focal point of the Berlin International Film Festival each June.

Bergamo   September 1969

Under the stalwart leadership of Nino Zucchelli, the Bergamo festival has grown in influence these past few years, chiefly on account of a new Section, whereby films directed and written, or overwhelmingly influenced by one man are screened and compete for a prize of 5 million Lire as well as Italian distribution via the festival. Another Section, for Documentaries and Shorts, has a Grand Prix of 1 million Lire. There is also a Round Table held during the festival to discuss contemporary problems in the cinema. *Inquiries to:* Rotonda dei Mille 1, 24100 Bergamo, Italy.

**AWARDS
1967**
Gran Permio (features): DAISIES (Czechoslovakia), Chytilová.
Best Actor: Bekim Fehmiu in PROTEST (Yugoslavia).
Best Actress: Macha Méril in AU PAN COUPE (France).
Best Short: UZKOST (Czechoslovakia), Kopac.

Berlin   June-July 1969

The Berlin festival enjoys an advantage unique to competitive European festivals: it takes place in a major city. It has thus become an acknowledged meeting place for film directors, stars, traders, critics, and producers during its 12 days at the end of June. There are 3 sections: the "Film Art" Competition for features and shorts, in which the winners qualify for major prizes; the Information Show, presenting out of competition films that for one formal reason or another could not be included in the first category; and the film market, which involves daily screenings of films hitherto unknown in Germany. A Week of Young Cinema is also now an integral part of the festival; in 1967 it was devoted to Italy; and in 1968 to Canada. This summer there were also excellent retrospectives of films by Abel Gance and Ernst Lubitsch (the latter's sound features). Several theatres and screening rooms are avilable free of charge for invited screenings of features, documentaries, and shorts. The festival is officially recognised by the Federal Government and by the Senate of West Berlin association with SPIO (the top organisation of the West German film industry). *Inquiries to:* Berliner Festspiele GmbH, Bundesallee 1-12, 1 Berlin 15.

XIX INTERNATIONALE FILMFESTSPIELE BERLIN 1969

Golden Bear (features): OLE DOLE DOFF (Sweden), Troell.
Silver Beurs (features): INNOCENCE UNPROTECTED (Yugoslavia), Makavejev; and COME L'AMORE (Italy), Muzii.
Best Actor: Jean-Louis Trintignant in L'HOMME QUI MENT (France).
Best Actress: Stéphane Audran in LES BICHES (France).
Best Direction: Carlos Saura for PEPPERMINT FRAPPE (Spain).

Competitive categories include:

Theatrical Feature Films. Short Subjects.
Industrial Films. Educational Films. Student Films.
International Television/Theatrical Commercials.
U.S. Television Commercials, Television Productions.

5th
Chicago
International
Film Festival

November 9-17

Write for complete details:

The Chicago International Film Festival
235 West Eugenie Street
Chicago, Illinois 60614
U.S.A.

196

Cambridge Animation November 1968

It is notoriously difficult to start a festival successfully, even in these days, but Richard Arnall managed to launch his festival at Cambridge last November with a real bang. Animators from many countries were there; there was a suberb retrospective of the Zagreb cartoons; and a memorable afternoon with Alexandre Alexeïeff and Claire Parker as they screened and commented on their work. This year the selection should be even better. Certainly this is the liveliest festival in Britain. It is sponsored and organised by the City of Cambridge, and is presented by the City in association with the British Film Institute. *Inquiries to:* Richard Arnall, Cambridge Animation Festival, The Corn Exchange, Cambridge.

Cannes May 1969

Anyone who has visited Cannes regularly during the past twenty one years will have been depressed and frustrated by the ridiculous events of May 1968, when the festival was closed not by unanimous decision but by the vicious machinations of a few extremists who felt that by interrupting or even abolishing an international event they could bring the sympathy of the world's press to their struggle for power in France. No respect was shown towards the thousands of foreigners attending the festival, and it seems unlikely that Cannes will ever be the same again. No awards were given in 1968. It is an enormous pity that such a well-organised and old-established event should have been brought down by what amounted to a few shouts, screams, and childish threats. *Inquiries to:* Madame Louisette Fargette, Festival International du Film, 25 rue d'Astorg, Paris 8.

Chicago November 1968

This 4th edition of the very successful Chicago festival consists of a series of events planned and co-ordinated to bring to the city a good sampling of international film products, and to give Chicago a recognised, full-scale comprehensive festival of art and communication in film. It is America's only competitive festival, and is organised as a non-profit corporation. The Student Film Competition has now been enlarged, and in 1968 there is an International TV Commercial Competition too. *Inquiries to:* 235 West Eugenie Street T-2, Chicago, Illinois 60614.

AWARDS 1967

Best Feature: HERE'S YOUR LIFE (Sweden), Troell.
Best Actor: Enrico Mario Salerno for THE SEASONS OF OUR LOVE (Italy).
Best Actress: Barbara Lubwizanka for SUBLOKATOR (Poland).
Best Direction: Jan Troell, for HERE'S YOUR LIFE (Sweden).
Best Short: AU FOU (Japan), Kuri.
Best Student Film: THE SEASON (University of Berkeley, California), MacDonald.

Australasia's most important fim event

11th Adelaide and Auckland International Film Festival Aug-Sept '69

Special Features:
Cash Awards
Connected with world famous
Festivals of Arts
Unique Trade and Cultural
outlets in two countries
Also organisers 2nd Australian
World Television Film Festival

Enquiries to Director:
Adelaide and Auckland Film Festival
79-80 South Terrace, Adelaide
South Australia 5000

Cork   September 1969

The aim of the Cork Festival, founded in 1956, is to present films in an unpretentious atmosphere in which audiences are sincere in their approach to the cinema.
New and outstanding features are screened daily, and competitions for shorts are
arranged. In 1968 Cork organised the Council of Europe Film Week. The International Competition for Television Commercials also takes place during the
festival period. At any time Cork is a holiday venue of note, but in September it
offers the added attraction of the festival. Each year two tribute programmes
honouring famous directors form an important part of the proceedings. *Inquiries
to:* Dermot Breen, 15 Bridge Street, Cork, Eire.

AWARDS *St. Finbarr Statuettes:* THE VOICE OF THE WATER (Netherlands); TEN
1967   TIES AND A HEART (Denmark); BY TRAIN FROM PARIS TO NICE
             (France); THE GROWING EDGE (U.S.A.); BASIC BLACK (U.S.A.);
             TRAWLER-FISHING (U.S.A.).

Cracow   June 1969

This is one of the better short film festivals, giving a particularly useful comparison
between Polish talent and international entries, as the Polish national short film
festival takes place immediately before the major gathering. This ancient city is
now a well-loved meeting place for anybody interested in documentaries or short
fiction films, not to mention animation. Films awarded prizes are purchased automatically for cinema distribution in Poland. *Inquiries to:* Jerzy Wittek, Festivals
of Short Films, Mazowiecka 6/8, Warsaw, Poland.

AWARDS *Grand Prix:* SANDCASTLE (U.S.S.R.), Bronsztein.
1968   *Special Jury Prize:* END OF A REVOLUTION? (Britain), Moser.
             FIPRESCI Prize: END OF A REVOLUTION? and I AM TWENTY (India).
             Grand Prix at Polish national festival: A YEAR IN FRANK'S LIFE, Karabasz.

Edinburgh   August 24 - September 7, 1969

This summer the Edinburgh film festival honoured Dr. John Grierson, and he was
awarded the Golden Thistle Award for Outstanding Achievement in the Art of the
Cinema. In a way, his presence symbolised the trend of the festival, which has
always been towards the committed documentary or experimental film. Next year,
there will be a Swedish film week with the co-operation of Svenska Filminstitutet.
16mm facilites have also been improved at Edinburgh, and stars and directors often
make a point of coming to the festival before going on to Venice and other events.
Murray Grigor is the enthusiastic Director. *Inquiries to:* Film House, 3 Randolph
Crescent, Edinburgh 3.

EDINBURGH INTERNATIONAL FILM FESTIVAL

FILM HOUSE
3 Randolph Crescent
Edinburgh 3
tel 031 225 1671

Festival of the Cinema of Commitment
features, shorts, documentaries
THE SWEDISH NEW WAVE a week devoted to Sweden

Aug 24 - Sept 7 1969

18th

MELBOURNE FILM FESTIVAL

June 1969

Non-competitive for feature films,
competitive for short films on 35 mm or 16 mm.

INFORMATION FROM: POST OFFICE BOX 62
CARLTON SOUTH, MELBOURNE, VICTORIA 3053, AUSTRALIA

AWARDS 1967

Diplomas of Merit: LA BATTAGLIA DI ALGERI (Italy); DESERT PEOPLE (Australia); DUTCHMAN (Britain); THE FAMILY OF MAN (Poland); HUNGER (Denmark/Sweden); HYPOTHÈSE BÉTA (France); THE LONGEST NIGHT (Bulgaria); KATHERINA ISMAILOVA (U.S.S.R.); LIGHT AND ARCHITECTURE (France); OPUS (Britain); SALTO (Poland); SEAS OF SWEET HATE (U.S.A.); SKY OVER HOLLAND (Netherlands); STORY OF A CONCERTO (West Germany); EN SOMMERKRIG (Denmark); THX 1138 4EB (U.S.A.); TORCH AND TORSO (U.S.A.).

Karlovy Vary   Every June

Although it has until now alternated with Moscow every other year, the Karlovy Vary festival now seems set to take place annually. This is partly due to the strength of the Czech film at the moment, and partly to the successful re-modelling of the festival's organisation. It now runs for only 11 days, and has 3 separate Juries, one consisting of film-makers and screenwriters, another of actors and actresses, and yet another of technicians. This festival is also rather more open-minded than many East European events about the kind of entries it accepts from the Western countries. So, an important venue for anyone wanting to see the best of both worlds. *Inquiries to:* Václavské námesti 28, Prague 1.

AWARDS 1968

Grand Prix: INDIAN SUMMER (Czechoslovakia), Menzel.
Best Actor: Nikolai Plotnikov for YOUR CONTEMPORARY (U.S.S.R.).
Best Actress: Carol White in POOR COW (Britain).
Special Jury Mentions: WHEN I AM DEAD AND GONE (Yugoslavia), Pavlovic; THE LONG JOURNEY (Chile), Caulen; IN COLD BLOOD (U.S.A.), Brooks; MEMORIES OF UNDERDEVELOPMENT (Cuba), Gutierrez.
FIPRESCI Prize: WHEN I AM DEAD AND GONE and MEMORIES OF UNDERDEVELOPMENT.

Leipzig   November 1968

The East German winter festival that maintains a competition for documentaries and shorts, whether made for cinema or television, and also includes information screenings, retrospective shows, trade projections, and conferences. The motto is: "Films of the World for the Peace of the World". *Inquiries to:* Burgstrasse 27, 102 Berlin, East Germany.

Locarno   September-October 1969

From 1968 onwards, Locarno is devoting its festival to competitive screenings of first and second films by young directors. The event is run by Sandro Bianconi and Freddy Buache (Curator of the Swiss Cinémathèque), who also organises an annual retrospective at Locarno. This year it was given in honour of Satyajit Ray. An international jury awards the following prizes: a Golden Sail and two Silver Sails for features; a Golden Sail and a Silver Sail for shorts. Seats are sold at reasonable prices for all screenings, and a holiday on Lake Maggiore can be combined with a visit to this stimulating festival. *Inquiries to:* C.P. 172, CH-6600 Locarno, Switzerland.

Two popular German actresses — Sabena Bethmann and Christa Linder — who visited the Cork Film Festival in 1967. They are shown here with (left), the Director of the Festival, Dermot Breen, and the Soviet director, Stanislav Rostosky, whose film BELLA was screened successfully at Cork.

London   November 1968

Members of the National Film Theatre and the general public have an unparalleled opportunity of making real discoveries at each new London Film Festival. Although it began with the aim of reducing the enormous time-lag that used to exist between production and eventual British distribution, the festival has now progressed beyond this stage (most of the directors it "discovered" have little trouble nowadays in placing their films) and can afford to promote talents like Korty, Berkovic, and Delvaux. It is non-competitive, and works in close liaison with the New York Film Festival (Richard Roud is Programme Director for both events). *Inquiries to:* British Film Institute, 81 Dean Street, London W.1.

Mannheim   Every October

This is an annual competition for short and feature-length documentaries, animated films, featurettes, and first features by short and documentary directors. Films must show the latest development in form and content along the theme, "Man in our Time". There are a number of attractive prizes: a Grand Prix of DM 10,000,— for the best "first feature"; the Josef von Sternberg Prize for the most original film, DM 2,000,—; four Mannheim Film Ducats, each accompanied by

DM 1,500,—; and the Prix Simone Dubreuilh (given by FIPRESCI) for the best short from among the winners of the year's earlier festivals. *Inquiries to:* Rathaus E5, 68 Mannheim, West Germany.

AWARDS 1967
Grand Prix: DAVID HOLZMAN'S DIARY (U.S.A.), McBride.
Josef von Sternberg Prize: THE AGE OF CHRIST (Czechoslovakia), Jakubisko.
Special Prize: HERBST DER GAMMLER (West Germany), Fleischmann.
FIPRESCI Prize: THE AGE OF CHRIST.
Prix Simone Dubreuilh: NAPALM (U.S.A.), Lenzer and Greenwood.

Mar del Plata   Every March

Now in its tenth year, the Mar del Plata festival, when it does take place (and there have been interruptions to the sequence!), is a valuable meeting place for South American film personalities, and is attended too by many buyers and distributors from Europe and the U.S.A. The town itself is some 250 miles south of Buenos Aires. *Inquiries to:* Enzo Ardigo, Lavalle 1943, Buenos Aires, Argentina.

AWARDS 1968
Grand Prix: BONNIE AND CLYDE (U.S.A.), Penn.
Best Actor: Tony Musante for THE INCIDENT (U.S.A.).
Best Actress: Annie Girardot for VIVRE POUR VIVRE (France).
Best Direction: György Revesz for THREE NIGHTS OF LOVE (Hungary).
Best Screenplay: Nicholas Baehr for THE INCIDENT.
Best Short: MAGIC LANTERN (Poland).
FIPRESCI Prize: BONNIE AND CLYDE.

Melbourne   June 1969

This outstanding festival is organised by the Federation of Victorian Film Societies in association with the Australian Film Institute and with the aid of the State Film Centre. It has been endorsed for the past ten years by F.I.A.P.F., and is competitive for features and shorts. There is usually a Guest of Honour in attendance. *Inquiries to:* Erwin Rado, 53 Cardigan Street, Carlton, Victoria, Australia.

XV. WESTDEUTSCHE KURZFILMTAGE OBERHAUSEN

"The Oberhausen Festival is the most important one in the world for short film makers."

The Times, 10.4.67.

23 - 29 March 1969

At MIFED'S 16th Ciné Meeting (October 1967), film producer Carlo Ponti saw his DOCTOR ZHIVAGO win a prize. With him at the Centre are Sophia Loren and the General Commissioner of MIFED, Cavaliere del Lavoro Dr. Michele Guido Franci.

AWARDS 1967

Grand Prix: PETROL (West Germany).
Silver Boomerangs (shorts): CHINA (Britain/China), and ROMANCE (Czechoslovakia).
Special Awards: AMERICAN ROULETTE (U.S.A.); BUSTER KEATON RIDES AGAIN (Canada); ELEGY (Hungary); INSTRUCTIONAL TECHNIQUE PART D - VISUAL AIDS (Britain); L'OISEAU DE LA SAGESSE (France); A SUNDAY ON THE ISLAND OF THE GRANDE JATTE (Netherlands); THE WINGS (Poland).

MIFED (Milan)   April and October 1969

MIFED — the International Film, TV Film and Documentary Market — was founded in 1960 at the time of the 38th Milan Fair. It is held twice a year: in April, to coincide with the Milan Fair, and in October. This film market is reserved solely for producers, renters, and distributors of feature and documentary films for cinema and tv presentation. MIFED offers several international film awards at its two annual sessions. Among these are the "Five Continents Trophy", and the "TV Pearl". The former goes to the best entertainment feature; the latter to the best full-length or serialised film, and to the best short produced for tv transmission. For clients who are unable to attend the entire meeting, there is a special assistance bureau which undertakes their interests. *Inquiries to:* MIFED, Largo Domodossola 1, Milan, Italy.

Moscow   July 1969

One of the big guns in the festival field. Every two years about 600,000 Muscovites flock to see a massive array of films from East and West, and twelve days are allotted to the screening of films in competition. Features are shown twice daily in the Kremlin Palace of Congresses, while shorts are on view at the Central Film Club (Dom Kino). Press conferences are held daily at 9 a.m. in the Moskva Hotel, which is also the centre for the festival management and the press office. An innovation in 1967 was the special prize for the best children's film. *Inquiries to:* 33 Vorovsky Street, Moscow, U.S.S.R.

New York   September 1969

This festival is now firmly established as a showcase for films in New York, and Amos Vogel and Richard Roud (who also directs the programmes at the London Film Festival) concentrate on developing a new taste in cinema. The event is open to the public, and at least 60,000 spectators attend each year. There is a programme of 32 special events, either symposia, lectures, interviews with visiting directors, or screening of films in progress, not to mention a retrospective section of significant old films rarely seen in the U.S.A. in recent years. Philharmonic Hall now has superb 16mm facilities, and this has widened the range of the festival considerably. *Inquiries to:* Amos Vogel, Director, New York Film Festival, Lincoln Center, 1865 Broadway, New York 10023.

Oberhausen   April 1969

Repelling a challenge similar to that flung at Cannes, this time by the Hamburg group of film-makers, Oberhausen continued in 1968 to emphasise its position as the major short film forum in Europe. When the films are bad, the festival is often blamed. But Hilmar Hoffmann and Will Wehling, by restricting the number of entries and the length of each viewing session, have now taken all the reasonable measures they can. This should guarantee that a prize at Oberhausen carries even more prestige next year. And April is a much better month in which to visit the Ruhrland! *Inquiries to:* Schwartzstr. 71, 42 Oberhausen/Rhld, West Germany.

AWARDS 1968
Grand Prix: OFF ON (U.S.A.), Bartlett, for Experimental Films; A FUNNY THING HAPPENED ON MY WAY TO GOLGOTHA (Belgium), Grapjos and de Hert, for Animated Films; WAITING FOR GODOT (Czechoslovakia), Jakubisko, for Fiction Films; RESPICE FINEM (Czechoslovakia), Spáta, and THE UNEMPLOYED (Yugoslavia), Zilnik, for Documentaries.
Documentary Awards: HOTEL IN KUKS (Czechoslovakia), Polak; SIXIEME FACE DU PENTAGONE (France), Marker; VIZKERESZT (Hungary), Sára.
Fiction Films: DET PERFEKTE MENNESKE (Denmark), Leth; MEDDIG EL AZ EMBER (Hungary), Elek; LETZTE WORTE (West Germany), Herzog.
Animated Films: HOBBY (Poland), Szczechura; THE FAIRY STORY (Britain), Cattaneo; CAPTAIN ARBANOS MARKO (Yugoslavia), Bourek.
FIPRESCI Prize: SIXIEME FACE DU PENTAGONE.

Pesaro   Every June

Violence and political in-fighting: the same story for Pesaro as for Cannes in 1968, although the extremists failed to stop the proceedings here, perhaps because Pesaro is essentially a "committed" event in any case, and the films shown there, though usually first features, are generally unconventional and experimental in nature. There are lively debates and addresses during the festival, which grows in influence year by year. *Inquiries to:* Mostra Internazionale del Nuovo Cinema, Via degli Uffici del Vicario 33, Rome.

Pula   July 1969

This is the most vital of Yugoslavian film gatherings, and over the past fourteen years Pula has become a traditional review of artistic quality in the Yugoslav cinema — particularly feature films. There are usually 15 films in competition, while the rest are screened in information programmes. Projections take place in the historic amphitheatre, for Pula dates back to ancient times. *Inquiries to:* Jugoslavija Film, Knez Mihailova 19, Belgrade.

**AWARDS
1967**

(Yugoslavian) Golden Arena: HAPPY GYPSIES, Petrovic.
Great Silver Arena: MORNING, Djordjevic; THE BIRCH TREE, Babaja;
PAPER PLANES, Klopcic; and THE RATS AWAKE, Pavlovic.
Best Actor: Bata Zivojinovic.
Best Actress: Milena Dravic.

San Sebastian   Every July

Another festival that seems to proceed by fits and starts. But San Sebastian can usually boast a good retrospective, and a useful film market under the direction of D. José C. Llorens Lacomba. Films entered for the competition proper must have been completed within the 12 months preceding the festival, and should not have been shown commercially in any European country other than their country of origin. Films are screened in their original version with Spanish or French sub-titles. *Inquiries to:* Miguel Echarri, Festival Internacional de Cine, Teatro Victoria Eugenia, San Sebastian, Spain.

San Francisco   October 1968

Over 30 countries take part in the non-competitive San Francisco festival (although there are awards to the winners of the "Films as Communication" and "Films as Art" sections). In addition to screenings of new films, there are useful "Director's Programmes", and homages to players (like Fred Astaire in 1966). Last year there was a large photographic exhibition on German Cinema. The attractive Masonic Auditorium provides fine facilities, including a 3,000 seat auditorium for the predominantly university audience, screening rooms, press rooms, and an exhibition hall. Albert Johnson is the Programme Director and handles the initial selection of the films. *Inquiries to:* Claude Jarman, San Francisco Film Festival, 333 Pine Street, San Francisco.

Sydney   June 1969

This flourishing Australian festival welcomed Satyajit Ray as its guest of honour this year, and has also moved forward by finding a new venue for the events themselves, away from the University. Foreign producers who doubt the interest in serious cinema in Australia should note that the Sydney festival is always heavily over-subscribed, even though there are approximately 30 programmes open to the public. *Inquiries to:* David J. Stratton, Box 4934, G. P.O., 2001 Sydney, Australia.

Tours   Every January

One wonders if the future of this admirable gathering in the Touraine will be affect-
ed adversely by the unfortunate incident of the Cinémathèque, whereby Pierre
Barbin, who founded and established the Tours festival, was installed by the Ministry of Culture as a replacement for Henri Langlois and was then later deposed
himself. It would be a pity if the festival were to languish, because it is the only
French-speaking short film forum and as such is important to overseas distributors
and film-makers as well as to the French cinema world. *Inquiries to:* A.F.D.C.,
21 rue de la Tour d'Auvergne, Paris 9.

AWARDS *Grand Prix:* YOU'RE HUMAN LIKE THE REST OF THEM (Britain),
Johnson.
1968 *Prix de la Première Oeuvre:* POZAR, POZAR, COS NARESSZCIE DZIEJE
SIE (Poland), Piwowski.
Special Jury Prizes: JIMMY O TIGRIS (Greece), Voulgaris; WHAT DO YOU
THINK? (Japan), Kuri; and THE GAME (U.S.A.), Hodes.
FIPRESCI Prize: SUICIDE (Hungary), Kosa.

Trieste   Every July

This is the only festival specialising in science-fiction films, although the appellation
has been stretched in the past year or two to fill out the programme. Screenings take
place in the 14th century Castle of San Giusto above the ancient port of Trieste.
There is a competition for short and documentary films, as well as a non-competitive
review of the best science-fiction features of the year. *Inquiries to:* Azienda Auto-
noma Soggiorno e Turismo, Castello di San Giusto, Trieste, Italy.

AWARDS *Grand Prix:* THE MACHINE STOPS (Britain), Saville.
Special Jury Prizes: WHAT ON EARTH (Canada), and THE FLY (Yugo-
1967 slavia).

Venice   August-September 1969

Still directed by Dr. Luigi Chiarini, who has resolutely put art above commerce in
his policy, the Venice Biennale maintains — but only just — its lead in the festival
field. It has, of course, been established since the thirties. An award at Venice, though
it does not necessarily carry box-office potentiality, probably procures more respect
for a film than any other award in the cinema. There are retrospectives and information programmes in addition to the closed competition. *Inquiries to:* Mostra
Internazionale d'Arte Cinematografica, Venice, Italy.

AWARDS *Leone d'Oro:* BELLE DE JOUR (France), Bunuel.
Best Actor: Ljubisa Samardzic for JUTRO (Yugoslavia).
1967 *Best Actress:* Shirley Knight for DUTCHMAN (Britain).
Special Jury Prizes: LA CHINOISE (France), Godard; LA CINA E' VICINA
(Italy), Bellocchio.
FIPRESCI Prize: LA CINA E' VICINA and REBELLION (Japan), Kobayashi.

Shorts of the Year

Lindsay Anderson at work.

Documentary and Fiction
by Peter Cowie and Charles Hedges

In Britain, it is still difficult for a quality short to obtain a circuit release, and the best that a budding director can hope for is a screening with a really successful first-run feature at a West End cinema. The Short Film Service and the Short Film-Makers Campaign battle on bravely, however, and one of the most hopeful signs for the future is the preparation, by distributors and organisations (like the New Cinema Club), of "short film shows", in which a well balanced programme can replace the familiar concept of a feature plus one or two shorts. The Museum of Modern Art in New York has a programme like this every Wednesday, while Janus Films circulates two popular "concerts" of short films on college campuses throughout the U.S.A. The charge that the public is not interested would seem to be defeated by the news that the Donnell Branch of the New York Public Library, which loans some 600 shorts on 16mm to any holder of a Library ticket, cannot cope with demand.

CZECHOSLOVAKIA: Jan Svankmajer's *The Garden* (Kratky Film) is the first film in which he uses real actors, and is an allegory about human relationships. A man places a hedge of silent people, literally under lock and key, around his house and garden. *Respice Finem* (Kratky Film) dwells touchingly on the plight of old widows living solitarily in village communities and hardly cared for,

Sensitive camerawork reveals the wealth of experience in the lined faces of these women who await death calmly but cannot bear to die alone. (Director is Jan Spáta.) Jakubisko's *Waiting for Godot* won the Grand Prix for Fiction Films at Oberhausen 1968. Here lovers, parties, students, fish in bathtubs all mingle in a web of dream and reality to form the last evening of some recruits before they don their responsibilities.

DENMARK: Laterna Film, under the guidance of Mogens Skot-Hansen, continue to produce excellent shorts. One of their recent prizewinners is *Det perfekte Menneske*, directed by Jørgen Leth, a witty observation on the place of the ideal person in Danish society, emanating from the wistful thinking of everyday life. Sune Lund-Sørensen's *The Drum* is as luminous a vision of childhood as his earlier work, and Laterna have also produced an affectionate record (in colour) of the last flea-circus in Copenhagen's Tivoli Gardens. *Kongens Enghave* (ASA Film Studios) is about an 80 year old man living on the fringes of the Danish capital and is directed by Claus Ørsted and Lars Brydesen.

FINLAND: Asko Tolonen's *Deck Passenger* follows the flight of a 16 year old schoolgirl to Germany by boat after the has "disappeared" from home. *Snow-Woman*, directed by Veli-Matti Saikkonen, won a State Prize in 1968 for its study of two boys who rebel against their school teacher and in so doing quarrel among themselves.

FRANCE: *Portrait of Orson Welles*, made by François Reichenbach and Frédéric Rossif, won the Golden Bear for Shorts at Berlin this year. Chris Marker's *La Sixième Face du Pentagon* builds up to a terrifying climax from quiet scenes of a sit-down demonstration in front of the Lincoln Memorial in Washington. Vampirism seems popular in French short films at the moment, and Pierre Philippe, a former critic on *Cinéma*, deals with an old landlady who "feeds" on her student lodgers, in *La Bonne Dame* (Les Films Armorial).

WEST GERMANY: *Exhibitionismus* is by Ottmar Schnepp. In this 12 minute piece, the actor films his actions from his own viewpoint with a hand-held camera. It was shot in a mere 36 hours. Schnepp is a name to watch for; he is currently a freelance television cameraman.

GREAT BRITAIN: One of the most widely-acclaimed British shorts of recent years is B. S. Johnson's *You're Human Like the Rest of Them* (BFI Production Board), which won the Grand Prix at both the Tours and the Melbourne Festivals in 1968. Made in part colour, it analyses a young schoolteacher's reaction to his imminent death (owing to a back injury), and his efforts to communicate the meaning and fear of his experience to pupils and fellow masters. Richard Taylor and Mostafa Hammuri also won a prize at Melbourne for *The Empty Quarter* (Orpheus Films and the Sahara Film Service), in which they reconstruct the journeys of Wilfred Thesiger through the South Arabian deserts. Peter Graham's *Edith Piaf* (Triangle Film Productions) won a "prime à la qualité" as an Anglo-French co-production, and was well received at Tours. It brings the life of the singer startlingly into focus, with a use of still photographs and archive material that is brilliantly imaginative, especially in the "Milord" sequence. *The White Bus*, Lindsay Anderson's 45 minute contribution to a now abandoned Woodfall trilogy, turns out to be a dazzlingly clever satire on Northern pride and stuffiness. Philip Trevelyan's second film *The Ship Hotel — Tyne Main* (Royal College of Art) is a vivid observation of an English pub and its habitués.

HUNGARY: *Twelth Night*, directed and photographed by Sándor Sára for Studio Béla Balázs, is an enchanting piece. It is winter on the Great Hungarian Plain; villagers arrive at the local hall by bus, tractor, or horse to see a production of the Shakespeare play. Later, in a beautiful sequence, the children skate home over the frozen canals, punting themselves along with cleft poles. György Kárpáti's *Sirtaki* was made when Mikis Theodorakis was in prison, as a brief tribute to the composer. Ference Kósa's *Suicide* won the Critics' Award at Tours, while Judit Elek's *Wher Life Ends* looks with compassion at the start of retirement for a worker after 40 years in his job.

U.S.A.: Satt Bartlett's interesting experimental prizewinner at Oberhausen, *Off-On*, is filmed from a television screen and consists of unrelated images, abstract and real, revolving round each other; colour reversal techniques are used effectively.

YUGOSLAVIA: Achievements this year have been primarily in animation (see our article on Zagreb Studios), but Dušan Vukotić's *Time* consists of one 50 second take, in which the first steps of a baby create an extraordinary sense of anticipation in the audience. One should also recognise the continued quality output of individual companies such as Dunav Film and Sutjesko Film, not to mention the group of talented short film-makers in Novi-Sad.

Note: Outstanding shorts from Canada and the Netherlands are mentioned in the national sections of those countries (see pages 51 and 118).

Still (left) shows Peter Hall snuffling at the magic mushrooms on the set of *Work is a Four Letter Word*, a scene reproduced in Derrick Knight & Partners' *Work – Is That What It's Called?* Britain's short film entry at the Berlin Festival in 1968, and scripted and directed by Paul Joyce. This documentary knits interviews with Hall into rehearsals and snippets of the finished film itself, recording the progress of the production.

Another remarkable Knight film this year is *Self Portraits*, sponsored by British Gypsum. The manufacture of plasterboard sounds like intractable material for any film-maker, but Stephen Cross has taken a revolutionary line, letting everyone involved in the process tell the camera how he works and just what gypsum does for industry. Enthralling, and, incidentally, an object lesson in how to blend black-and-white sequences with colour ones.

The Knight partnership celebrates its tenth anniversary this year, and embarks on its biggest production schedule ever, including a colour tv documentary on Samuel Palmer, a major film for IBM, and a co-production with France on kinetic art. Then the firm has completed the first in a series of educational pictures on the Arthurian legends for America, as well as promotion documentaries on *Villa Rides!* and *Barbarella*. Knight himself (photo at left) has been in South Africa shooting a film on apartheid for Human Rights Year, and co-directed another African film with Patrick Garland for Christian Aid. This is *Reaching Out*, focusing on the need for sophisticated farming to bridge the gap between the old and the new life in Kenya.

213

knight films 1968

Derrick Knight
& partners Ltd.,
8/12 Broadwick St.,
London W.1.
GER: 0761

Care "Stress - Parents with a handicapped child"
  "Reaching out" - the problems of aid in Africa

Impact "Marketing is the link"
  "The youth wave"

Education "The learning revolution"
  "King of the round table" - the poetic legends

Action "Work - is that what it's called?"
  "Pancho Villa - the myth or the man"
  "The movement movement" - Kinetic art today

knight films make news

From Bruno Bozzetto's new cartoon, VIP — MY BROTHER SUPERMAN, which is being distributed throughout the world by Atlantic Film of Zürich.

Animation

A New Visual Language   by John Halas

It has taken animation ten years to get rid of its old realistic appearance and acquire a new pictorial graphic look. It has taken even longer to change from a routine story narrative to a sophisticated, philosophical statement. Nevertheless, during the last five years animation has not advanced or expanded in any significant direction. It has repeated itself again and again. Where do we go from here?

A new partnership with the technical wizards of the Western world could very well provide the answer. Today it is possible to programme animation in terms of simple mathematics and process it through the graphical display of a computer.

Animation will never be the same again. The performance of the Stromberg Carlson 4060 Computer has injected the inevitable mark of the Electronic Age into animation which, for decades, has searched for a new formula. The computer's greatest asset is that it can perform long, arduous and repetitive calculations at a very high speed.

The "Fortran" System, developed for animation, permits animators to produce movements by joining designated points on the screen, rather in the manner of a simple game where a sequence of numbers are joined to produce a picture. In this case, however, the points number up to millions instead of a couple of dozen and complex forms and shapes can be achieved.

The film experiments and achievements of Stan Vanderbeek, Ken Knowlton, Edward Zajac and the Witney brothers are inspiring and deeply satisfactory. There is no turning back, unlike *musique concrète*, which has run into a cul-de-sac with gimmicky scores of little relevance. Computer-made films have great practical application as well as exciting artistic potential.

At this moment the process of computerised animation can only be carried out in the form of moving images, live action cannot yet be considered. Consequently, the technique needs the participation of animators, designers and layout artists.

The game is played with new tools. The graphite pencil becomes electronic, the storyboard turns into a sensitive cathode ray tube, capable of generating thousands of electronic signals per second. The new language must be learned just like the skill of flying or driving a combustion engine or tapping the keys of an Olivetti. The reward is a widening of vocabulary in visual language and experience. The keyboard is already in existence and widely approved both by artists and scientists.

Nothing as important has happened in animation for a very long time.

215

FOR
OUTSTANDING
ANIMATED FILMS
CONTACT

HALAS & BATCHELOR

3-7 KEAN ST. LONDON W.C.2
TELEPHONE 01/240-3143-5

International Survey   by Richard Arnall

BELGIUM: *Sirène*, directed by Raoul Servais, chronicles the love between a mermaid and a cabin-boy in a Dantesque commercial port; it very successfully combines a modern graphic style for the environment with a more classic one imparting "depth" to the heroes. A satire in collage, Robbe de Herte's *A Funny Thing Happened On My Way To Golgotha* (Fugitive Cinema) involves a little man with a cross crusading through contemporary society.

BULGARIA: The delightful film by Doniu Donev, *Sharpshooters*, awarded a Grand Prix at the Mamaia Animation Festival, is a wry comment on the true nature of courage. Apart from a weak ending, it is excellently paced and utilises an inventive and original soundtrack.

CANADA: The National Film Board of Canada maintains its high standard of animation production over a variety of fields. In *The Cruise*, the latest film by John and Faith Hubley, the satirical message (about the role of the individual in society) becomes a little lost. But on the way, one is captivated by fresh stylisation and some novel technique. Including vestiges of "Jack and the Beanstalk", *The House That Jack Built* is the tale of a small man who, having built a splendid new house with money stolen from a giant, still aches for something better; the whimsical dialogue by Don Arioli is as important as the vigorous drawing. Directed by Ron Tunis. Pierre Hebert continues his significant investigation of pure visual sensation, in films such as *Opus 3*.

CZECHOSLOVAKIA: For *Historia Naturae*, one of three highly sardonic works from Kratky Film, Jan Svankmajer uses medieval prints and live creatures to illustrate animal evolution. Awarded the Max Ernst prize at the Oberhausen Festival, it brilliantly suggests the destruction of nature by man, and finally shows that he too is temporary. *The Gossips*, directed by Josef Kluge, is a sad but pointed story of true love wrecked by caluminators, cleverly depicted here in grotesque cut-out form.

Below: Jan Svankmajer's HISTORIA NATURAE.

Ivan Renc's *The Sword* deals with perception; he depicts the psychological reactions to a beautiful sword-hilt of a variety of people, none of whom can see that the sword itself is still stuck in a human back!

FRANCE: *The Spider Elephant* (Les Films Armorial) is Piotr Kamler's best work to date, a droll saga of a spider-legged elephant which walks in a straight line back and forth across the world. Its superb animation and fabulously-textured surface justly gained it the 1968 Emile Cohl award. Arresting graphics also contribute to *Uuivers* (Cinemation), by Otero and Leroux, who present visually the paradox of "worlds within worlds".

HUNGARY: *Koncertissimo* (Studio Pannonia) by Jozsef Denes makes a skilful attack upon vain and ostentatious concert-goers, who do not notice, until they are mown down, that the assembling "orchestra" is composed of armed soldiers.

JAPAN: Puppet animation can be tedious stuff unless it is directed by one of the few masters of the craft; now another has been added to this select category. With his first film *Breaking of Branches Is Forbidden*, in which the stylised movement is developed from traditional Japanese theatre, Kihachiro Kawamoto has proved that he possesses the requisite control and sensitivity. The best of Yoji Kuri's three latest films is *The Room:* a variety of miscellaneous happenings in a womb-like environment provide the quintessential Kuri elements of sex, sadism and surrealism. A private world invaded, destroyed and then rebuilt is the theme of his *Deux Poissons Grillés*, particularly remarkable for its stunning visuals. Finally, *What Do You Think?* is an experimental film involving animated and live action chaos, in which Kuri makes a Hitchcockian personal appearance.

NETHERLANDS: Wim van der Linden's brief experimental film on the fringes of animation, *Hawaian Lullaby* (Dodgers Syndicate), hilariously parodies a film genre and the whole Hawaian myth. But the incorporation of a (near nude) hula dancer before the screen induces contemplation on the very nature of cinematic experience itself.

POLAND: Across a 'scope screen, sculpted in three-dimensional, free-flowing oil paint, a man attempts to subjugate a proud wild stallion. Even if the style of Witold Giersz's film is not altogether original, the form and technique rightly gained *Portrait Of A Horse* (Warsaw Animation Studio) a Grand Prix at Mamaia. *Hobby* (Se-Ma-For) is probably the most genuinely surrealistic animated film of the year. Daniel Szczechura has conceived, amidst an almost Giacomettian universe, a bizarre wom n who lassoes bird-men and imprisons them in cages; a formidable and haunting work. In Stefan Schabenbeck's second film, a philisophical story entitled *Exclamation Mark* (Se-Ma-For), here is again a fascination for mathematical/graphic punning. People create a ball in flat geometry, only to be crushed as it rolls down a hill; their remains form a huge exclamation mark.

ROMANIA: At last Romanian animation, from the Animafilm Studios, has lost much of the selfs-consciousness and the sterility of ideas that troubled it, and has also gained in self-control and timing. *Along The Thread Of The Tale*, by Constantin Mustetea, is a simple, unpretentious and highly amusing piece of whimsy, in which the characters and their adventures are all outlined by an unravelled ball of wool. Sabin Balasa comments coherently in *The Wave* upon the relationship between the artist's temporal life and the immortality of his work; once again his drawing is superb.

SWITZERLAND: A man loves a woman from within the society that he shuns; for his crime he is chased and ultimately hanged — *The Ravens* gather. Ernest and Gisèle Ansorge have drawn in carbon to create an exceptionally free and expressive style.

U.S.A.: Herbert Kosower investigates *The Face* of womankind with a rapid and multifarious assemblage of photos, and proves that in true film absurdity a female face can be simultaneously bizarre *and* beautiful. *You Can*, by Rose Neiditch, is a splendid sequence of sharp vignettes in which the characters can do anything — except smoke! A significant and promising phenomenon that has recently appeared in America is the excellent animation being produced by students. For example, from the University of Southern California, *The Resurrection Of Mr. Man* which was made specially for Human Rights Year, and *Marcello, I'm So Bored* about the emptiness of modern life, are both remarkably sensitive interpretations of their themes. And although the New York Institute of Cinematography cheats slightly in *Calypso* by "pirating" a famous musical parody, their drawings are quite equal to Stan Freeberg's brilliant send-up of "Banana Boat Song".

U.S.S.R.: Why is it that the Russians, with lavish financial backing and super-competent technique so rarely satisfy with their animation, so rarely transmit any creative excitement, any feeling of any sort? This year's only exception is *The Bench* (Soiuzmultfilm), in which L. Atamanov uses the observations of Danish cartoonist Herluf Bidstrup to depict a day's cycle of events around a park seat. Impeccably animated, it should also be of interest to students of the "Cold War" for its inclusion of a sizeable chunk of Beatle music.

218

Zagreb Round Up

The Zagreb harvest this year includes two really outstanding cartoons. Zlatko Bourek's *Captain Arbanas Marko* is based on an old folk song about a powerful knight who woos three sisters and comes to a dramatic end. Bourek's shaded figures look like Renaissance princes, and there is an element of anguish in the imagery that reminds one also of Goya. *Diogenes Perhaps* confirms the massive talent of Nedeljko Dragic. A lonely individual wanders about in an absurd world searching for happiness. He enters a hotel to find the dining room crowed with a reproduction of "The Last Supper" . . . Every scene is illuminated a visual gag: the hero pushes a stone down a hill with tremendous efforts, only to find that it then runs "up" the slope again; and when he opens his window at night, darkness and stars leak like ink through the window. *Tolerance*, directed by Zlatko Grgic and Branko Ranitovic, follows a running fight between four men and one midget who continually interrupts their harmonious life. Like most of the Zagreb cartoons, *Tolerance* is built on a succession of incidents and wicked jokes, although the final pay-off, in Heaven, may not be as clear as it should be to some audiences.

Krek introduces a comparative newcomer to the studios — Borivoj Dovnikovic-Bordo, and gives a very funny picture of Army life as it traces the humiliating service of a young conscript whose pet frog enrages the local Sergeant. Some Zagreb work this year is perhaps rather too ambitious in concept and fails to have more than a mildly amusing impact. The disappointing *Sisyphus*, by Aleksandar Marks and Vladimir Jutrisa (who made *The Fly*), uses just one background as a melancholy man is reduced to suicide by a revolt among his furniture and fittings. Ante Zavinovic uses the single scene method much more successfully in *Of Holes and Corks*, an arresting and witty account of a man whose complacency angers the volcano on which he is unknowingly seated. Boris Kolar's latest cartoon, *Discoverer*, starts with an excellent gag as an invisible man stumbles round a darkened room but then drifts into a series of obscure interludes. A Grand Prix winner at Mamaia, Zlatko Grgic's *Inventor of Shoes* is a bouncy little children's story with a commentary in English, while Pavao Stalter's *The Boxes* deals uncannily well with the efforts of two men to locate each other, and the prolific Zavinovic's other 1968 cartoon, *Feet*, uses comic figures to illustrate a story of short-sighted bickering.

From a long-term point of view, however, the greatest achievement of the year must be *A Stain on his Conscience*, in which Dusan Vukotic combines live action with animation to create a weird and terrifying surrealist atmosphere. A man sitting in a café is suddenly harried by a lump of noxious matter. Try as he may, he cannot shake it off or dispel it. It grows larger and cuts off his lines of retreat. Finally he imprisons it in a bottle, but in the concluding scene he shrinks from opening the

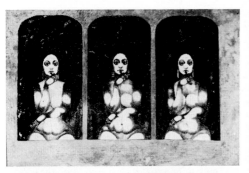

beer that a waiter brings him . . . Colour and music are used with remarkable intelligence in this film, and perhaps Vukotic will develop the combination technique still further in his future work.

It is often forgotten that Zagreb produces documentaries as well as cartoons (not to mention about 200 commercials a year), and among the 1968 titles the most suitable for international audiences would seem to be *The Violin Maker*, directed by Bogdan Lizic.

Richard Taylor, formerly with Larkins, has been striking sparks on his own at 49 Rathbone Street, W.1., for some time. *The Rise of Parnassus Needy* has won awards that matter, and so has *The Princess and the Wonderful Weaver*, an excellent *risqué* cartoon for the National Wool Export Corp.

Taylor's personal film, *Revolution* (still at left) has taken him 4 years. It's an entirely visual (no words) study of governmental power: people try to change the speed and direction of the official machine, but they are simply absorbed into its tempo. Taylor calls it an anarchist film, and there are some hallucinatory goings-on in a labyrinth of dungeons . . .

Still (left) from *The Trendsetter*, one of Biographic's recent films directed by Vera Linnecar from a storyboard by Stan Hayward. The Biographic studio divides its time almost equally between animation and live-action, and this year the team has been working on instructional films for the Women's National Cancer Control Campaign, and the COI among other sponsors. *Living Tomorrow* (for the COI) makes life easier for the exporters by selling British technology to the world. Meanwhile, television commercials have to be done too, many of them in colour so that advertisers can insure themselves against a bottleneck at the labs when every channel goes gaudy.

LARKINS
IS GOOD
FOR YOU

16 HENRIETTA STREET, LONDON, W.C.2—COV 2733
IN ASSOCIATION WITH THE FILM PRODUCERS GUILD

4 scenes from YELLOW SUBMARINE. This 85 minute film was made by T.V.C. London, directed by George Dunning, with animation directors Jack Stokes and Bob Balser, design by Heinz Edelmann, special sequences by Charlie Jenkins, and production supervision by John Coates, and a group of animators and other helpers totalling 185 people in all.

Stills (left) from Richard Williams's highly-praised animation effects for *The Charge of the Light Brigade*. His studio now wants to move beyond the titles stage into the full-scale production of special effects and animation features. Williams is co-conceiving a screen version of John Bowen's *After the Rain* with designer Tony Walton, and this will give them more freedom to "doctor" every phase of the script before shooting even begins. Also in the pipeline are the special effects and animation for *Pax?*, the prestige film issued for the Mexico City Olympiad.

Stills (right) from the latest Richard Williams production, MULLA NASRUDIN

Right: Dick Williams watches his boyhood hero, Ken Harris, at work on NASRUDIN. Harris was one of the great animators in Hollywood, and probably the finest talent involved in BUGS BUNNY.

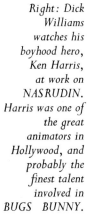

Familiar scenes and figures from commercials designed and animated by
Wyatt-Cattaneo Productions.

Still (below) from *The Fairy Story*, directed by Tony Cattaneo from a story by Stan Hayward and told by Kenneth Griffith. The shaggy dog pattern of *Fairy Story* is given a fresh look by Cattaneo's blending of fantasy and deadpan observation (the father shifting, twitching in his chair before beginning the tale), and was roundly applauded at the last Cambridge Animation Festival.

Ron Wyatt and Tony Cattaneo have now been operating as a unit for over 3 years, yet already the large majority of British tv cartoon commercials come from their studio. They've done plugs for Ovaltine, Tom Piper, Nescafé, Sunfresh, and umpteen for Spillers flour. Both men have a background in advertising, but Cattaneo was trained as a painter. Most animators are too obsessed with the artistic side to cope with the detailed demands of the agencies, but W-C make an analysis of every project from an agency angle. They're engaged on a descriptive cartoon of the Carnival of the Animals for Decca, who are keen on the idea of a series to illustrate their records for children; and they also plan to expand their "combination" work (live action and animation together) in the future. Their new large studios are at 24 Charing Cross Rd.

Still (left) from *Flurina*, a new film for children by Halas & Batchelor, based on Alois Carigiet's book. It has been made in association with Condor Films of Zürich, and has music by the Swiss composer Paul Burkhard. This 12 minute colour cartoon has been released simultaneously in 4 languages, English, German, French, and Spanish. H & B have also completed a series of 3 television commercials in colour promoting the new German colour service, under the general title of *Flora*, and are working with Encyclopaedia Britannica Films on a group of 6 one-reel colour cartoons based on classical fairy tales.

RICHARD TAYLOR CARTOON FILMS

49 RATHBONE STREET, LONDON W1

TELEPHONE 636 2805·6

Still (below) from *Refining*, a cartoon for British Petroleum by Larkins, the lively studio in Covent Garden that churns out Talkie strips and still manages to make films for the COI (on automation), and Barclays (those one-minute cinema jokes that tickle local audiences), as well as a 6-minute affair called *Small Boats* ("more a happening than a film," comments Beryl Stevens, sparkling head of the studio). The Talkie strip revolution has changed lives at Larkins. "It's an arduous, time-consuming process, fraught with problems," says Miss Stevens, but the results are wickedly effective, especially one for BOAC about the Caribbean, and another called *Right First Time*, on women's internal infections . . .

Project Shell

Eight new films you can borrow

You can see the titles and brief details below. For full information about them and about the many other Shell films, please write to your local Shell company or, in the U.K., to Petroleum Films Bureau, 4 Brook Street, London, W.1.

The Threat in the Water	*30 minutes*	Progress report on world attempts to defeat bilharzia, the debilitating disease.
The Land Must Provide	*25 minutes*	The importance of fertilisers in raising world food production, particularly in less-developed regions.
'Capshell'	*8 minutes*	Operation of the deep-diving-bell 'Capshell' off the coast of Italy.
Tanker Journey	*11 minutes*	Impressions of life aboard tankers on journeys to Scandinavia, the Middle East and the Caribbean.
Paint	*25 minutes*	The history of paint from the Stone Age to the present day.
Engine Lubrication	*10 minutes*	Re-edited version of Part IV of 'How the Motor Car Works'.
Defensive Driving	*13 minutes*	How to drive more safely by adopting the 'Defensive Driving' technique.
Mountain Driving	*14 minutes*	The principles of 'Defensive Driving' applied to driving in the Swiss Alps.

Sponsored Films

British Transport

Edgar Anstey's team at British Transport has won over a hundred awards since its inception twenty years ago, and about a dozen films are produced annually. *Next Stop — Scotland* (*d* Kenneth Fairbairn, *ph* Ronald Craigen and Trevor Roe *in colour*, 30 mins) begins as a bright advertisement for Motorail and then slowly develops into one of the most splendidly photographed travelogues of the year. Two couples, one newly wed, the other elderly, tour Scotland by different routes. The commentary is informative and leavened with just a touch of humour. Some of the scenery in the Western Isles is very imaginatively recorded here. *Eighth Rail Report — The New Tradition* (*d* Nick Nicholls, *ph* Trevor Roe *in colour*, 13 mins) lays the emphasis on the container revolution — even special cargo ships are being built so as to accept stacked containers. This change is symbolic of British Rail's general efforts to modernise their activities, from signalling to station catering.

Container Port (*d* Ian Woolf, *ph* Jack West *in colour*, 13 mins) is a survey of the new port built at Tilbury on reclaimed land, where a wide variety of cargoes can now be handled in bulk. The film was made for the Port of London Authority, and it is interesting to note that the British Transport Unit is undertaking more outside work than ever before.

Ford

Far and away the most ambitious and sophisticated film made by a sponsor this year, *9 Days in Summer* (*d* Philip Bond, *ph* Vic Francis, Alan More *et al in colour, mus* Jeff Wayne, 50 mins) traces the progress of the Lotus-Ford engine from drawing board to U.S. and Mexican triumphs on the Grand Prix circuit. Every shot in this production is carefully chosen in relationship to the theme as a whole, and Philip Bond's inspired direction catches the smell and the poetry of motor racing far better than many a feature film. Special effects are legion, but all belong intimately to the idea of the film (such as the immaculate dissolves from sketched cars to real cars lined up for the start). *9 Days in Summer* is not afraid to admit the failures of the Lotus-Ford combination either, and it pays tribute to the driving skill of Graham Hill and, appropriately, Jim Clark. This film must be the most impressive produced by Norman Vigars during his long period at the Ford Film Unit. Editor Peter Gold and titles designer Michael Graham-Smith should also be congratulated. P.S. As a lead-in to the main film, there is also *First Time Out* (d Philip Bond, 10 mins), which relates the Lotus-Ford victory at Zandvoort.

A dramatic close-up of the late Jim Clark in one of the Grand Prix events featured in 9 DAYS IN SUMMER.

Imperial Chemical Industries

Over twenty films have been produced at ICI during the past year, most of these being made by the Millbank Unit, which is permanently attached to the big company. *Dead Safe* (d Ronnie Whitehouse, *ph* Peter Grimwood and Ken Rodwell *in colour*, 27 mins) has won a Screenwriters' Award for its casual but informative dialogue about the dangers of shooting. There is some outstanding photography on East Anglian locations, and the absence of a commentary allows the

How to treat 100 people to the movies for 7/6d.

The Ford Film Library at Hendon has the answer.

Whilst we've been maintaining our stock, we've come up with a few new ideas lately.

Films like '9 Days in Summer', a 50 minute colour documentary on last year's Grand Prix season.

Then there's our movie magazine. The first edition features articles on films about the Escort in Rallycross, the work of the fire brigade, helicopter stunts in Zurich, the Escort in San Remo and the World Ski-Bob championships in the Italian Alps. We're issuing it three or four times a year and calling it 'Motoring Scene'.

But we don't concentrate solely on motoring. We've got films on anything from student explorations in the Sahara to the story of a Midland football team.

And there's one thing we haven't changed. Our handling charge.

You can still treat your friends and your friends' friends to an evening at the movies – and it's still only 7/6d.

Ford

hazards and suspense to emerge from the action itself. *Making Reservoirs with Polythene Sheeting (prod* British Visqueen Ltd. *in colour*, 14 mins) was shot largely in the Spanish province of Alicante, and demonstrates how waterproof polythene lining does not deteriorate and works out at less than one third of the price of concrete. Spain is not the only country whose crops languish for lack of water, and this film will have a significance for many overseas audiences.

Finally, *The Laws of Disorder — Part 1, "Entropy" (in colour,* 20 mins) features Nobel Prize winner Professor George Porter, FRS, who outlines a fundamental principle of thermodynamics with a lucid address and several demonstrations. This sensible film, which reached the BISFA Finals in June, is the first in a series made in collaboration with the Royal Institution.

National Coal Board

There is a staff of about forty attached to the NCB Film Unit, which was founded in the early fifties (although *Mining Review*, first shot by the Crown Film Unit, has now celebrated its 21st anniversary and is screened in some 700 cinemas every month. It is even made in colour about 4 times a year). One of the best NCB films of this or any other year is *The Cathedral in a Village (d* Robin Carruthers, *ph* Cyril Arapoff *in colour*, 30 mins), a paean to Southwell Cathedral, Nottinghamshire. Every May, miners from the surrounding collieries gather for a choral festival at Southwell, and Robin Carruthers uses this occasion as an excuse to reveal the architectural wonders of the minsters — the strength and balance of the 12th century nave, the stone carvings and statuary of the 13th century chapter house. This graceful, beautifully modulated documentary is an achievement by any standards.

The Longhirst Story (d Peter Pickering, *ph* John Reid, 17 mins) is a story of enterprise and hard work. It shows how and why productivity at a Northumberland colliery was boosted to over a thousand tons per shift; while *Helping Learners to Learn (d* Nestor Lovera, *ph* Eddy Tilling, 17 mins) urges a more business-like approach to teaching in the coal industry, emphasising the need for visual aids at a time when highly complex techniques and machines have to be mastered. These titles are but a few from the large NCB library, and in fact the Unit completes between 60 and 80 reels of 35 mm film each year.

Ordered your copy?

The 1968 ICI Film Catalogue contains some 180 titles covering the interests of virtually any type of audience. The catalogue gives synopses and running times for the films in ICI's library. All are 16 mm, all with sound — and all available free of charge.

Please write to: ICI Film Library
Thames House North, Millbank, London SW1

KS1

Shell

An above-average year for Shell, with one title virtually assured of classic status among sponsored films. It is *The Threat in the Water* (*d* Richard Bigham, *ph* Alan Fabian *in colour*, *mus* Edward Williams, 30 mins), which was made for the 20th Anniversary of the World Health Organisation. It deals with a terrible but usually unpublicised disease, bilharzia, and the aggressive quality of the film is in admirable contrast to the scenes it has to show — men slumped in lethargy and thus in poverty, polluted rivers, dying villages. Even with the help of the recently developed molluscicide dose, it is formidably difficult to intercept the danger. A fearless film, and a timely one. *The Land Must Provide* (*d* Philip Owtram, *ph* Gus Coma and K.G. Prabhaker *in colour*, *mus* Otto Ketting, 24 mins) stresses the need to bridge the gap between research and the farmer, by showing him how to exploit chemical fertilisers. This far-ranging production includes sequences in Guatemala, Japan, and Turkey.

Paint (*d* Michael Heckford, *ph* Alan Fabian *in colour*, 26 mins) is a visual delight, tracing the history of paint back to prehistoric times while pointing out that the raw materials involved have changed

236

more in the last 30 years than they did in the previous 30,000. The Egyptians and the 15th century Flemings are said to have had the greatest influence on the history of painting. Shell have also issued two excellent instructional films, *Mountain Driving* and *Defensive Driving* (both *d* Michael Barden, *ph* Peter Hennessey *in colour*, and both 13 mins), shot in Germany and Switzerland.

U.K. Atomic Energy Authority

An extremely popular prize-winning film recently added to the UKAEA Library is *On the Safe Side* (*d* Lawrence Crabb, *ph* Frank North *in colour*, 20 mins). This enumerates the hazards of careless handling of electricity in a research laboratory, and describes one potentially lethal situation in a taut and dramatic way that ensures reception of the film's message by any audience. It emphasises the mnemonic S.I.D.E. — Switch off, Isolate, Dump, and Earth — as a safeguard against disaster. *Water for Life* (*d* Phil Dennis, *ph* Charles K. French *in colour*, 15 mins) starts with the fact that only 1% of the world's water is available in a fresh state, and goes on to discuss the

A drawing specially made for the UKAEA film, WATER FOR LIFE, illustrating the ancient method of distillation.

How to borrow films on atomic energy

types (and advantages of) desalination plants, of which Britain supplies some 60% to the world. Much pleasing photography in Kuwait and elsewhere.

An instructional film in the reliable UKAEA tradition is *Radio Isotopes in Medical Diagnosis and Investigation* (*d* Denis Ward, *in colour*, 30 mins) which tells how renography depends on radio isotopes for its effective analysis of ailments such as pernicious anaemia. The importance of the gamma spectrometer is also underlined. Finally, *Transport Ability* (*d* John S. Green, *ph* Michael Nunn *in colour*, 20 mins) has been brought into the Library as an expanded version of *Return Journey* (reviewed in IFG 1968). This new film describes two journeys, one from Canada to Windscale in Cumberland, the other between Marseilles and Latina. Both show how irradiated fuel, properly stored, can be transported safely through any kind of environment.

Other Outstanding Titles

During 1967, some 2,843 sponsored films were made by 476 production companies in the U.S.A., Canada, Europe, Latin America, the Middle East, Africa, Australia, Japan, and Malaysia, and one notes that the Film Producers Guild of London topped the list with 58 films. The Guild was also responsible for last year's most honoured documentary, *Indus Waters* (*in colour*, 25 ½ mins), a report for the World Bank on the biggest engineering project in history, affecting one in sixty of all the world's peoples. Two films about insurance made their mark in 1968: *The Risk Takers* (*d* Anthony Pelissier, *prod* R. H. Riley and Associates for The Chartered Insurance Institute, *in colour*, 17 mins), which aims to explain the industry to young people thinking of an insurance career, but which suffers from a commentary rather too overweighted with information; and *In the Dark* (*d* David Eady, *ph* Martin Curtis, *prod* R. H. Riley and Associates for The British Insurance Association), an inventively shot account of an industrial accident and its aftermath, though again hampered by rhetorical dialogue. Films on North Sea gas continue to appear. John Laing Construction have sponsored *Pipeline through the Fens (in colour)*, which describes the complex laying of a 33 mile pipe under the Fens as part of the Feeder Main for North Sea gas from the Norfolk Coast to the Rugby area. Also concerned with the sea is the Random Film Production of *The Demanding Sea* (*in colour*, 30 mins) for the King George's Fund for Sailors, which displays the sea and its ships in a number of moods.

The Gas Council sponsored *Shapes of Progress* (*d* John Mollinson, *ph* Edwin Hillier *in colour*, 22 mins) so that several top designers could give their own views on the factors affecting design in a wide range of commodities. *World of Clay — A Portrait of an Industry* (*d* Alexander C. Ricketts, *ph* John M. Gresty and Derek Alltree *in colour*, 27 mins) provides a picture in depth of the china clay industry, centred on St. Austell, Cornwall, the HQ of the English China Clays Group. Vickers's *Centenary* is an excellent compilation of film clips from 1909 onwards, showing the range of the contribution the company has made to British growth during the past hundred years. *Self Portraits* (*d* Stephen Cross for British Gypsum) is an unusual and effective promotion film for plasterboard products, even if it is primarily intended for building industry audiences. BP's *Divertimento* (*in colour*, 7 mins) uses microphotography to discover patterns of beauty in oil, while *Swordcraft* (*in colour*, 23 mins) succeeds in showing how sword-making is at once an ancient and a highly advanced manufacturing organisation. *Stay Still While I Hit You* (*in colour*, 28 mins) is a fine film for general audiences, focusing as it does on the Alcan Golfer of the Year Championship. Finally, a word for Richard Taylor's *The Princess and the Wonderful Weaver*, a delightful and witty cartoon aimed at boosting the sale of British wool cloth abroad.

Film Schools

Subtitling

Improvements in their own chemical process have enabled that reliable firm *Cinetyp* (Grünaustrasse 10, 3084 Wabern-Bern, **Switzerland**) to enlarge their scope of operations and to subtitle more films these past two years. Among the titles they have worked on recently are: *Vargtimmen, Un Homme et une Femme, Vivre pour Vivre, Belle de Jour, A Man for all Seasons, Guess Who's Coming to Dinner,* and *Thoroughly Modern Millie.* The brothers H. and J. Weber, who are at the head of Cinetyp, have been together in the business for more than thirty years, and they employ more than twenty titlers and engineers, not to mention a number of outside translators. Write with our recommendation.

In **Germany** the leading firm in this field is *Neue Mars-Film Peters KG* (Friedrichstrasse 235, Berlin 61), and they also have a branch in Paris being directed by Mr. Peters himself (at 4 rue Christophe Colomb, Paris 8). It is now over ten years since this energetic man took over the firm and highlights of its progress have been the introduction of ultrasonics and the installment of "Lichtsatzgeräten", as well as the Dow-caustic machine for the production of clichés. There is a team of qualified translators and technicians under Mr. Peters, and among the more important films subtitled for cinemas and television this year have been *A Man for all Seasons, Barrier, Don Quixote* (by Pabst), and Pasolini's *La Ricotta.* Neue Mars-Film Peters are always interested in satisfying customers from abroad.

The acknowledged authority as far as subtitling in Britain is concerned is **Mai Harris** (at 26-27 d'Arblay Street, London W.1.). She is always busy with work for cinema and tv, and she also prepares spots and master titles for companies like Fox, Paramount, Columbia, and Universal. Recently she has subtitled several Czech films, the Yugoslav *Rondo,* and the Swedish *Woman of Darkness.* Miss Harris is interested to hear from new clients overseas and will quote for their requirements.

Title and Copyright Research

In an age of specialists, few in the film world are more useful than the Entertainment Copyright Research Co., Inc., 225 West 57th Street, New York City 10019. This remarkable firm will, for Copyright Research, locate the origin of the basic work, the U.S. copyright registration(s), the assignment(s), renewal(s), renewal assignment(s), foreign copyright, and dramatisations, picturisations, radio and tv

Ultrasonic equipment for achieving clear bright titles on a finished film has long been installed in the premises of Neue Mars-Film Peters KG, Berlin.

NEUE MARS-FILM
PETERS KG
UNTERTITELUNG

Friedrichstraße 235
1 BERLIN 61
Tel. 180865/66

Branch:
4 rue Christophe Colomb
75 PARIS VIII
Tel. 225-2768

presentations based on the original. For General Title Research, they cover periodicals and all literature published in the U.S.A. and Britain from 1938 onwards; as well as filmstrips and films from 1900 up to date, and original foreign language titles and translation titles from 1950 onwards, covering France, Italy, Spain, Japan, and West Germany. They can also offer original titles of films from Argentina, Brazil, Bulgaria, Czechoslovakia, Holland, India, Israel, Mexico, Poland, Portugal, Scandinavia, and the Soviet countries. Go to this firm too for biographical research, cartoon titles, music titles, fictional characters, property verification, log surveillance search, and obituary research. Radio, tv, and theatre are also covered.

Film Insurance

A useful contact for producers who plan to work in Europe is the firm of Jauch & Hübener, Gr. Reichenstr. 2, Hamburg 11, West Germany. This old established business, with branches in Berlin, Mülheim, Frankfurt, Munich, Vienna, and Zürich, now handles all the production insurance for the second television channel in Germany, and for a majority of the features produced in that country. Note that Jauch & Hübener maintains links with Lloyd's of London.

Film Transport

Our research has shown that each country has one or at most two transport firms *specialising* in film work. In the U.S.A., the leader is clearly Barnett International Forwarders Inc., 543 West 43rd Street, **New York**, N.Y. 10036. Here is the largest freight forwarder and customs broker in the continent, with a network of agents throughout the world. There are offices in Los Angeles and at John F. Kennedy Airport. Norman Barnett, currently President, manages the enterprise (which goes back some 80 years) with his brother Alan Barnett. Both men are sons of the founder.

Then in **London,** Wm. H. Müller & Co, 58 Old Compton Street, W.1., are well known for their reliability in transporting not only films and film stock, but also entire crews when they depart for overseas location work. Müller's branch here was set up in 1934, and there is an office at London Airport.

At 18 Barter Street, **London** W.C.1., Bob Burge Ltd. have some 19 years' experience in film shipments, import and export. They have offices in the new "freight village" at London Airport, and correspondents in every major country.

The firm of Franz Kroll & Co., Lindenstr. 39, 1 **Berlin** 39, is an outstanding specialist in this field, with a network of international contacts as well as branches in Hanover and Düsseldorf. Radio and television shipments are also handled by Krolls, who have been in existence for over 35 years. Our recommendation.

In **Hamburg** (at Chilehaus C), Hagens, Anthony & Co. can trace their origins back to the nineteenth century. For many years now they have been IATA agents in air-freight traffic, with a non-stop service at Hamburg Fuhlsbüttel Airport, as well as at Bremen.

In the Netherlands, Aeronaut's Bonded Stores for Films has its headquarters in the magnificent new **Amsterdam** Schiphol Airport. It handles, at low prices, all kinds of films and associated items such as mother-tapes. Documents are transported direct and automatically to customs, airlines, and freightsheds, and Aeronaut deals with 300 shipments of general merchandise every day. A staff of 68 people are employed in air freight here. Contact Mr. Y. Oldenburg with mention of this book.

Finally, Scandinavia. H. Melchior Jensen, of Copenhagen Forwarding Agency A/S, is well known in several countries, and now has new offices at **Kastrup** Airport. His company is the only one in Europe that handles *film* and nothing else. For speedy service in or out of Denmark, get in touch with the enterprising Mr. Jensen.

And in Stockholm, we recommend AB Transportkompaniet (postal address: Fack, Hornsbruksg. 28, Stockholm 9), which has 40 years' experience in the management of film and film units. Crews from abroad can be cleared at the border towns with minimum delay. The company has branches in Göteborg, Malmö, Hälsingborg, Norrköping, Trelleborg, Borås, and Örebro, and their own offices at the main domestic airports of Stockholm, Göteborg, and Malmö. Inquiries to Mr. H. Söderberg.

245

Film Transporters

AUSTRIA
Frey & Co., Lindengasse 43, Vienna.
Karl Vrablitz, Neubaugasse 36, Vienna.

BELGIUM
F. van de Moortel, 17 Av. Galilee, Brussels.
Import Film Service, 13 Bvd Badouin, Brussels.

FINLAND
International Transport AB, Glogatan 3, Helsinki.

FRANCE
Michaux, R. et Cie., 2 & 5 Rue de Rocroy, Paris X. Tel. 878 72-72.
Donot, Paul et Cie., 175 Rue de Courcelles, Paris XVII.
Express Transport, 27 Rue de Flandres, Paris.

DENMARK
Copenhagen Forwarding Agency a/s, Copenhagen Airport, Kastrup. Tel. 503555.

GERMANY
Hagens, Anthony & Co., Chilehaus C, (P.O. Box 966), Hamburg 1. Tel. 322426.
Kroll, Franz & Co., Lindenstr. 39, Berlin 61. Tel. 185051.
Kroll, Franz & Co., Airport Freight Centre, Düsseldorf-Nord. Tel. 422671 & 4216565.
Kroll, Franz & Co., Mainzer Landstr. 168, Frankfurt/Main 9. Tel. 253029.
Kroll, Franz & Co., Airport Freight Centre, Hannover. Tel. 7735407.

Kroll, Franz, & Co., Schertlinstr. 10, München. Tel. 789986.

GREAT BRITAIN
Air Express Ltd., 15 Macklin Street, London W.C.2.
Bob Burge Ltd., 18 Barter Street, London W.C.1. Tel. 242. 6481.
Film Transport Specialists (G.B.) Ltd., Fairfield House, N. Circular Rd., London N.W. 10.
Howlett, B. J. & Co. Ltd., 83 New Bond Street, London W.1.
Müller, Wm. H. & Co. (London) Ltd., 58 Old Compton Street, London W.1. Tel. GER 8131.

GREECE
Greca Transport, 96 Academy Street, Athens.

ITALY
Cippolli & Zanetti, Via Nomentana 257, Rome.

NETHERLANDS
NV Aeronaut, Vrachtgebouw Schiphol Airport, Freight Bldg., Rooms 900-920. Tel. 170922.
NV Netrov, (Mr. Burns), Building 114, Schiphol Airport.

SPAIN
Ferrer Y Cia, Almirante 5, Madrid.

SWEDEN
AB Transportkompaniet, Hornsbruksgatan 28, Stockholm 9. Tel. 680580.

U.S.A.
Barnett International, Forwarders Inc., 543 West 43 St., New York, N.Y. 10036.

Leading European and American Studios

AUSTRIA
Wien-Film GmbH, Sievering Studios, Sieveringstr. 135, Wien 19. Tel. 362153.

CZECHOSLOVAKIA
Barrandov Studio, Krizeneckeho nám 322, Prague-Smichov.

Bratislava Feature Film Studio, Bratislava-Koliba.

DENMARK
Nordisk Film, Mosedalvej, Copenhagen.

FRANCE
Studios de Boulogne, 137 Av. Jean Baptiste Clément, Boulogne (Seine). Tel. MOL 6580.

Studios Eclair, Av. de Lattre-de-Tassigny, Epinay-sur-Seine. Tel. PLA 39.60.

Franstudio, 4 Rue des Reservoirs, Saint-Maurice (Seine).

Paris Studios Cinema, 50 Quai du Pont-du-Jour, Billancourt (Seine).

GERMANY
Bavaria-Atelier GmbH, Bavaria-Filmplatz 7, München-Geiselgasteig. Tel. 47691.

Studio Hamburg, Tonndorfer Hauptstr. 90, Hamburg-Wandsbek.

GREAT BRITAIN
Associated British Elstree Studios, Boreham Wood, Herts. Tel. ELS 1600.

M-G-M British Studios, Elstree Way, Boreham Wood, Herts. Tel. ELS 2000.

Pinewood Studios, Iver, Bucks. Tel. IVER 700.

Shepperton Studios, Shepperton, Middx. Tel. CHE 2611.

HUNGARY
Mafilm Studios, Lumumba utca 174, Budapest XIV.

ITALY
Cinecittà, Via Tuscolana 1524, Roma.

De Laurentiis Studios, Via Medina, Rome. Tel. 607913.

Titanus Studios, Via Del Villini 5, Rome. Tel. 841217.

JUGOSLAVIA
Avala Central Film Studios, Film Town, Belgrade. Tel. 58-080.

NETHERLANDS
N.V. Cinecentrum, P.O. Box 508, Hilversum.

Cinetone Studios, Duivendrechtsekade 83-87, Amsterdam. Tel. 020-54404, 51971 and 020-56567.

SPAIN
C.E.A., Arturo Soria 99, Madrid. Tel. 2-45-76-00.

Sevilla Films, Pio XII, 2, Madrid. Tel. 2-59-03-00.

U.S.A.
Columbia, 1438 North Gower St., Hollywood, Calif. 90028. Tel. 642-3111.

Metro-Goldwyn-Mayer, 10202 W. Washington Blvd., Culver City, Calif. 90230. Tel UP 0-3311.

Paramount, 5451 Marathon St., Hollywood, Calif. Tel. HO 9-2411.

Twentieth Century-Fox, 10201 W. Pico Blvd., Los Angeles, Calif. Tel. CR 7-2211.

Universal, Universal City, Calif. Tel. Tel. 877-1211.

Warner Bros.-Seven Arts, 4000 Warner Blvd., Burbank, Calif. Tel. HO 9-1251.

Film Archives

ALBANIA
Film Arshiva e Republikes Popullores Te Shqiperise, Tirana. Director: V. Aristidhi.

AUSTRALIA
*National Library of Australia Films Division, 113 London Circuit, Canberra A.C.T. Director: Harold White.

AUSTRIA
*Osterreichisches Filmarchiv, Galileigasse 3, Vienna 1090. Director: Dr. Ludwig Gesek. *Stock: 1,100 films. Also publishes useful brochures.*

*Osterreichisches Filmmuseum, Augustinerstr. 1, Vienna. Directors: Peter Kinlechner, Peter Kubelka.*6,500 members are entitled to attend daily showings at the Albertina Gallery.*

BELGIUM
*Cinémathèque Royale de Belgique, Palais des Beaux Arts, 23 rue Ravenstein, Brussels. Conservator: Jacques Ledoux. *Stock: 5,000 films, 200,000 stills, 8,000 books, and large collection of posters. Also publishes useful brochures, and screens three films daily.*

BULGARIA
*Bulgarska Nacionala Filmoteka, 50 Rue Gourko, Sofia. Director: G. Stojanov-Bigo.

CANADA
*Canadian Film Institute, 1762 Carling, Ottawa 13, Ontario, Curator: Peter Morris. *A growing collection of films and related materials as well as regular film screenings. Owns approx. 1,700 films and 50,000 stills.*

*Cinémathèque Canadienne, 1015 Vanier Street, St. Laurent, Montreal. President: Guy L. Côté.
Especially noted for its fine collection of early animated films.

CHILE
*Cineteca Universitaria, Huerfanos 1117 Of. 407, Santiago. Director: P. Chaskel. *Stock: 220 films, 10,000 stills, 200 books.*

COLOMBIA
*Cinemateca Colombiana. Apartado Nacional 1898, Bogota. Director: Hernando Salcedo Silva.

CUBA
*Cinemateca de Cuba I.C.A.I.C., Calle 23 No. 1155, Havana. Director: Hector Garcia Mesa. *Stock: 950 films, 110,000 stills. Has organised nearly 800 programmes in its own theatre.*

CZECHOSLOVAKIA
*Ceskoslovensky Filmowy Ustav — Filmoteka, V jàme 1, Prague 1 (Nové Mesto). Director: Dr. Bohumil Brejcha. *Stock: 16,000 films, 200,000 stills, 70,000 books. Specialities: early short fiction films and cartoons.* *

DENMARK
*Det Danske Filmmuseum, Store Sondervoldstraede, Copenhagen. Director: Ib Monty. *Stock: 4,500 films, 700,000 stills, 13,000 books. Also a collection of about 300 instruments, including magic lanterns, epidiascopes, film projectors etc. The Museum contains a virtually complete Dreyer collection, and also publishes "Kosmorama". It now shares an excellent 157 seat cinema with the Danish Film School and operates like a National Film Theatre.*

FINLAND
*Suomen Elokuva Arkisto, Eriksgatan 12A 9, Helsinki. Director: Peter von Bagh. *Stock: 500 films, 3,300 books, 150,000 stills.*

FRANCE
La Cinémathèque Française. *Following its dispute with the Centre National du Cinéma in early 1968, the Cinémathèque is now an independent body, relying on private support to continue its excellent work of showing old films in the two cinemas at Rue d'Ulm and Palais de Chaillot. The Cinémathèque has a collection of around 50,000 films, more than 8,000 books, and over a million stills.*

*Cinémathèque de Toulouse, 3 rue Roquelaine, Toulouse. Conservator: Raymond Borde.

GERMANY (EAST)
*Staatliches Filmarchiv der D.D.R., Kronenstrasse 10, Berlin W.8. Director: Herbert Volkmann. *Stock: 26,000 films, 90,000 stills, 1,370 books. Also over 6,000 posters. Fosters an excellent series of retrospectives.*

GERMANY (WEST)
*Deutsches Institut für Filmkünde eV., Wiesbaden-Biebrich, Schloss. Director: Ulrich Pöschke. *Stock: 450 films, 252,000 stills; 12,000 books. Also over 13,000 posters.*

Deutsche Kinemathek, Schlüterstr.41, Berlin 15. *Holds regular seasons of specialised films. Good collection of pre-1914 films. Permanent exhibition of film history. Now has a small theatre for regular screenings.*

249

GREAT BRITAIN

*National Film Archive, 81 Dean Street, London W.1. Director: Ernest Lindgren. *Stock: 8,500 films approx., over 650,000 stills, 15,000 books. Noted for its good Information and Stills reproduction services. Founded in May 1935 and believed to be the oldest surviving film archive in the world.*

GREECE

Tainiotheke tes Hellados, 9 Av. Reine Sophie, Athens. General Secretary: Mme A. Mitropoulos.

Hellenike Tainiotheke, 5 Plateia Dexamenis, Athens 136, President: R. Coundouros.

HUNGARY

*Magyar Filmtudományi Intezet Es Filmarchivum, Népstadion ut. 97, Budapest XIV. Director: Szilard Ujhelyi. *Stock: 8,000 films, 12,000 stills, 5,000 books.*

INDIA

National Film Archive of India, Law College Road, Poona 4. Conservator: P. K. Nair.

ISRAEL

*Archion Israeli Leseratim, 142 Hanassi, Haifa. Director: Mrs. Lia van Leer. *Stock: 500 films, 1,000 stills, 300 books. Founded in 1961.*

ITALY

*Cineteca Italiana, Villa Reale, Via Palestro 16, Milan. General Secretary: Gianni Comencini. *Stock: 4,000 films, 10,000 stills, 2,000 books.*

*Cineteca Nazionale, Via Tuscolana 1524, Rome. Director: Dott. Leonardo Fioravanti. *Stock: 6,000 films, 15,000 stills, 6,000 books. Has close connections with the Centro Sperimentale, and publishes "Bianco e Nero".*

*Museo Nazionale del Cinema, Palazzo Chiablese, Piazza S. Giovanni 2, Turin. Director: Prof. Maria Adriana Prolo. *Opened in 1958, although the collection was started in 1941.*

JAPAN

Japan Film Library Council. Dir.-General: Mrs. K. Kawakita. *Has organised retrospective season of Ichikawa's works in London, Paris,* New York and many other cities in recent years. Museum of Modern Art, Kyobashi, Tokyo. *Founded in 1952.*

JUGOSLAVIA

*Jugoslovenska Kinoteka, Knez Mihailova 19, Belgrade. Director: Vladimir Pogacic. *Stock: 11,000 films, 85,000 stills, 6,500 books.*

KOREA

Fédération Coréene des Archives du film, Pyong-Yang. Director: Kim Han Kyoo.

NETHERLANDS

*Stichting Nederlands Filmmuseum, Paulus Potterstraat 13, Amsterdam-Z. Director: Jan de Vaal. *Stock: 5,000 films, 90,000 stills, 4,400 books. Also publishes books and organises projections. Founded in 1952, with the amalgamation of the Netherlands Historic Film Archive and The Outlook Cinema's Archive.*

NORWAY

*Norsk Filminstitut, Aslakveien 14, Oslo. Director: Bo Wingard. *Stock: 1,500 films, 40,000 stills, 2,300 books.*

POLAND

*Centralne Archiwum Filmowe, Ul. Pulawska 61, Warsaw. Direction: W. Barnaszkiewicz. *Stock: 8,000 films, 170,000 stills, 5,200 books. Also over 12,000 posters.*

PORTUGAL

*Cinemateca Nacional, Palacio Foz Restauradores, Lisboa, Director: F. Ribeiro. *Stock: 850 films, 20,000 stills, 5,500 books.*

ROMANIA

*Archiva Nationala de Filme, 1 Chaussée du Sabar, Bucharest. Director: N. Balcescu. *Stock: 16,000 films, 84,000 stills, 18,000 books. Also 3,000 posters.*

SPAIN

*Filmoteca Nacional de Espana, Joaquin Costa 43, Madrid. Director: Carlos F. Cuenca.

SWEDEN

*Filmhistoriska Samlingarna, Tekniska Museet, Stockholm No. Director: Nils-Hugo Geber. *Stock: 1,300 films, 1,000,000 stills, 3,200*

---

books. Also over 26,000 posters. *Integrated with Svenska Filminstitutet.*

SWITZERLAND

La Cinémathèque Suisse, Case Ville 850, Lausanne. Director: Freddy Buache. *Over 100,000 references available for consultation. Nearly 700 features in stock: over 5.000 stills and 2,000 books.*

Filmmuseum Zürich, Ausstellungstr. 60, Zürich. Secretary: Hans Heinrich Egger.

TURKEY

Sinematek Dernegi, Mis Sokak 12/3, Galatasaray, P.K. 307 Beyoglu, Istanbul. Director: Onat Kutlar.

URUGUAY

*Cine Arte Del S.O.D.R.E., Andes y Mercedes, Montevideo. Director: Eugenio Hintz.

U.S.A.

George Eastman House, 900 East Avenue, Rochester 7, N.Y. Director: James Card.

*Museum of Modern Art Film Library, 11 West 53rd. Street, New York, N.Y. Director: Willard Van Dyke. *Stock: 3,000 films, 1,000,000 stills, 1,000 books. Also collection of over 500 shooting scripts. Publishes monographs and runs extensive seasons of rare films. Present theatre holds 480 people. Altogether the Department has 15 million feet of film from all countries and periods.*

U.S.S.R.

*Gosfilmofond, Stancia Bielye Stolby, Moscow (Oblast). Director: Victor Privato. *Stock: 35,000 films, 180,000 stills, 8,250 books. Also over 25,000 posters. The Gosfilmofond owns 3 cinemas and has a varied programme of publications, lectures and exhibitions.*

denotes full Member of F.I.A.F. (38 Avenue des Ternes, Paris 17).

THE BARNES MUSEUM OF CINEMATOGRAPHY

Fore Street, St. Ives, Cornwall.

The Barnes Museum of Cinematography is the only museum in the British Commonwealth devoted entirely to the history and origins of the cinema. It has been established in St. Ives since 1963 and has already been visited by over 100,000 people.

The collection is a private one gathered together over a period of thirty years and forms one of the most comprehensive collections of its kind. It is extensively used by students of film history and items from its collections have been featured in numerous books and periodicals.

The collection can be divided into three main headings: Precursors of the Cinema; Pre-Cinema; and Cinematography. The first section traces the history of shadowgraphy, panoramas, dioramas, and peepshows in their relation to the history of the cinema. The second illustrates the three main streams of discovery which culminated in the invention of cinematography, viz. optical projection, persistence of vision, and photography. The third section deals with the early achievements in cinematography.

The interior of the "national film theatre" of Denmark, sited at the Danish Filmmuseum, St. Sondervoldstraede, Copenhagen.

Films on 16 mm

The section consists of a list of those feature-length films considered likely to be of interest to readers that have been added or restored to the catalogues of 16mm distributors in Britain during the approximate period, June 1967 to June 1968. A similar list was published in last year's INTERNATIONAL FILM GUIDE and provides further titles that are generally still available for hire. Some of the films appearing below can also be booked on 35 mm. Catalogues, giving further details including hire fees, can be obtained by British readers from the distributor at the address given below, the charge for such catalogues being indicated in brackets after the address.

Adams Films, Film House, Muscott St., Northampton (2s.).

British Film Institute, Distribution Dept., 81 Dean St., London W.1.

Columbia Pictures, 16mm Division, 142 Wardour St., London W.1. (2s.6d.).

Connoisseur Films Ltd., 54-58 Wardour St., London W.1. (3s.6d.).

Contemporary Films Ltd., 55 Greek St., London W.1. (5s).

ETV Films, 164 Shaftesbury Ave., London W.C.2 (1s.6d.).

Embassy Films, 1-2 Berners St., London W.1 (free).

Film Distributors Associated (16mm) Ltd., P.O. Box 2JL, Mortimer House, 37-41 Mortimer St., London W.1 (free).

Hunter Films Ltd., 174 Wardour St., London W.1 (2s. 6d.).

Intercontinental Films, 90 Merthyr Mawr Road, Bridgend, Glamorgan (free).

John King (Films) Ltd., Film Library, Film House, East St., Brighton (2s.6d.).

Kingston Film Hire, 16 Bridge Ave., Hanwell, London W.7 (2s.6d.).

Rank Film Library, 1 Aintree Rd., Perivale, Greenford, Middlesex.

Ron Harris Cinema Services Ltd., Glenbuck House, Surbiton, Surrey (2s.6d.).

Sound-Services, Wilton Crescent, London S.W.19 (free).

United Artists, 16 mm Division — now part of **Film Distributors Associated.**

Warner-Pathe, 16 mm Division, 135 Wardour St., London W.1 (3s.6d.).

Watso Films, Film House, Charles St. and Vine, Coventry, Warwickshire.

hunter films limited

the 16mm film distributors

TITLES FOR YOUR 1968/9 SEASON INCLUDE:

THE GOSPEL ACCORDING TO ST. MATTHEW
SWITCHBOARD OPERATOR
THE THEATRE OF MR. & MRS. KABAL
CHIMES AT MIDNIGHT (FALSTAFF)
SIMON OF THE DESERT
OLE DOLE DOFF   :   HUGO & JOSEPHINE
DUTCHMAN   :   WARRENDALE
RED BEARD
WITCHFINDER GENERAL
REBELLION   :   KWAIDAN
DER JUNGE TORLESS
LES BICHES   :   HERE IS YOUR LIFE
I AM CURIOUS   :   I, A WOMAN

FURTHER DETAILS OF THESE
AND MANY MORE ARE
CONTAINED IN OUR
ILLUSTRATED CATALOGUE (2/6)

HUNTER FILMS LIMITED
182 WARDOUR STREET,
LONDON W.1V 4 BH.
TEL: 01-734 8527/8

To present as much information as possible within a limited space, the following abbreviations have been adopted to identify the distributor of each film: **A** Adams Films; **BFI** British Film Institute; **C** Columbia; **Cnr** Connoisseur; **Cty** Contemporary; **E** Embassy; **ETV** ETV Films; **FDA** Film Distributors Associated; **H** Hunter; **I-C** Intercontinental; **JK** John King; **K** Kingston; **R** Rank; **RH** Ron Harris; **S-S** Sound Services; **W** Watso; **W-P** Warner-Pathe. An asterisk * preceding the title denotes colour; a dagger † indicates that prints are anamorphic (cinemascope). Where alternative black-and-white and non scope versions are available, the symbols are enclosed in brackets. Year date ('61 for 1961 etc.) and the surname of the director follow the title in brackets, then the running time in minutes plus in some instances EST for English subtitles or ED for English dialogue (dubbed prints or commentary), and finally the key to the distributor.

Accattone ('61, Pasolini) EST 115 Cnr
*Accident ('67, Losey) 105 K
Ace of Aces ('33, Ruben) 75 K
*(†)*Actor's Revenge, An* ('63, Ichikawa) EST 113 Cty
Actress, The ('53, Cukor) 90 RH
Adventures of Werner Holt, The ('63, Kunert) EST or ED 120 Cty
*(†)*After the Fox* ('65, de Sica) 102 FDA
*(†)*Agony and the Ecstasy, The* ('65, Reed) 139 FDA
Alphabet Murders, The ('65, Tashlin) 85 R
*(†)*Anastasia* ('56, Litvak) 105 RH
Angel of Merciful Death ('66, Skalsky) EST 85 ETV
Angel Who Pawned Her Harp, The ('54, Bromly) 83 H
Annabel Takes A Tour ('38, Landers) 68 K
*Arabesque ('66, Donen) 105 R
*(†)*Assault on a Queen* ('66, Donohue) 106 RH
**Autumn Afternoon, An* ('62, Ozu) EST 113 Cty
Bachelor Girl Apartment ('66, R. E. Miller) 85 W-P
Bad and the Beautiful, The ('52, Minnelli) 118 RH
Ballad of a Soldier, The ('60, Chukhrai) EST 87 Cty
**Barefoot in the Park* ('67, Saks) 106 RH
Barrier ('66, Skolimowski) EST 81 Cty
Battle Inferno ('59, Wisbar) ED 76 Cty
**Battle of the Bulge* ('65, Annakin) 128 W-P
**Beautiful Blonde from Bashful Bend, The* ('49, P. Sturges) 77 H
Beware Automobile ('66, Riazanov) EST 92 Cnr
Beyond A Reasonable Doubt ('56, F. Lang) 80 Cty
Bezhin Meadow (Yutkevitch from Eisenstein) EST 31 Cty
Big Deal at Dodge City ('66, Cook) 96 W-P
*Black Sabbath ('63, Bava) 96 K
Blob, The ('58, Yeaworth) 83 H
Blonde in Love, A ('65, Forman) EST 82 Cty

Blood on the Sun ('45, Lloyd) 94 H or K
*Blow Up ('67, Antonioni) 111 R
*(†)*Blue Max, The* ('66, Guillermin) 155 FDA
Bundle of Joy ('56, Taurog) 100 W
*†*Casino Royale*, ('67, Huston, etc.) 131 C
*†*Cast A Giant Shadow* ('66, Shavelson) 135 FDA
Champion ('49, Robson) 96 E
(*)*Chelsea Girls* ('66, Warhol) 120 Cnr
Chimes at Midnight ('66, Welles) 119 H
Changing Village ('63, Peries) EST 105 Cty
*Chuka ('67, Douglas) 105 RH
Clash by Night ('51, F. Lang) 107 Cty or W
*†*Cleopatra* ('63, Mankiewicz) 192 FDA
Clouded Yellow, The ('50, Thomas) 95 K
†*Cold Days* ('66, Kovács) EST 101 Cty
(†)*Company of Cowards*? ('64, Marshall) 86 RH
**Countess from Hong Kong, A* ('67, Chaplin) 120 R
Crime in the Girl's School ('65, Novak, Rychman, Menzel) EST 111 ETV
**Dead Heat on a Merry Go Round* ('67, Girard) C
Death Comes in the Rain (Czech film) EST 94 ETV
**Deep Blue Sea, The* ('55, Litvak) 99 RH
*(†)*Demetrius and the Gladiators* ('54, Daves) 100 RH
Départ, Le ('67, Skolimowski) EST 90 Cty
(†)*Desire in the Dust* ('60, Claxton) 102 H
Destination Moon ('50, Piche) A (also K, W)
Diamonds of the Night ('64, Nemec) EST 64 Cty
(*)*Diane* ('55, Miller) 101 RH
Diary of Anne Frank, The ('58, Stevens) 150 RH
Dimples ('36, Seiter) 78 H
**Disorderly Orderly, The* ('64, Tashlin) 89 RH
**Divorce American Style* ('67, Yorkin) 108 C
Don Quixote ('57, Kozintsev) EST 107 Cty
**Double Man, The* ('67, Schaffner) 105 W-P
**Drop Dead, Darling* ('67, Hughes) 100 RH
Dutchman ('67, Harvey) 57 H

Man With a Gun, A ('38, Yutkevitch) EST 85 ETV
Marseillaise, La ('37, Renoir) EST 130 Cty
Martyrs of Love ('66, Nemec) EST 73 Cty
*Meet Me After the Show ('51, Sale) 87 H
(†)*Meet Whiplash Willie* ('67, Wilder) 123 FDA
Moment to Moment ('67, LeRoy) 108 R
Mouchette ('67, Bresson) EST 90 Cnr
Mr. Hulot's Holiday ('52, Tati) Cnr
Murder Inc. ('51, Windust, Walsh) 84 H or K
My Way Home ('65, Jancsó) EST 82 Cty
Naked Hearts ('66, Luntz) EST 93 Cty
*Naked Prey, The ('57, Wilde) 95 RH
*†Nevada Smith ('66, Hathaway) 120 RH
Night in Casablanca, A ('46, Mayo) 85 A, H, K or W
Nightmare in the Sun ('63, Lawrence) 81 E or H
*Not With My Wife, You Don't ('66, Panama) 119 W-P
*Old Man and the Sea, The ('58, Sturges) 86 W-P
*(†)One Born Every Minute ('67, Kershner) 104 FDA
One Potato, Two Potato ('63, Peerce) 79 R
*(†)Our Man Flint ('65, Daniel Mann) 108 FDA
Outlaw, The ('42, Hughes) 100 W
Overlanders, The ('46, Watt) 120 BFI
Pacific Destiny ('56, Rilla) 97 K
Pad and How to Use It, The ('67, Hutton) 86 R
Panama Flo ('32, Murphy) 72 K
Patch of Blue, A ('65, Green) 105 R
*Patsy, The ('64, Jerry Lewis) 101 RH
*Parapluies de Cherbourg, Les ('63, Demy) 92 Cnr
Pawnbroker, The ('63, Lumet) 115 Cty
*Penelope ('67, Hiller) 98 R
Persona ('65, Bergman) 85 FDA
Philosopher's Stone, The ('57, Ray) EST 90 Cty
Pornographer, The ('66, Imamura) EST 90 Cnr
Port of New York ('49, Benedek) 82 I-C or K
*†Professionals, The ('66, Brooks) 117 C
Promise Her Anything ('66, Hiller) 82 RH
(*)*Proud Ones, The* ('56, Webb) 94 RH
*Quiller Memorandum, The ('66, Anderson) 103 R
*Quo Vadis ('51, LeRoy) 166 RH
*Rare Breed, The ('67, McLaglen) 97 R
Rebellion ('67, Kobayashi) 120 H
Rebound ('34, E. H. Griffith) 92 K
Reign of Terror ('49, A. Mann) 99 I-C or K
*(†)Remarkable Mr. Pennypacker, The ('58, Levin) 87 RH
*Return of the Gunfighter ('67, Neilson) 88 R
*(†)Return of the Seven ('67, Kennedy) 95 FDA
Roar of the Dragon ('32, Ruggles) 77 K
Run of the Arrow ('57, Fuller) 92 W
*(†)Russians are Coming, The Russians are Coming, The ('66, Jewison) 125 FDA
*†Sand Pebbles, The ('67, Wise) 180 FDA

†*Saragossa Manuscript, The* ('56, Has) EST 124 Cty
*Scarlet Coat, The ('55, Sturges) 99 RH
Secret Service ('31, Ruben) 70 K
Seduction of Julia ('67, Weidenmann) ED 96 E
Seventh Veil, The ('45, Bennett) 95 K
She and He ('64, Hani) EST 115 Cty
*(†)633 Squadron ('66, Grauman) 94 FDA
*Silver Horde, The ('30, Archainbaud) 76 K
Simon of the Desert, The ('65, Bunuel) EST 42 H
Sky Giant ('38, Landers) 82 K
So Ends Our Night ('41, Cromwell) A
Soldier and the Lady, The ('37, Nichols) 86 K
(†)*Sound and the Fury, The* ('58, Ritt) 115 RH
Southwest to Sonora ('66, Furie) 98 R
*(†)Stagecoach ('66, Douglas) 114 FDA
Star of Midnight ('35, Roberts) 92 K
St. Elisabeth's Square ('66, Bahna) EST 85 ETV
Strada, La ('54, Fellini) EST 104 Cty
Stromboli ('49, Rossellini) 81 Cty
*(†)St. Valentine's Day Massacre, The ('67, Corman) 99 FDA
*Such Men are Dangerous ('55, Hathaway) 92 RH
Suicide Fleet ('31, Rogell) 82 K
Switchboard Operator ('67, Makavejev) EST 78 H
Take the High Ground ('53, Brooks) 100 RH
*Tall Men, The ('55, Walsh) 122 RH
Task Force ('49, Daves) 85 W
10th Victim, The ('65, Petri) 92 H
This Property Is Condemned ('66, Pollack) 110 RH
*Thousand Clarinets, A ('6 , Rohac, Svitacek) EST 132 ETV
Thousand Clowns, A ('65, Coe) 115 FDA
Three Secrets ('50, Wise) 98 K
Tiger Makes Out, The ('67, Hiller) C
Tillie's Punctured Romance ('14, Sennett) 42 I-C
(†)*Tirez sur le Pianiste* ('60, Truffaut) EST 80 Cty
T Men ('47, A. Mann) 90 E
*Tobruk ('67, Hiller) 109 R
To Die in Madrid ('62, Rossif) ED 85 Cty
*Tonite Let's All Make Love in London ('67, Whitehead) 72 Cnr
*(†)Tony Rome ('67, Douglas) 110 FDA
*Torn Curtain ('67, Hitchcock) 128 R
*Trap, The ('66, Hayers) 106 R
Trapped by Fear ('60, Dupont) ED 70 E
Twenty Hours ('65, Fabri) EST 112 Cty
*(†)Two for the Road ('67, Donen) 111 FDA
Voyage to the End of the Universe ('62, Polák) 84 K
Vierges, Les ('63, Mocky) EST 90 Cty
Village Tale ('35, Cromwell) 82 K
*(†)Viva Maria ('65, Malle) 113 FDA
*Wabash Avenue ('50, Koster) 93 H

257

Brandon Films presents
A Special Listing from:

THE MOST SIGNIFICANT REPERTOIRE OF WORLD CINEMA

available for nontheatrical exhibition in the U.S.A.

IKIRU	POTEMKIN
ACCATTONE	LA STRADA
LE MILLION	THE TRIAL
L'ATALANTE	SHE AND HE
WAGES OF FEAR	THE BAILIFF
POIL DE CAROTTE	BWANA TOSHI
THE THREE SISTERS	CASQUE D'OR
THE BICYCLE THIEF	BALTIC EXPRESS
SALT OF THE EARTH	KAMERADSCHAFT
LA GUERRE EST FINIE	THE GIVEN WORD
ALEXANDER NEVSKY	AGE OF ILLUSIONS
ZERO FOR CONDUCT	THRONE OF BLOOD
THE GOSPEL ACCORD-ING TO ST. MATTHEW	THE WORLD OF APU
	NOTHING BUT A MAN
KNIFE IN THE WATER	SAWDUST AND TINSEL
PASSION OF JOAN OF ARC	THE CRANES ARE FLYING
IVAN THE TERRIBLE, PART I	UCCELLACCI E UCCELLINI
IVAN THE TERRIBLE, PART II	NOBODY WAVED GOODBYE
THE THREE PENNY OPERA	DIARY OF A COUNTRY PRIEST

Special announcement: available 1969

THE RED AND THE WHITE   HERE'S YOUR LIFE
THE CRY OF SILENCE

FREE WORLD CINEMA LIST WRITE: DEPT. IFG *(USA only)*

BRANDON FILMS, INC.
221 West 57th Street, New York, N.Y. 10019 212-CIrcle 6-4867

FILM CENTER, INC.
20 East Huron Street,
Chicago, Ill. 60611
312-DElaware 7-2855

WESTERN CINEMA GUILD, INC.
244 Kearny Street,
San Francisco, Calif. 94108
415-EXbrook 7-4255

Wages of Fear, The ('52, Clouzot) ED 128 Cnr
*(†)*Warlock* ('59, Dmytryk) 120 RH
Warning Shot, The ('67, Kulik) 100 RH
Warrendale ('66, King) 100 H
Way Back Home ('31, Seiter) 82 K
*(†)*Way West, The* ('67, McLaglen) 112 FDA
*(†)*What Did You Do in the War, Daddy?* ('66,
Edwards) 115 FDA
Whisperers, The ('67, Forbes) 105 FDA
Who Are You, Polly Maggoo? ('65, Klein) EST

102 Cty
Who's Afraid of Virginia Woolf? ('66, Nichols)
133 W-P
*(†)*Woman of Summer* ('62, Schaffner) 94 H
Yesterday Girl ('66, Kluge) EST 90 Cty
Young Have No Morals, The ('60, Mocky) EST
77 E
Young Torless ('66, Schlöndorff) EST 85 H
You're a Big Boy Now ('67, Coppola) 97 W-P
Zorba the Greek ('64, Cacoyannis) 141 FDA

News from Brandon Films

One of the last of the truly independent specialised distributors in the U.S.A.,
Brandon Films has added some excellent titles to its library this season, and forth-
coming titles include Miklós Jancsó's *My Way Home*, *The Red and the White*, and
Silence and Cry. Catalog 29 has just been published, again in two volumes, one for
English language features and the other for foreign language features. Another new
development is that in 1969 Brandon expect to be able to supply a substantial
number of the features and shorts they distribute in the U.S.A. to Canadian outlets.
Among the best of the 1968 additions to Brandon's library are the following: *La
Guerre est Finie*, *Accattone*, *The Hawks and the Sparrows*, *Love Affair* (Makavejev),
Der Untertan, *The Bell*, *Bwana Toshi*, and *She and He*.

Swedish Documentaries for Hire

In Great Britain, a number of 16mm short films about Sweden are available through
Sound-Services Ltd., Kingston Road, Merton Park, London S.W.19.

A Place to Live (Colour, 19 mins.) — about architecture and modern living.
Like Rings on Water (Black-and-white, 16 mins.) — about town planning.
The Quiet Revolution (Black-and-white, 20 mins.) — how Sweden changed in
50 years from an agrarian society with widespread poverty into a modern
industrialised and affluent society with far-reaching social reforms.
Souvenirs From Sweden (Colour, 22 mins.) — an unconventional view of
Sweden through the eyes of Danish director Henning Carlsen.
Johan Ekberg (Black-and-white, 21 mins.) — an excellent study of the loneliness
of old age by Jan Troell (director of *Here's Your Life*).
The Reindeer Herders (Colour, 23 mins.) — follow an authentic Lapp family
and its reindeer herd during the course of a year.
Ferrum (Colour, 14 mins.) — a lyrical documentary on iron mining by Gunnar
Höglund. No commentary, only music by Karl-Erik Welin.
Glass (Colour, 12 mins.) — made at the Kosta Glass Works, shows the pro-
duction of both art glass and beautiful everyday glass.
A Summer Day in Sweden (Colour, 20 mins.) — scenes of animal life, directed by
the talented Jan Lindblad.
Vasa (Colour, 18 mins.) — the proud warship Vasa sank in the harbour of
Stockholm in 1628 and was lifted from the muddy depths 333 years later.
The Drottningholm Court Theatre (Colour, 28 mins.) — Inaugurated 200 years
ago, the theatre has been preserved in its original form, and every summer
performances are given there with the original stage settings and old stage
machinery. The film includes scenes from a performance of Gluck's "Iphi-
genia in Aulis" with Elisabeth Söderström,

WOMAN IN THE DUNES, distributed throughout the U.S.A. by Contemporary Films.

Film Services

Academy of Theatre & Film Arts, Budapest

The theatrical section of the Academy dates back to 1865, while the film classes have been active since 1947. Directors, cameramen, and editors are trained for both film and television. Each course occupies 4 years (8 terms). Because of the high number of applicants, a high school certificate ("matura") is the minimum qualification, and applicants should really have a university degree. The top 40 to 60 people who do best in the theoretical entrance examinations are given a 6 months basic course with 16mm cameras and will shoot their own film, which is the basis for the second and final round of the entrance test. The Budapest Academy is probably the only film school that selects its students on such a complex and rigorous examination basis, all stemming from the film actually made by the applicant. All costs involved are paid by the Academy.

All Hungarian students who graduate here can be assured of a job in the industry subsequently. Foreigners are also going to be catered for in the near future. Lectures in their class will be held in English or French or both. This course will last 3 years, and applicants should contact the Academy direct (see address in List of Film Schools).

The director of the film section is János Herskó, and among the lecturers are Károly Makk, Félix Máriássy, Márton Keleti, and György Illés.

The curriculum is divided into theoretical and practical sessions. There are lectures on literature, the history of fine arts, music, aesthetics, film history, dramaturgy, and production planning. Students learn *directing*, including scriptwriting and editing; *camerawork*, including photography, lighting, lenses, trick effects; and *sound*. In the first year every student shoots his own 16mm sound film; in the second and third year he shoots a 35 mm sound film; and in the fourth year he completes his diploma film, in one of the professional studios, or in the television studios.

Tuition at the Academy is free of charge (for Hungarians), and the students obtain scholarships. There is a college and mensa in the same building, where the students can get board and lodging — **György Kárpáti.**

Note: The motion picture curriculum at San Francisco State College has been brought to our notice. There are around 34 classes, a faculty of 12, and approximately 150 graduate and undergraduate majors. Address: 1600 Holloway Avenue, San Francisco, California 94132.

Key European Film Schools

Akademie für Musik und Darstellende Kunst in Wien, & Schule für Fernsehgestaltung, 111/40 Lothringerstr. 18 & Türkenstrasse 4, Wien IX. *President:* Prof. Dr. Hans Sittner.

INSAS (Institut National Supérieur des Arts du Spectacle et Techniques de Diffusion), 54 Rue de Namur, Brussels. *Director:* Raymond Ravar.

Hochschule für Gestaltung, (Abteilung Film), Kuhberg, Ulm, Germany. *Director:* Dr. Alexander Kluge.

London School of Film Technique, 24 Shelton Street, London W.C.2. *Director:* Robert Dunbar.

The Danish Film School, St. Søndervoldstraede, Copenhagen K. *Director:* I. C. Lauritzen.

Deutsche Film- und Fernsehakademie Berlin G.m.b.H., Pommernallee 1, 1 Berlin 19. *Directors:* Erwin Leiser, Dr. Heinz Rathsack.

Hochschule für Film und Fernsehen, Geschwister Scholl Platz (Universität), München 22. *Director:* Dr. Pleister.

Institut des Arts de Diffusion, 15, avenue de Tervueren, Brussels IV. *Director:* José Jolet.

Ministère de la Culture Académie des Arts, Section des Hautes Ecoles Artistiques, Faculté du Film, Valdstejnska ulice, Prague III. *Director:* Anton-Martin Brousil.

L'Institut des Hautes Etudes Cinématographiques (I.D.H.E.C.), 92, Champs Elysées, Paris VIII. *General Director:* Rémy Tessonneau.

Izdala Akademija za pozorište, film, radio i televiziju, Uskočka 2-a, Belgrade. *Director:* Dejan Kosanovic.

Nederlands Filminstituut, Oost Indisch Huis, Oude Hoogstraat 24, Amsterdam. *Director:* Dr. Anton Koolhaas.

Panstwowa wyzsza Szkola Teatralna Filmova, Ul Targowa 61, Lodz & A1 Armü, Ludowej 6 m 165, Warszawa 10.

Escuela Oficial de Cinematografia, Ciudad Universitaria, Carretera de la Dehesa de La Villa, Madrid 20. *Director:* Antonio Cuevas.

Centro Sperimentale di Cinematografia (C.S.C.), Via Tuscolana 1524, Rome. *Director:* Dr. Leonardo Fioravanti.

Dept. of Film and Television, Royal College of Art, Queen's Gate, London S.W.7. *Reader:* Keith Lucas.

Swedish Film School, c/o Svenska Filminstitutet, Kungsgatan 48, Stockholm. *Director:* Rune Waldekranz.

Szinház és Filmmüvészeti Fóiskola, Vas u. 2/c, Budapest VIII. *Director:* László Vadász.

Film Magazines

L'AVANT-SCÈNE DU CINÉMA. Ed: Jacques-G. Perret, 27 rue Saint-André des Arts, Paris 6. 11 n.p.a.: 38 francs (or 69s. from British agents, The Tantivy Press, 7 Sedley Place, London W.1.). 60 pp. approx. *The only monthly magazine devoted specifically to film scripts, reproduced in every detail with a cluster of fine photographs to illuminate the text. Attractively produced. For a combined subscription of 52 francs (84s.), readers can also obtain the unique series of pamphlets on directors, ANTHO-LOGIE DU CINÉMA, together with each issue of L'AVANT-SCÈNE.*
Number 72-73: Carné's *Les Enfants du Paradis*.
Number 74: Eisenstein's *October*.
Number 75: Roullet's *Le Mur* with Baratier's *Le Désordre à Vingt Ans*.
Number 76: De Sica's *Bicycle Thieves*.
Number 77: Rocha's *Terre en Transe*.
Number 78: Lang's *Fury*.
Number 79: Godard's *A Bout de Souffle*.
Number 80: Bresson's *Mouchette*.
Number 81: Carné's *Nogent, Eldorado du Dimanche* and *Les Jeunes Loups*.
Number 82: Bertolucci's *Prima della Rivoluzione*.

BIANCO E NERO. Ed: Ernesto G. Laura, Via Tuscolana 1524, Rome. 12 n.p.a.: 6,800 Lire (92s. or 11.50 dollars). 60 to 140 pp. *This erratic magazine (double and even triple numbers compensating for the lack of a prompt monthly publication) has long been regarded as the leading Italian film journal, and it began in 1937. But it has sadly failed to change its image and looks more and more esoteric and theoretical as the years go by.*
Oct-Nov-Dec. 1967: "Fascicolo speciale su cinema e futurismo", including many valuable texts and manifestoes.
Jan-Feb. 1968: Devoted mainly to festival reports.

CAHIERS DU CINÉMA. Ed: Jean-Louis Comolli, Jean-Louis Ginibre, 63 avenue des Champs-Elysées, Paris 8. 12 n.p.a.: 75 francs (130s. or 16 dollars). 76 pp. approx. *Lavish, excitingly designed monstre sacré among French film magazines. Essential on account of its long interviews and filmographies, but not above the petty parochial squabbling that disfigures all contemporary French culture.*
Sept. 1967: Focus on Samuel Fuller and G. W. Pabst.
Dec. 1967: Excellent interviews with Renoir, Penn, and Allio.
Jan. 1968: Jerry Lewis number, including a disc recording (in English) on one of his press conferences.
Feb. 1968: Ernst Lubitsch number. Also interview with Chytilová.
Mar. 1968: Dossier on Tati, *plus* all the "facts" on the Langlois affair.

CHAPLIN. Ed: Stig Björkman, Svenska Filminstitutet, Kungsgatan 48, Stockholm. 9 n.p.a.: 25 Kr. (42s. or 5 dollars). 32 pp. *In many ways a model for any aspiring film monthly, and certainly better informed and more enthusiastic about the world movie scene than most English- or French-speaking magazines. Indispensable, if you read Swedish (still attractive to leaf through if you don't).*
Number 74: Interview with Widerberg about *Elvira Madigan*.
Number 75: Interview with Robbe-Grillet.
Number 76: Interview with Rocha on Brazil's "Cinema Novo".

S&S

SIGHT AND SOUND 5/-

MFB

MONTHLY FILM BULLETIN 2/-

Published by The British Film Institute
81 Dean Street London W1

Number 77: Interview with Godard.
Number 78: Interview with Makavejev and dossier on Yugoslav cinema.
Number 79: Very revealing interview with Bergman.
Number 81: Hollywood issue: Jan Aghed reporting talks with Ford, Fuller, Peckinpah, and Wayne.
Number 82: Elia Kazan index.

CINEFORUM. Ed: Francesco Dorigo, Casella Postale 414, 30100 Venezia. 10 n.p.a.: 5,000 Lire (65s. or 8 dollars). 84 pp. approx. *Enlarged in format and incorporating several new features, CINEFORUM is one of the most searching and committed of the Italian monthlies.*

Jan. 1968: "Violenza come Modello di Evasione", by Sandro Zambetti.
Feb. 1968: Dossier on *La Chinoise*, including the complete scenario.
Mar. 1968: "Cinema libertà e liberazione", by Fiorenzo Viscidi.
May 1968: "Sartre di fronte al cinema", by Jean-Paul Sartre.

CINEMA CANADA. Ed: Art C. Benson, 2533 Gerrard St. East, Scarborough, Ontario. 6 n.p.a.: 3 dollars (25s.). 24 pp. *The most business-like of Canadian film periodicals, strong on points of technique, issues like censorship, and extended interviews with Canadian film personalities.*

Sept.-Oct. 1967: "Film Censorship in Canada", by Ian McLaren.
Nov.-Dec. 1967: "Film Censorship in Canada", part two.
Jan.-Feb. 1968: "Film Censorship in Canada", part three. Also an interview with Susan Clark.

CINEMA NUOVO. Ed: Guido Aristarco, Capo Santa Chiara 6, 16146 Genoa. n.p.a.: 6,000 Lire (78s. or 9,50 dollars). 64 pp. approx. *The reflective, distinguished successor to the famous CINEMA of the forties (and the Marxist view of the film still predominates). Poorly illustrated.*

Number 185: "Monologo e nulla, tragedia della persona bergmaniana," by Guido Aristarco.
Number 186: "L'ateismo borghese nell Bergman de 'silenzio'", by Guido Aristarco.
Number 192: "Cinema et teatro nell'opera di Ingmar Bergman", by Elisabetta Chicco. "Partito, opposizione e muri nel film ungherese d'oggi", by András Kovács.

CINEMA 68 . . . 69. Ed: Pierre Billard, C.I.B., 7 rue Darboy, Paris 11. 10 n.p.a.: 37 francs (approx. 63s. or 8 dollars). 128 pp. *Petite but often underrated organ of the French ciné-clubs, excellent for festival reports, inquiries in depth, and balanced reviews.*

Jul-Aug. 1967: Special issue on Czech cinema.
Sept-Oct. 1967: "Jeune Cinéma: Belgique", by Paul Davay.
Nov. 1967: Dossier on *Bezhin Meadow*.
Dec. 1967: "Petite Planète du Cinéma: Yougoslavie", by Marcel Martin. Also an interview with Truffaut.
Jan. 1968: "Petite Planète du Cinéma: Jeune Cinéma Suédois", by Marcel Martin. Also an interview with Chytilová.
Feb. 1968: Conversation between Luis Buñuel and Glauber Rocha.
Mar. 1968: First part of a detailed re-evaluation of Harold Lloyd, by Roland Lacourbe. Also an interview with Zinnemann.
Apr. 1968: Interview with Penn. "Harold Lloyd", continued.
May 1968: Spotlight on new Czech films. "Harold Lloyd", concluded.
Jun. 1968: Extracts from Vilgot Sjöman's diary of shooting *I Am Curious*.

CONTINENTAL FILM REVIEW. Ed: Gordon Reid, 71 Oldhill St, London N.16. 12 n.p.a.: 30s. (6 dollars). 32 pp. *CFR pursues a formula that has pleased tens of thousands of readers for some 15 years now: enticing stills on glossy paper interspersed with serious, informed, and always very up-to-date articles on the foreign cinema.*

Nov. 1967: Articles on new films from Sweden, Romania, India, Italy, and the Netherlands.
Dec. 1967: The only complete transcription in English of Bergman's important press conference on *The Shame*.

Mar. 1968: "Hungarian Renaissance", by Peter Cowie. "Notes on the new Dutch and Belgian Cinema", by Albert Steeman.
Apr. 1968: Notes on films from Poland, Canada, Germany, Sweden, France, and Yugoslavia.
May 1968: Detailed report on Oberhausen by Charles Hedges.
Jun. 1968: Notes on films from Czechoslovakia, the U.S.S.R., Italy, and the Netherlands.
Jul. 1968: "Chabrol 1958-1968".

FILM. Ed: Peter Armitage, 14 Sherlies Avenue, Orpington, Kent. 3 n.p.a.: 6s. (1 dollar). 44 pp. *Tightly packed with offbeat interviews and criticism, this is the organ of the British Federation of Film Societies, and has improved its design these past 12 months.*
Number 49: "Raoul Walsh", by Kevin Brownlow.
Number 50: "Irvin Willatt", by Kevin Brownlow. "Honest to Godard", by Peter Armitage.
Number 51: "'Labyrinth' and Multiscreen", by Walter Lassally. "Eric Rohmer", by Nicoletta Zalaffi and Rui Noguiera. "B. P. Schulberg", by Kevin Brownlow.

FILM. Ed: Werner Kliess, Erhard Friedrich Verlag, 3001 Velber bei Hannover, West Germany. 12 n.p.a.: DM 44,— (90s. or 11 dollars). 52 pp. approx. *A large format German monthly with a wide grasp of world cinema and a penchant for scripts, by the extract or in toto.*
Nov. 1967: Interview with Godard.
Dec. 1967: "Der Western", by Georg Alexander.
Jan. 1968: Interview with Glauber Rocha.
Feb. 1968: Interview with Arthur Penn. Analysis of *La Passion de Jeanne d'Arc*, by Martin Schaub.
Mar. 1968: Complete script of Makavejev's *Love Dossier (Ein Liebesfall)*. Also re-assessment of Harry Langdon, by Klaus Eder.
Apr. 1968: Interview with Fellini.
May 1968: "Andy Warhol, Super-Artist — Porträt des Filmmachers". Also interview with Truffaut, and the script of May Spils's *Zur Sache Schätzchen*.
Jun. 1968: "Eisensteins Abstieg zur Klassizität", by Ernst Schmidt and Peter Weibel.

FILM COMMENT. Ed: Gordon Hitchens, 838 West End Avenue, New York, N.Y. 10025. 4 n.p.a.: 3.75 dollars (U.S.A. and Canada) or 5 dollars (elsewhere). 96 pp. approx. *A responsible periodical that aims to solicit significant comment on films from its readers and contributors, comment that may be all the better for being controversial.*
Volume 4, Numbers 2 & 3: Conversation with Mark Lane and Emile De Antonio on *Rush to Judgement.*
Volume 4, Number 4, and Volume 5, Number 1: Double issue focusing on Catholic censorship and Catholic film education.
Volume 5, Number 2: Interviews with Polanski, Skolimowski, and Jires.
Volume 5, Numbers 3 and 4: Double issue devoted entirely to Swedish cinema.

FILM CULTURE. Ed: Jonas Mekas, G. P. O. Box 1499, New York, N.Y. 10001. 4 n.p.a.: 4 dollars (U.S.A.) or 4.50 dollars (elsewhere). 80 pp. approx. *This maverick among American film magazines is rather irregular in its publishing habits these days (only two issues since our last round-up). But Number 44 contains a vast amount of material, including a speech by Len Lye, a prognostic statement by Gregory Markopoulos, and a dossier on Lev Kuleshov.*

FILMKRITIK. Ed: Enno Patalas, Ainmillerstr. 7, 8 Munich 13. 12 n.p.a.: DM 33.50 (70s. or 8.80 dollars). 60 pp. *As more pictures creep into the conservative layout of FILMKRITIK, so the magazine looks and reads somewhat better. The very up-to-date reviews are admirable; the lengthy articles on the aesthetics of cinema are tolerably pretentious.*
Aug. 1967: "Fellini, il poeta und das Horn des Stiers", by Peter M. Ladiges.

Dec. 1967: "Zum Selbstverständnis des Films. VI: Joseph Losey".
Jan. 1968: "Die Kamera in Augenhöhe: Howard Hawks in Gesprächen".
Feb. 1968: Analysis of *Bezhin Meadow*, by Ulrich Gregor.
Apr. 1968: "Underground Cinema . . .Gespräch mit Jonas Mekas".
May 1968: Three texts by Carl Th. Dreyer.
Jul. 1968: Underground cinema: articles by Susan Sontag and Parker Tyler.

FILM QUARTERLY. Ed: Ernest Callenbach, University of California Press, Berkeley, California 94720. 4 n.p.a.: 4 dollars (U.S.A. and Canada) or 7.20 dollars (elsewhere). 64 pp. *Only a quarterly, but FQ manages to wield a hefty influence in the American film world. Long articles and inquiries are favoured by the editor.*
Winter 1967-68: "The Films of Sidney Lumet. Adaptation as Art", by Graham Petrie. "Question Marks on the New Czech Cinema", by Jan Zalman.
Spring 1968: "The Danger is Seduction: An Interview with Haskell Wexler", by Ernest Callenbach and Albert Johnson. "Masquage: The Multi-Image Film", by Robert Siegler.

FILMRUTAN. Ed: Björn Norström, Lars Olsson, Bo Heurling, Kungsgatan 65, 3 tr., Stockholm. 4 n.p.a.: 10 Kr. (18s. or 2.50 dollars). 64 pp. approx. *Ten years old this year, FILMRUTAN is the organ of the film society movement in Sweden, and has some highly commendable articles every quarter.*
Number 4, 1967: "Lester Speaks. Bo Heurling och Björn Norström intervjuar Richard Lester". "Tjeckisk sextett", by Arne Svensson.
Number 1, 1968: "Bonnie & Clyde --- en idédiskussion", by Orjan Roth Lindberg, and also an interview with Penn.

FILMS AND FILMING. Ed: Robin Bean, 16 Buckingham Palace Road, London S.W.1. 12 n.p.a.: 60s. (8.50 dollars). 60 pp. approx. *Peter Baker in his most enthusiastic period lifted F. & F. to the level of the world's best cinema magazines. Recently the sparkle has diminished, and one hopes that under Robin Bean's guidance this informative monthly can really improve once more.*
Sept. 1967: "The Private War of Robert Aldrich", by Allen Eyles.
Oct. 1967: "The House that Jack Built", by Douglas McVay (on Clayton).
Dec. 1967: "Underground Subversion", by Raymond Durgnat.
Jan. 1968: Interview with Paul Wendkos.
Feb. 1968: Interview with Michael Winner.
Mar. 1968: "Myrna Loy on Comedy", by Eric Braun.
May 1968: "Out for the Kill", by David Austen (on Don Siegel).
Jun. 1968: "Out for the Kill", part two. "The Three Ages of the Musical", by George Sidney (interview).
Jul. 1968: "A Wajda Generation", by David Austen.

FILMS IN REVIEW. Ed: Henry Hart, National Board of Review, 31 Union Square, New York, N.Y. 10003. 10 n.p.a.: 7 dollars (U.S.A.) or 7.50 dollars (elsewhere). 64 pp. *The recipe as usual — career articles of (primarily) Hollywood stars and directors; films on tv and 8 and 16mm; caustic reviews; and columns of erudite readers' mail.*
Aug-Sept. 1967: "Bernard Herrmann", by Page Cook.
Oct. 1967: "Walt Disney's Films", by Leonard Maltin. "Harry Langdon", by Vernon L. Schonert.
Nov. 1967: "Ramon Novarro", by DeWitt Bodeen. "Anatole Litvak", by Jack Edmund Nolan.
Dec. 1967: "Laurence Olivier", by Henry Hart. "Constance Talmadge", by DeWitt Bodeen.
Feb. 1968: "Ingrid Bergman", by Ronald L. Bowers.
Apr. 1968: "Tim McCoy", by Anthony Thomas.
May 1968: "Theda Bara", by DeWitt Bodeen. "Mark Robson", by Herbert G. Luft.
Jun-Jul. 1968: "Bing Grosby", by Alvin H. Maritt.

KOSMORAMA. Ed: Øystein Hjort, Det Danske Filmmuseum, Store Søndervold-straede, Copenhagen K. 6 n.p.a.: 25.60 Kr. (30s. or 3.80 dollars). 40 pp. approx.

Not many magazines have dared to change their format and frequency so dramatically as KOSMORAMA, for years a staid, official quarterly and now a bright, big bi-monthly sporting some excellent articles.

Number 81: Interview with Henning Carlsen.
Number 82: Interview with Truffaut.
Number 83: "Filmkritikkern. Opgaver og metoder", by Soren Kjorup.
Number 84: Interviews with Demy and Skolimowski.
Number 85: Dreyer memorial number. "Ingmar Bergman og 'Sjaelens morke nat'", by Johannes Fabricius.

SCREEN FACTS. Ed: Alan G. Barbour, Screen Facts Press, P.O. Box 154, Kew Gardens, N.Y. 11415. 6 n.p.a.: 5.50 dollars (U.S.A.) or 7 dollars (elsewere). 64 pp. *A distinct cut above the average fan magazine, Alan Barbour's bi-monthly features exhaustive career articles and interviews. He also issues SERIAL QUARTERLY, SCREEN ADS MONTHLY, SERIAL PICTORIAL, and even 300 page books like "The Serial", Volumes One and Two, 10.95 dollars each (abroad).*

Number 6: "Bela Lugosi".
Number 7: "Mae West".
Number 9: "Bette Davis".
Number 10: "Busby Berkeley".
Number 13: "Maria Montez".
Number 17: "Rudolph Valentino". "Wini Shaw".

SIGHT AND SOUND. Ed: Penelope Houston, British Film Institute, 81 Dean St, London W.1. 4 n.p.a.: 22s. (4 dollars). 54 pp. *35 years old and as accurate as anyone could wish for. Articles are sometimes too lofty, and the preferences too marked, but each issue is still wide-ranging and informative enough to prove vital for students in the future.*

Summer 1967: "Dukinfield meets McGargle", by David Robinson (on W.C. Fields). Interview with Fritz Lang.
Autumn 1967: "Buñuel's Golden Bowl", by Elliott Stein (on *Belle de Jour*). "North Light and Cigarette Bulb", by Charles Higham and Joel Greenberg (on vintage Hollywood cameramen).
Winter 1967-68; "Bellocchio", by Christian Braad Thomsen, "Meet Whiplash Wilder", by Charles Higham.
Spring 1968; Interview with Renoir, by Rui Nogueira and François Truchaud.
Summer 1968: Interview with Jean-Pierre Melville. "Godard and the US", by Claire Clouzot.

Some Other Magazines

Restrictions of space prevent us from listing full details of more than about a score of the hundreds of film magazines in existence. But here are the addresses of some useful periodicals. In Canada, **Take One** (Box 1778, Station B, Montréal 2) is perky and internationally-minded; and a similar, though lavishly produced magazine in Holland is **Skoop** (Sarphatipark 92, Amsterdam), the mouthpiece of the young Dutch cinema. In Britain, **Monthly Film Bulletin** (British Film Institute, 81 Dean St, London W.1.) provides full and commendably correct credits, synopses, and reviews of all new films released in the U.K., while **Movie** (21 Ivor Place, London N.W.1.) has risen again for the third time, as a quarterly, and one hopes it will survive for good. **The British National Film Catalogue** (55a Welbeck St, London W.1.) gives essential particulars of a non-fiction films (British and foreign) becoming available in British each years. **The Journal of the Society of Film & Television Arts** (80 Great Portland St, London W.1.) is a distinguished quarterly edited by Roger Manvell, with each issue reserved for one film or tv subject.

Magazines that are hampered from attaining a wide circulation outside their own language area include **Film a doba** (Václavské nám. 43, Praha 1), the renowned Czech monthly; **Fant** (Frognerveien 29, inng. Baldersgt., Oslo), a well-designed but occasional Norwegian periodical; and **Filme Cultura** (Praça da República 141-A, 2° andar, ZC 14, Rio de Janeiro, Guanabana), whose March 1968 issue is just about the most comprehensive dossier yet compiled on Brazilian cinema.

In French, there is **Positif** (14-16 rue de Verneuil, Paris 7), a rival to *Cahiers du Cinéma* that spews its entertaining polemics out by fits and starts, with Benayoun, Thirard, and Tailleur among its liveliest writers; **Dossiers Art et Essai** (47 quai des Grands Augustins, Paris 6), Jeander's guide to the films and the cinemas that matter in France; and **Cinéma International** (Château d'Echandens, Vaud, Switzerland), award-winning and attractive in design, but becoming a little irregular in its schedule. Then in Austria, the official, scholarly, and sober publication is **Filmkunst** (Rauhensteingasse 5, 1010 Vienna), and in Italy, **Cinema e Film** (Via Prenestina 395, Rome) is worth consulting for the latest trends in "new cinema".

American magazines that should be better known in Europe are **Film Fan Monthly** (77 Grayson Place, Teaneck, New Jersey 07666), first-class on Hollywood hagiography and abundant in useful pieces like "Hitchcock's TV Films" (in number 84); **American Cinematographer** (ASC Agency Inc., 1782 North Orange Drive, Hollywood, California 90028), a technical monthly that devoted its entire June 1968 issue to the know-how behind *2001: A Space Odyssey;* and **CTVD** (Hampton Books, Hampton Bays, N.Y.), which digests writings on cinema and tv from magazines all over the world.

Readers may like to know where to obtain the principal "trade" magazines. For Britain, there is **Kine Weekly** (161 Fleet St, London E.C.4.), and **The Daily Cinema** (Film House, Wardour St, London W.1.); for France, **Le Film Français** (40 rue du Cherche-Midi, Paris 6); for Germany, **Filmblätter** (Verlag für Kultur und Wirtschaft GmbH, Tauntzienstr. 16, 1 Berlin 30); for Sweden, **Film & bio** (Stureplan 13 (III), Stockholm); for Norway, **Film og Kino** (Stortingsgt. 16, Oslo 1); and for the U.S.A., of course, the invaluable **Variety** (154 West 46th St, New York, N.Y. 10036).

Book Section

ANTHOLOGIE DU CINÉMA, Tome 3 (Editions de L'Avant-Scène, Paris, 1968). Third volume in the unique collection of dossiers on dead directors (Disney, Fescourt, Lubitsch, DeMille,Mizoguchi, Munk, Rossen, Sennett, Stiller, Stroheim). Bound together attractively. Some 300 photos spread over the 542 pages. 72s.6d. *

ART OF W.C. FIELDS, THE, by William K. Everson (Bobbs Merrill, New York, 1967). The usual, thorough job of research by Everson — closely descriptive, warmly written, less penetrating in analysis. Well chosen pictures.

BRITISH CINEMA, An Illustrated Guide, by Denis Gifford (Zwemmer, London; Barnes, New York, 1968). An alphabetical companion to the British work of over 500 directors, actors, and actresses, with an enormous index for cross-reference to the text. 12s.6d. *

CINEMA OF ALAIN RESNAIS, THE, by Roy Armes (Zwemmer, London; Barnes, New York, 1968). A sober, extremely illuminating account of all R's films, with copious quotations from the director's own comments, and a very detailed reference dossier. 12s.6d. *

DICTIONARY OF THE CINEMA, A, by Peter Graham (Zwemmer, London; Barnes, New York, 1968). Second, revised edition of *the* standard small dictionary in this field. 20,000 references; index to 6,000 films; 620 filmographies; 144 portraits. 12s.6d. (paperback); 25s. (hardback). *

DIETRICH, MARLENE, by John Kobal (Studio Vista, London; Dutton, New York, 1968). Kobal has one of the world's finest collections of Hollywood stills. Over 100 pictures of Dietrich decorate an adulatory text in this paperback.

FILM CENSORS AND THE LAW, by Neville March Hunnings (Allen & Unwin, London, 1967). An exhaustive probe into the business of censorship and its legal implications and precedents. Scholarly and useful for reference.

FILMGEGNER VON HEUTE — FILM FREUNDE VON MORGEN, by Hans Richter (Verlag Hans Rohr, Zürich, 1968). A facsimile of Richter's classic plea for the film as a basically new art form, first published in 1929 and beautifully illustrated. A full, up to date filmography of R himself is appended. A limited edition of 1,000 copies. Essential for libraries still without it. 60s. *

FILM MAKERS ON FILM MAKING, Edited by Harry M. Geduld (Indiana University Press, Bloomington and London, 1968). The first English-language compendium of director's comments on their work that looks really comprehensive. 30 contributors, from Lumière and Hepworth to Satyajit Ray and Kenneth Anger. An invaluable source book.

Feature books on the film — its art and its artists

THE MOVING IMAGE
A Guide to Cinematic Literacy. ROBERT GESSNER. The shooting script as the key to the secrets of cinema. "Explores with analytic sweep and probing authority the unique nature of the movies."—LEWIS JACOBS. Illustrated.
Cloth $8.95

JEAN-LUC GODARD
A Critical Anthology. Edited, and with an Introduction, by TOBY MUSSMAN. An in-depth study with 18 articles covering about 15 feature Godard films; 3 scenarios; 5 pieces by Godard. Chronology; bibliography. Illustrated.
DP 229   Paper $2.45

FILM: A MONTAGE OF THEORIES
Edited, and with an Introduction, by RICHARD DYER MacCANN. Pudovkin, Eisenstein, Hitchcock, Bergman, Langer, Fellini, Truffaut, and 30 other leading filmmakers and critics present exciting, often conflicting, ideas. Illustrated.
DP 181   Paper $2.45

THE LUBITSCH TOUCH
A Critical Study. HERMAN G. WEINBERG. Analyzes the genius of Lubitsch in such masterpieces as *The Marriage Circle, Trouble in Paradise,* and, using the entire scenario for discussion, *Ninotchka.* Complete filmography. With 76 photographs.
DP 221   Paper $2.25

Write for free descriptive brochure:

published by dutton

JOSEF VON STERNBERG

A Critical Study. HERMAN G. WEINBERG. Critiques of all of Sternberg's films, how he works, his discovery of Marlene Dietrich, a lively Sternberg interview, and critical reviews. With 50 illustrations.   DP 206   Paper $1.95

THE NEW AMERICAN CINEMA

A Critical Anthology. Edited, and with an Introduction, by GREGORY BATTCOCK. Critics and film-makers discuss the various aspects of "underground" films. Included are Jonas Mekas, Susan Sontag, Stan Brakhage and 26 others. Illustrated.   DP 200   Paper $1.75

AN INTRODUCTION TO THE AMERICAN UNDERGROUND FILM

SHELDON RENAN. Introduction by WILLARD VAN DYKE. The subject matter, elements of style, technique, general history, the makers, the "stars" and the "establishment" of the underground film and latest developments. Nearly 100 photographs.   DP 207   Paper $2.25

THE AMERICAN CINEMA

Directors and Directions, 1929-1968. ANDREW SARRIS. About 200 sound film directors are discussed, their virtues, their vices, their output—from Chaplin and Griffith to Mike Nichols and Arthur Penn. Index of films, 1929-1968; film and performance chronology.   DP 227   Paper $2.95

 **dutton**
201 Park Avenue South New York, N.Y. 10003

>>>Cinema One

New Titles

BUSTER KEATON by David Robinson
A critical revaluation made possible by the recent comprehensive retrospective at the National Film Theatre in London.

BILLY WILDER by Axel Madsen
The work of Hollywood's foremost satirist, director of innumerable harsh comedies, **Sunset Boulevard, Ace in the Hole, The Apartment** and **One Two Three** being perhaps the best known.

SIGNS AND MEANING IN THE CINEMA by Peter Wollen
A critical study which looks at the cinema as a system of signs and leads to a re-examination of film aesthetics and the work of specific directors, notably Hawks, Ford and Eisenstein.

Also available:
JEAN-LUC GODARD by Richard Roud
JOSEPH LOSEY ON LOSEY
LUCHINO VISCONTI by Geoffrey Nowell-Smith
HOW IT HAPPENED HERE by Kevin Brownlow
THE NEW WAVE: CRITICAL LANDMARKS
        selected by Peter Graham
ALAIN RESNAIS, OR THE THEME OF TIME by John Ward
HOWARD HAWKS by Robin Wood

CINEMA ONE: ''Well-produced, attractively designed books, with illustrations carefully related to the text'' — David Robinson, **Financial Times.** "A handsomely produced and illustrated series" — Dilys Powell, **Sunday Times** "All are eminently well-presented" — Sheridan Morley, **Films & Filming.**

Paperback 15s/Hardcover 30s

Published by Secker & Warburg in association with the British Film Institute

FILM REVIEW, Edited by F. Maurice Speed (W. H. Allen, London; Barnes, New York, 1968). Another edition of the long-established annual that is readable, well illustrated, and contains a useful list of all films released in Britain during the year. Features this time include articles by Bryan Forbes on directing, and by Ivan Butler on picture palaces. Much else.

FILMS AND FEELINGS, by Raymond Durgnat (Faber & Faber, London, 1967). A series of articles, many based on a post-graduate research thesis at the Slade School, that reveals Durgnat at his most infuriating, incisive, and provocative.

FILMS AND FILM-MAKERS, by Jan Zalman (Orbis, Prague, 1968). The only detailed survey of the young Czech cinema yet available in English, and as the author is really Antonín Novák, editor of *Film a doba*, it is perceptive as well as informative. Filmographies.

FILM UND FILMWIRTSCHAFT IN DER SCHWEIZ (Verlag Hans Rohr, Zürich, 1968). A superbly printed survey of the Swiss film and film industry, on the 50th anniversary of the Allgemeine Kinematographer A.G., Zürich. Several rare stills and posters are reproduced, and as this is the only up to date account of Swiss cinema it should be in all libraries.

FORD, JOHN, by Peter Bogdanovich (Studio Vista, London; University of California Press, Los Angeles, 1968). Philippe Haudiquet's book is still the most penetrating analysis of F's work, but this slim paperback yields some entertaining interviews and an annotated filmography.

4 GREAT COMEDIANS, by Donald W. McCaffrey (Zwemmer, London; Barnes, New York, 1968). The author earned his Ph. D. with this trenchant thesis on Chaplin, Lloyd, Keaton, and Langdon, discussing all their films and several other comedies too. Rare illustrations. 12s.6d.*

FRANJU, by Raymond Durgnat (Studio Vista, London, 1968). Durgnat at his best on a director often ignored by critics. He interprets and tests F's psychological commitments as well as his extraordinarily sensitive style. The chapter on *Thérèse* is brilliant.

FRANJU, GEORGES, by Gabriel Vialle (Editions Seghers, Paris, 1968). An original analysis of F's films, with the author claiming that F has created a world of his own, in the sense of Eluard's "Il y a un autre monde, mais il est dans celui-là." Script extracts, texts by F himself and by various critics bulk out the volume.

HAWKS, HOWARD, by Robin Wood (Secker & Warburg, London; Doubleday, New York, 1968). After his controversial book on Hitchcock, Wood elects Hawks to his pantheon. The close-reading, Leavisite method works well with some films and rather ludicrously with others. That *The Big Sleep* is relegated to the Appendix as a "failure" should prepare readers for a lively study.

HOLLYWOOD IN THE TWENTIES, by David Robinson; **HOLLYWOOD IN THE THIRTIES,** by John Baxter; **HOLLYWOOD IN THE FORTIES,** by Charles Higham and Joel Greenberg (Zwemmer, London; Barnes, New York, 1968). A major 3-volume re-evaluation by experts of the most crucial and fruitful decades in Hollywood's history. Virtually every film of significance made in America between 1920 and 1950 is discussed here. Each vol. 12s.6d.*

HOLLYWOOD, THE HAUNTED HOUSE, by Paul Mayersberg (Allen Lane, The Penguin Press, London, 1967). An idiosyncratic and often illuminating series of interviews with Hollywood directors, but very thin for its high price.

HORROR MOVIES, An Illustrated Survey, by Carlos Clarens (Secker & Warburg, London, 1968). A far-reaching and luxuriously presented study of the genre, including science-fiction. Emphasis on film-makers like Chaney, Browning, Castle, Lewton, and Corman.

HOW IT HAPPENED HERE, by Kevin Brownlow (Secker & Warburg, London; Doubleday, New York, 1968). A thoroughly entertaining account of the trials and tribulations of *It Happened Here*, the independently-made film about a Nazi occupation of England. This is a film book with a difference, almost unbearably readable, and it proves what an elaborate team operation even the cheapest picture can be.

INTRODUCTION TO THE AMERICAN UNDERGROUND FILM, AN, by Sheldon Renan (Dutton, New York, 1967,). As complete and sympathetic a guide through the underground cinema as any enthusisast could wish for. Much good analysis of the films, but also a surprising amount of reference material, including a section telling readers how and where to rent each title.

LAUREL & HARDY, by Charles Barr (Studio Vista, London, 1968). Unquestionably the best book on L & H to date. Excellent descriptions of their better shorts and features, illuminated by learned literary quotations but hampered by the minute frame reproductions.

MOTION PICTURES FROM THE LIBRARY OF CONGRESS PAPER PRINT COLLECTION, by Kemp R. Niver (University of California Press, Los Angeles; Cambridge University Press, London, 1967). An expensive but inexhaustible mine of information about the nursery years of the cinema (1894-1912). In effect, a descriptive catalogue of all the films deposited with the L of C for copyright purposes, divided by genres and indexed. Endless patterns can be discerned in this material, which includes foreign films as well.

NEW AMERICAN CINEMA, THE, A Critical Anthology, Edited by Gregory Battcock (Dutton, New York, 1967). 29 critics and film-makers talk about what is otherwise known as the American "underground cinema". Some nonsense, some shrewd blows at the movement itself, some lively theorising.

NEW WAVE, THE, by Peter Graham (Secker & Warburg, London; Doubleday, New York, 1968). By far the best translations ever made of the seminal writings of Bazin, Godard, Astruc, Benayoun *et al*, linked with an articulate commentary by Graham.

NEW CINEMA IN THE USA, by Roger Manvell (Studio Vista, London; Dutton, New York, 1968). A companion volume to the same author's *New Cinema in Europe*. The text is brief but informative on postwar American films and their directors. Stills in abundance.

PHILIPE, GÉRARD, by Georges Sadoul (Editions Seghers, Paris, 1967). A moving account of P's career and early death, made doubly sad by the fact that Sadoul, father of French critics, is no longer there himself. The first in this "Cinéma d'Aujourd'hui" series to deal with a personality rather than a director.

RENOIR, JEAN, by Pierre Leprohon (Editions Seghers, Paris, 1967). Studies of R are still scarce, and Leprohon's long treatment here deals well with the thirties period — films known and unknown in the career of the greatest French director.

RESNAIS, ALAIN, Or the Theme of Time, by John Ward (Secker & Warburg, London; Doubleday, New York, 1968). An essay on the philosophical content of R's feature films, with particular reference to Bergson. Esoteric, theoretical: but R's work withstands the treatment.

SEVENTY YEARS OF CINEMA, by Peter Cowie (Barnes, New York; Yoseloff, London, 1968). A table companion chronology of the cinema, with 235 individual reviews (with full credits), checklists of several hundred other important features and shorts, and more than 250 stills. 105s.*

SUSPENSE IN THE CINEMA, by Gordon Gow (Zwemmer, London; Barnes, New York, 1968). A readable, perceptive, and coherent examination of the thriller genre, by a distinguished BBC critic and journalist, with reference to many films.

SVENSKA STUMFILMER 1896-1931 OCH DERAS REGISSÖRER, and SVENSKA LJUDFILMER 1929-1966 OCH DERAS REGISSÖRER, by Sven G. Winquist (Svenska Filminstitutet/Proprius Förlag, Stockholm, 1967). An accurate list of all Swedish films, with their directors, production companies, and release dates. A useful preliminary to what one hopes will be a complete filmography of the Swedish cinema. Some English text.

SVENSK FILM PÅ VAG, by Kenne Fant (Bokförlaget PAN/Norstedts, Stockholm, 1968). The head of Svensk Filmindustri provides a carefully researched and revealing picture of the Swedish cinema industry — how it has developed during the past few years, economic trends, prospects for the future. Essential for libraries and students of Swedish film.

VIGO, JEAN, by Pierre Lherminier (Editions Seghers, Paris, 1967). The 50th in the most sustained and admirable series of French film books. Appropriately, it is the general editor Pierre Lherminier who has composed this tribute. A rounded picture of V the man and of his films emerges not only from Lherminier's essay but also from the invaluable mass of reference material.

WHAT IS CINEMA? by André Bazin, Essays selected and translated by Hugh Gray (University of California Press, Los Angeles; Cambridge University Press, London, 1967). The first time that the real core of B's criticism has been available in English. His Gallic logic translates uneasily here, and several of the essays are mild and forgettable. The pieces on Chaplin and Bresson, though, are still biting and original.

WORD AND IMAGE, A History of the Hungarian Cinema, by István Nemeskürty (Corvina Press, Budapest, dist. by Kultura, P.O.B. 149, Budapest 62). Fine and thorough study of Hungarian films from 1912 to 1966, written from the standpoint of the cinemagoer. Extremely valuable for reference. 48 pages of illustrations.

MADE IN USA, LE PETIT SOLDAT, LA GRANDE ILLUSION, THE BATTLE-SHIP POTEMKIN, THE BLUE ANGEL (Lorrimer Publishing, London; Simon and Schuster, New York, 1967 and 1968). These 5 paperbacks are the latest in a sleek new series devoted exclusively to film scripts. Each has about 100 pages and 20 pages of stills. There is the occasional introduction of note (like von Sternberg's, specially written for *The Blue Angel*). The more "literary" scripts, such as *La Grande Illusion*, tend to make the most absorbing reading, and, with many more titles in preparation, these Lorrimer books will soon fill an essential shelf in any enthusiast's library.

Round the Film Bookshops

Zwemmers, of 78 Charing Cross Rd, **London** W.C.2., are the distributors of the "International Film Guide" series and also offer one of the country's most comprehensive selections of books on the cinema in many languages. Magazines and pamphlets on the film are stocked too, and regular catalogues are issued.

A short distance away is Foyle's (119-125 Charing Cross Rd, London W.C.2.), where on the 3rd floor Alfred Rogers manages a lively and wide-ranging display of film literature. Items are rarely allowed to go out of stock, and of course Foyle's are famous for their mail-order service.

Over the road is Better Books (94 Charing Cross Road, London W.C.2.) In the basement there is a well-known cinema section, and film posters are often available here.

One man's interest in the cinema can often create a book department where one did not previously exist. So with Fred Zentner, whose enterprise at the Atlantis Bookshop (49a Museum Street, London W.C.1.) has resulted in a fine selection of stills, posters, new and rare books, magazines, and press books. Our recommendation.

The enthusiastic firm of Motley Books (10 Westminster Palace Gdns, Artillery Row, London S.W.1 – by appointment only) recently sold the remarkable Paul Rotha Archive, and offers cinema and pre-cinema material of every description, from optical toys to new foreign books in unusual languages. Early periodicals are another of Barbara Cavanagh's specialities. Write to her for one of her splendid annual catalogues.

Milton Luboviski

... A SHOP

TO SET STORE BY

By Vince Ducette

TIME WAS WHEN certain members of our industry, needing assistance of a specialized form, shouted — "Get Geisler!" The form was legal in nature, the man sought was a specialist by reputation. . . .

Today when film makers seek a specialist the order is — "Get Luboviski!" The man, Milton Luboviski, is not only a specialist by reputation, he is regarded as a world authority on motion picture memorabilia wherever films are lensed, edited, or planned. At 6658 Hollywood Boulevard he operates the world's largest establishment specializing in the books, stills, magazines, programs and scripts that involve the motion picture industry.

The name of the store — Larry Edmunds Bookshop — is a place bursting with bindings with the memorabilia of a great film industry. Mr. Luboviski is both founder and original partner of the man on the storefront title sign. And since the latter's death in 1941, he has been sole owner of a specialty premised upon a hunch. . . .

Although Luboviski's reputation as world authority is as recognized in Europe and Asia as it is domestically, (he holds an honorary Delta Kappa Alpha from USC) of equal importance is his knowing from memory the detailed history of an industry that is intricate at best. And what doesn't come to mind is but fingertips away — in his currently 249 page catalogue containing more than 7,000 publication entries. They represent what the store *has on hand*, not what he can readily secure upon request.

This catalogue, representing 7,000 book titles alone, also includes 10,000 magazines, thousands of programs, posters and scripts. In a companion index are more than three quarters of a million stills — also in stock.

In essence, most of what has ever been placed upon paper concerning the motion picture industry, whether here or abroad, can be smoothly secured.

But of equal significance is that the catalogue has grown more over the past two years than in all the previous years combined.

"This, I regard as a symbol of the upsurge in motion picture interest on the part of the moviegoing public," Luboviski states. Soft spoken by nature, he cites a curious fact of Hollywood in light that has been the pace setter across the globe. . . .

"Out of the thousands of books on the industry, a very minor percentage have been written by Americans. Most have been authored by writers of England, France, or Italy. . . ."

Luboviski declares that the reason for this is because writers of Europe and England have found it profitable to author such books — while our own writers have always had a ragged time of it, especially when the work is of a technical nature.

But this world authority contends that the American writers' situation is changing — that a good book on the American film industry is now a recognized need and would find rapid publisher acceptance.

In this publishing vein, he projects reissuing several out of print classics later this year with the assistance of Gene Ringgold, an associate who has edited previous publications on the motion picture theme.

Luboviski, Milwaukee-born and son of a musician, first entered the world of books some 29 years ago, but did not specialize in motion picture material until 1949.

"I was what you might call a motion picture buff ever since seeing my first film at the age of three," he asserts. "But obviously my interest in motion picture writings and the like were some time in crystalizing."

He feels the U.S. Army helped the occurance during World War II — "Because I was from Hollywood, they put me to work on combat films in the Signal Corps." It proved to be a partial catalyst for the Luboviski specialty-to-be, still hovering in the wings. Upon discharge he turned to the bookstore business, and with the help of his wife, set to work on specialization in the late forties.

"I decided to concentrate on this field because I had become increasingly aware of the great shortage of stills, scripts, and associated memorabilia of the industry. The studios have always maintained a remarkable laxness in saving such material after they have used it," he says.

"Also, I sensed a coming interest in motion picture production on the part of the universities and training institutes," he adds.

His belief in the upsurge of interest is reflected in his first catalogue when compared to the size of the one current:

". . . Seven pages compared to today's 249 — and my wife has compiled every one of them."

The demand for the bookstore's wares has increased in intensity since the start. A routine day now involves phone calls from throughout the world, all requesting orders from stock.

In addition, requests of a different nature are lodged — for Luboviski to speak at universities, on England's BBC, on Japanese television. The requests are satisfied as his schedule — and search tours — allow. The latter is another reason why the store's stock of memorabilia is second to none, and why his advice is constantly sought by persons seeking appraisal, or recently, as it happened — by Paramount seeking New Orleans interiors and exteriors circa 1930. The studio had none in stock. . . .

But private parties have proven the greatest source of the Hollywood material, as they have also proved to be the greatest consumers of the store's stock.

Either in person or through mail orders, still-shot requests pour in on a daily basis, with the photos of Garbo, Harlow, Chaplin, W. C. Fields and Laurel and Hardy heading the most wanted list.

Because Luboviski has made such an exhaustive study of the film industry and its eras of growth, he says that on the whole, the American film maker is not as studious as his English, French, or Italian counterpart.

"But I believe this situation is undergoing change now that the major universities are gradually granting proper status to the art of film making. This increased capability for proper training will ultimately lead to a more realistic product than we presently have," he feels.

Luboviski, who made his own important niche in the industry's structure by choice rather than by persuasion, has found that the true "motion picture buff" — those captivated by filmdom and its trappings — have no age group or occupational category.

"From eight to eighty they are enthralled by the magic that is motion pictures — and the magic of those stars with whom they identify.

"For these millions, the name and the face of a Valentino will live forever, for that name, that face, is a part of their own personal dream in a distant past." — Is the belief of this man who made his own personal involvement with a great industry become his life's work.

And without exactly saying so, Luboviski hints that nostalgia may play a part in it, too. . . .

Another postal business is that of **A. E. Cox, 21 Cecil Rd, Itchen, Southampton,** which issues monthly lists, offering mainly out of print items — books, annuals, foyer posters, stills, magazines, even souvenir theatre programmes. Send 6d for a current issue, with mention of our book.

In **New York,** the Mecca for film bibliophiles is the Gotham Book Mart, at 41 West 47th St, which is packed to the roof with literature of every kind on the cinema. Philip Lyman is the Manager, and he is just about to issue his Film File no. 6, which lists many thousands of items. If you have really *scarce* books or runs of magazines on the subject, Mr. Lyman may acquire them from you.

Two further rewarding calls in New York are Cinemabilia, 10 Cornelia St, N.Y. 10014, deep in the heart of Greenwich Village, and The Drama Bookshop, upstairs at 150 West 52nd St, N.Y. 10019. Ernest Burns's Cinemabilia is crammed with back issues of magazines, lobby posters, stills and autographed photos, and, of course, new and out-of-print books on the cinema. His catalogue is excellent value at 1 dollar, and patrons are sent supplements two or three times a year. Mr. Burns requests overseas clients to send 20 or 30 cents more with any order to speed delivery through the mails.

Arthur Seelen and Allen Collins run The Drama Book Shop, founded in 1921 by the New York Drama League. It is no exaggeration to say that this establishment houses virtually every book in print pertaining to the theatre. But cinema is now given its own flourishing department too, and there is an excellent mail-order service. Write with your wants, with the recommendation of this book. Catalogues are issued.

In the same state of N.Y., but north in **Hampton Bays,** is the famous Hampton Books establishment run by Ben and Muriel Hamilton. Their house is overrun with books, more than 25,000 of them, and this is a treasure trove indeed for anyone interested in cinemabilia. The Hamiltons are experts in the mail order business, so write with a list of your wants. (They also specialise in books on *aviation!*)

In the real home of movies, the Larry Edmunds Bookshop (6658 Hollywood Bd, **Hollywood,** California 90028) is recognised as one of the best film bookshops in the world. Milton Luboviski and his wife work without pause in their efforts to find rare out of print titles and runs of magazines, not to mention a vast quantity of stills.

Their massive catalogue (costing 1 dollar) is a reference book in its own right. Even original shooting scripts can be obtained from Larry Edmunds.

Another address worth noting in the U.S.A. is that of Modern Times Booksellers, 600 South Webster St, **Taylorville,** Illinois 62568. They offer books and magazines on all aspects of the cinema, and on radio and television too. They supply the very useful *Feature Film Source Book*, including details of over 12,000 films.

In **Paris** there are two rewarding specialists in film literature. Le Minotaure, at 2 rue des Beaux Arts, Paris 6, is overflowing with lore and literature about the cinema, and there are scarce back numbers of *Cahiers du Cinéma* and other magazines. Language, for once in France, is no barrier here, for M. Roger Cornaille's colleague speaks excellent English. Postal inquiries welcomed.

Then at 24 rue du Colisée, Paris 8, just behind the Champs-Elysées, is the attractively designed shop known as Librairie Contacts. Again there is a large selection of film magazines, but there are books too in French, English, German, Spanish, Italian, and even Portuguese! Lists are issued occasionally, and mention this book when writing to the proprietress.

In Switzerland, Hans Rohr's International Library of Motion Picture Books, Oberdorfstrasse 5, CH 8024 **Zürich,** is exactly what it says, and it was from here that the indispensable "Internationale Filmbibliographie 1962-65" appeared under the editorship of Hanspeter Manz. As well as selling books and magazines, Rohr's *publish* books on the cinema, and two of these are mentioned in our reviews section. Again, postal business is welcomed.

The Low Countries are well represented in this Tour. In **Amsterdam,** at Damrak 62, is the basement film department of Allert de Lange, replete with all kinds of cinema books and also works on photography; while in **Brussels,** La Jeune Parque, 55-57 rue des Eperonniers, has some 15 years' of experience in selling film literature in French, German, and English language, as well as titles devoted to the theatre; and Librairie Lefebvre, at 7 rue des Colonies, is especially strong on French film publications and magazines in its recently expanded premises.

In **Stockholm** you can visit one of the world's most sophisticated and up-to-date bookshops — Sandbergs, on the corner at Sturegatan 8 (there is also a new paperback shop opposite). And at the far end of the shop ask for Mr. Neumann or his assistant, who speak excellent English and can show you shelf after shelf of film literature from a dozen countries. The firm's mailing list is admirable, sending to clients every few weeks a complete annotated list of all acquisitions. Write if you cannot call, with mention of this book.

Finally, in Germany, there are two establishments in **Berlin** worth contacting. Antiquariat Carl Wegner, Martin-Luther Str. 113, Berlin 62, is always anxious to build up his collection of rare books on film and theatre history, so if you have any items of this description, be sure to write with details to Herr Wegner, citing this paragraph.

If you are visiting Berlin, a call at the upstairs film department of M. Schoeller, Kurfürstendamm 130, will be rewarding.

But it will be best to *write* to "Proszenium", Postfach 41, 8584 **Kemnath-Stadt**, in southern Germany, where a dedicated family business issues catalogues of literature on film, music and theatre, and specialises in items pertaining to the period of Nazi persecution.

Lorrimer

Modern and Classic Film Scripts

A series of books created for the increasing number of people who wish to possess a permanent record of the most famous films in the world. *(All illustrated)*

Already published:

Alphaville
Jean-Luc Godard 9s 6d

Made in USA
Jean-Luc Godard 12s 6d

Le Petit Soldat
Jean-Luc Godard 12s 6d

The Battleship Potemkin
Sergei Eisenstein 12s 6d

La Grande Illusion
Jean Renoir 12s 6d

The Blue Angel
Josef von Sternberg 12s 6d

M
Fritz Lang 12s 6d

Jules and Jim
François Truffaut 12s 6d

Forthcoming:

Les Enfants du Paradis
Marcel Carné 20s

The Seventh Seal
Ingmar Bergman 12s 6d

L'Age d'Or & Un Chien Andalou
Luis Bunuel 12s 6d

Ikiru
Akira Kurosawa 12s 6d

The Third Man
Graham Greene & Carol Reed 12s 6d

Bicycle Thieves
Vittorio De Sica 12s 6d

Pierrot le Fou
Jean-Luc Godard 12s 6d

Pandora's Box
G. W. Pabst 12s 6d

Lorrimer Publishing Ltd 47 Dean Street London W1

Directory of Film Booksellers

BELGIUM
Librairie Lefebvre, 7 Rue des Colonies Brussels 1. Tel. 131391.
La Jeune Parque, 55-57 Rue des Eperonniers, Brussels 1. Tel. 122305.

DENMARK
Busck, Arnold, Fiolstraede 24, Copenhagen K. (Also at: Kobmagergade 43).

ENGLAND
Atlantis Bookshop Ltd., 49a Museum St., London W.C.1.
Better Books Ltd., 94 Charing Cross Rd., London W.C.2. Tel. TEM 6944.
Cox, A. E., 21 Cecil Rd., Itchen, Southampton. (Postal business only)
Foyle, W. & G., 119-125 Charing Cross Rd., London W.C.2.
Motley Books Ltd., 10 Westminster Palace Gdns, Artillery Row, London S.W.I. Tel. 928 8931.
Zwemmer, A., 78 Charing Cross Rd., London W.C.2.

FRANCE
Minotaure, Le, 2 Rue des Beaux-Arts, Paris 6ème. Tel. ODE 73-02.
Terrain Vague, Le, 14-16 Rue de Verneuil, Paris VII.
Contacts, 24 Rue du Colisée, Paris VIII.
"La Joie de Lire", 40 Rue Saint-Séverin, Paris V.

GERMANY
Gielow, Wolfgang, Theatinerstr. 35 (im Zierhof), Munich 2. Tel. 227214.
Proszenium, Ernst-Max Hacke (Peer Baedeker), Postfach 41, 8584 Kemnath-Stadt.
Schoeller, M., Kurfürstendamm 30, Berlin 15.
Wegner, Antiquariat Carl, Martin-Luther Str. 113, Berlin 62.

NETHERLANDS
Stichting Inst. voor Filmdocumentatie, Postbox 5102, Amsterdam.
Allert de Lange, Damrak 62, Amsterdam-C. Tel. 246744.

SPAIN
Miessner Libreros, José Ortega y Gasset 14, Madrid.
Buchholz, Calvo Sotelo 1, Madrid.
Aguilar, Generalisimo 44, Madrid.

SWEDEN
Sandbergs Bokhandel, Sturegatan 8, Stockholm Ö.

SWITZERLAND
Rohr, Hans, Oberdorfstr. 5, Zürich. Tel. 245839.

U.S.A.
Cinemabilia, 10 Cornelia St, New York 10014
Drama Book Shop, 150 West 52nd St, New York 10019
Gotham Book Mart Inc., 41 West 47th Street, New York.
Hampton Books, Hampton Bays, New York.
Larry Edmunds Bookshop, 6658 Hollywood Blvd., Hollywood, California, 90028.
Modern Times Booksellers, 600 South Webster St., Taylorville, Illinois 62568.

Tour of Cinemas

introduction

by Walter Talmon-Gros

President of CICAE

Founded in 1955 on the initiative of three film critics, Delcorde from Brussels, Jeander from Paris, and myself from Munich, the International Confederation of Art Houses (known by its French initials, CICAE) now links cinemas in 18 countries in Europa, Africa, Asia, and North America. In spite of all the different conditions pertaining to the various art houses, it is the quality of their programmes that unites them. The art houses have always been in the forefront of the exhibiting side of the cinema. They have never been afraid to take risks and to screen films that are reputedly box-office "poison". And developments have proved them correct: what seemed a precarious innovation ten years ago now attracts an ever-increasing public. Happily the cinema continues to evolve, and thus there is the need to cultivate new generations of audiences and enthusiasts. Not surprisingly the art houses are essentially devoted to "young cinema", and we search for these new films all over the world. It is obvious that this search for quality films and this cultivation of the public requires a constant exchange of information between the art houses, and a sharing of experiences. This is why we see our major task as being the preparation of monthly bulletins (which appear at the moment in German and French), and the organisation of national and international meetings that will allow our members to exchange views. This internal action is complemented by our appeals to all the appropriate authorities to abolish once and for all the obstacles in the way of a free distribution and circulation of art films. All inquiries concerning the CICAE should be addressed to the General Secretary, Monsieur Henri Ginet, at 92 Avenue des Champs-Elysées, Paris 8.

new
cinema
club

only members risk
tomorrow's films today

"Like a continuous
London Film Festival"
The Times

Subscription one guinea

Free illustrated programme — 122 Wardour St., London W.1. 01 - 734 5888

FESTIVAL DIARY

——*the only monthly guide to forthcoming festivals*

Film Festivals are still multiplying. Soon there will be three hundred a year.

The only up-to-the-minute guide to the festival scene is the Festival Diary, published once a month by the Short Film Service. The Diary gives details of dates, locations, themes, awards, deadlines, addresses for all festivals for more than a year ahead. And every month the latest information from the festivals themselves brings the picture up-to-date.

Festival Diary, recommended by International Film Guide, is essential for everyone who makes films, uses films or writes about films.

Subscription: £3 a year (£4 airmail outside Europe)

122 Wardour Street, London W.1. 01-734 5888

288

Britain

All visitors to London should purchase *What's On in London* (price 1s.6d.), the weekly magazine that gives up-to-the-minute details of programmes at the cinemas described below.

✻✻✻✻   **ACADEMY CINEMAS, Oxford St, London W.1.** Three impeccable cinemas under one roof, each with its own distinctive atmosphere, each showing either a brand new film or an exclusive revival from the past. A première at the Academy remains the highest compliment that a foreign director can be paid in Britain, and many films that could disappear after a week elsewhere do astonishingly well here: *Ulysses*, *The Round-Up*, *Elvira Madigan*, and *Mouchette* for example. Other interesting programmes this year have included *Rondo* and *My Way Home*. The policy of the Academy has not wavered for over twenty years, and owes its success to the proprietor, Mr. George Hoellering, and his colleague Ivo Jarosy.

✻✻✻✻   **CURZON CINEMA, Curzon St, London W.1.** This luxurious first-run cinema in the heart of Mayfair offers the last word in comfort and sophistication. The projection is exceptionally good, and the short films accompanying the main feature are always chosen with flair *(Au Fou* with *In Cold Blood*, *The Fly* with *Closely Observed Trains*, *You're Human Like the Rest of Them* with *Petulia)*. Unlike most British art cinemas, the Curzon often programmes English-language films when their quality warrants it. There are 542 seats (including two boxes) in the air-conditioned Curzon, and the décor is dominated by patterns of grey, setting off the attractive blue velvet of the armchairs.

✻✻✻✻   **CAMEO-POLY, Upper Regent St, London W.1.** Now under the aegis of the Classic group, the Cameo-Poly continues its policy of showing high-class foreign-language films on their première run in this country — *Happy Gypsies*, *Vivre pour vivre*, *The Hour of the Wolf*, *Kwaidan*, etc. Once again, shorts are carefully selected, and the central position of this cinema (only 2 minutes from Oxford Circus tube station) makes it a regular rendezvous for overseas visitors as well as English film enthusiasts. Other theatres in the group include the Cameo-Royal in Charing Cross Rd, and the Cameo-Victoria.

✻✻✻✻   **PARIS PULLMAN, Drayton Gardens, London S.W.10.** Under the new management of Contemporary Cinemas Ltd., this petite cinema in South Kensington has regained its reputation as one of the

Star rating: ✻✻✻✻ first-run cinema of international quality.
✻✻✻ excellent all-round programmes.
✻✻ high standard repertory programmes.
✻ above average.

National Film Theatre 01 928 3232

"The best film club in London" ALEXANDER WALKER
EVENING STANDARD

most offbeat of London's first-run houses. Not only are the films of a high standard *(Father, Mahanagar, Le Départ, Hugs and Kisses)* but the whole atmosphere radiates enthusiasm for the cinema. In the club at the rear there are film evenings, lively discussions with visiting film-makers like Renoir, Franju, Forman, and Passer, and morning previews for members. Any cinephile living in London should join this club, for in addition to its activities, it offers seats at reduced rates to members as well as a bar where drinks, coffee, books, and magazines are all on sale at reasonable prices. Late night shows every Saturday too.

✳ ✳ ✳   **THE EVERYMAN, Hollybush Vale, London N.W.3.** For close on 35 years the Hampstead Everyman has been a symbol of good cinema, a meeting place for enthusiasts from every part of London. Jim Fairfax-Jones has a wide-ranging taste, and a gift for linking together in seasons films barely screened after their West End première. Programmes change weekly, and among the most intriguing of 1967-68 have been a Polanski series, a quartet of classics from both Japan and India, and 5 controversial features by Godard. The Christmas programme is usually well worth catching (last year *The General* and *M. Hulot's Holiday* in a double-bill!) and the shorts are always of high calibre. Note that seats are bookable by telephone, and that performances start at 2, 4, 6, and 8 p.m. Exhibitions of paintings and drawings are on show regularly in the foyer.

✳

INSTITUT FRANÇAIS, 25 Queensberry Place, London S.W.7.
The French Institute in London (Queensberry Place, off Cromwell Rd.) runs an excellent "Ciné-Club" at 8 p.m. every Monday evening. Not only does this society screen many French films that are unavailable in commercial cinemas; it also invites the director concerned to speak about his film in some instances, and René Clair and René Clément have been among the guests in recent years. Membership of the Institute costs 4 guineas per annum, and is open to all (the fee includes other facilities, of course). There is also a vast film library of shorts and documentaries on hire.

✳ ✳ ✳ ✳
NATIONAL FILM THEATRE, South Bank, London S.E.1. With its range of seats from 5s. to 10s. (7s. and 10s. bookable by telephone), its small membership fee, and intimate clubroom and bar, the NFT has become the most vital cinema in London. It comes under the wing of the BFI, and its Controller, Leslie Hardcastle, is now realising new plans for increasing the Theatre's activities. The greatly varied programmes are divided into seasons — like the Godard retrospective, the highly successful Langdon week, and the tributes to Ustinov, Don Siegel, and Rouben Mamoulian. Quarterly booklets provide detailed information of the 600 or so films shown per year at the NFT, as well as details of lectures and discussions with international directors.

293

From

ALDEBURGH

to YORK

RFT*

are springing up all over!

---

* Regional Film Theatres, jointly sponsored by The British Film Institute and local authorities.

✳✳✳   **NEW CINEMA CLUB, 122 Wardour St, London W.1.** Derek Hill's Short Film Service has given birth to an outstanding enterprise, the New Cinema Club, which shows to members a sparkling collection of new films, even if (like Makavejev's *Love Dossier/The Switchboard Operator*) they have been banned by the censor, or, like Chytilová's *Something Different*, they have been ignored by commercial distributors. There are regular programmes of American underground cinema, and the quarterly booklets are well documented and informative. Most shows take place at Nash House, The Mall, S.W.1. but prospective members should telephone 01-734 5888 for details first. Annual membership only costs one guinea. Shorts, of course, are legion.

✳✳   **THE STARLIGHT CLUB, May Fair Hotel, London W.1.** John Hickey has been running this club for some 5 years, and has combined vintage Hollywood films with more recent, popular titles in order to please the diverse tastes of members, and, at the same time, to screen worthwhile programmes. The membership fee is two guineas a year or one guinea for 6 months. There is no admission charge to the cinema, which has two performances nightly, but drinks and sandwiches are on sale in the club bar. The work of great stars like Judy Garland, Bette Davis, and Spencer Tracy is very much welcomed here. The cinema itself is available for hire outside normal club hours at 5 guineas per hour.

✳✳   **THE CLASSICS (for addresses see Directory).** This rapidly expanding group now virtually constitutes a "third circuit" in Britain for the revival of quality films from America and the continent, but also for first-run seasons of specialised and popular titles. The Classics in London are the most famous, those at Baker St, Chelsea, and Notting Hill Gate being particularly good, and their activities are detailed in a monthly booklet. There are late night shows at some of the theatres, and at Chelsea and Notting Hill there are adjacent branches of Clare's confectionery shops, where fine hand-made chocolates are available. Individual managers work hard to give atmosphere and attraction to certain seasons, while one of the best *coups* achieved by the Classics in the past year has been the revival of several M-G-M classics of the thirties, not to mention an interesting Soviet season.

✳ ✳ ✳   **ARTS CINEMA, Market Passage, Cambridge.** Sustained by a faithful and constantly changing University audience, the Arts, founded in 1933 by Norman Higgins MBE, is one of the finest cinemas in Britain. Over the past year it has shown the following (among others) on their first run in Cambridge: *Un Homme et une Femme, Masculin Féminin, Chimes at Midnight, Persona, Tell Me Lies, La Marseillaise, Mouchette, My Way Home*, and *Belle de Jour*. The usual revivals have been shown on Sundays, and there was an Ingmar Bergman season during the Easter Term. Most of the new shorts available are included in the programmes. There are separate performances, for which all seats are bookable. Programme booklets are sent to subscribers at 3s.6d. per annum.

✳ ✳ ✳   **SCALA CINEMA, Walton St, Oxford.** As the double-bill dies a slow death in England, one learns to cherish those at the Scala more than anywhere else. No Scotland Yard second features for Mr. Eric Bowtell: instead, an intelligent pairing of continental films like *The Silence* and *Ballad of a Soldier*, or *La Règle du Jeu* and *The Eavesdropper*, or *The Round-Up* and *Le Deuxième Souffle*. The Scala is also the home of Oxford University Film Society. Programme leaflets are available on request, and they conveniently list the precise time of the close of the last performance. The best time to visit this excellent cinema is during Term, when the programmes cater for the student population.

✳ ✳   **THE CAMEO, Home St, Tollcross, Edinburgh.** This cinema, founded in 1949 by Mr. J.K.S. Poole, is the traditional venue for the film section of the Edinburgh Festival, and for the remainder of the year it maintains an admirable series of programmes, including continental productions but also a good many British and American successes. Especially popular this year have been *A Man for all Seasons, Fahrenheit 451, The Taming of the Shrew*, and the Olivier *Othello*. There is a licensed bar for patrons and admission prices are 5s.6d. and 6s.6d.

✳ ✳ ✳   **REGIONAL FILM THEATRES:** Over twenty Regional Film Theatres have been established in Britain during the last three years, with many more to come. They are sponsored jointly by the British Film Institute and local authorities, and present the best of the new (*Herostratus, Hugs and Kisses, Mouchette*) alongside exclusive revivals (*Pandora's Box* and the uncut *Eve*, comedies of Buster Keaton and Mauritz Stiller). In brief, they narrow the gap — of time and scope — between what can be seen in London and in the provinces. Extended tributes to such directors as Godard and Buñuel alternate with theme seasons — Garbo, Shakespeare on film, thrillers, Human Rights, and Eastern Europe. Short films of outstanding quality support most features and a shorts festival was held in eight theatres last October. Compilation programmes on opera and theatre, trains and canals, flying and mountaineering are regularly presented to large audiences, and educational schemes are steadily gaining ground. Most performances are open to the public, except at Bristol; however, members are numbered in their thousands and are able to attend special screenings of very old or very new films, many of which have never been passed for public exhibition.

No list of theatres can remain up-to-date for long, so rapid is the rate of growth; several that started part-time are likely soon to become full-timers. At the time of writing theatres are operating or about to open in the following towns and cities: Aldeburgh, Bradford, Basildon, Bristol, Colchester, Dartington, Edinburgh, Exeter, Malvern, Manchester, Middlesbrough, Newcastle-upon-Tyne, Newport, Norfolk & Norwich, Nottingham, Petworth, Prestatyn, St. Albans, St. Austell, Sheffield, Southampton, Street, York.

A New Approach to Art Cinemas in Britain

Under the name of Cinecenta, a new company has been formed to distribute and exhibit a wide selection of prestige films that cinemagoers rarely have a chance to see — and its first step is the building of a new nation-wide chain of cinemas. Each Cinecenta will be a complex of from 2 to 4 cinemas seating from 100 to 250 people each. (The design enables Cinecenta to offer many additional facilities to cinemagoers.) The first will open in London's West End (just off Leicester Square) by the beginning of 1969, and will contain 4 cinemas. It will be followed almost immediately by Cinecentas in Bradford, Sheffield, and Leicester. And negotiations are under way for another 9 sites throughout the country.

On the other front, Cinecenta begins distributing films this year too. Titles include *Les Biches, Ole Dole Doff* (Golden Bear at Berlin 1968), *Hugo and Josefin, Tu seras terriblement gentille, Engelchen, Mahlzeiten,* and *Tatowierung*. All these films, like the others in the initial batch of 18 to be handled by Cinecenta, have won numerous awards at festivals in recent months. Yet they were all bought prior to their winning prizes. An excellent start for an enterprising company.

France

★ ★ ★ ★   **LE BIARRITZ, 22 rue Quentin Bauchart, Paris 8.** Just off the Champs-Elysées (although there is an entrance to the cinema about halfway up this broad avenue), Le Biarritz is a U.G.C. first-run "salle", offering exceedingly comfortable seats at 9F and 10F each. A long line of important films have been given their French première here — *Viridiana, The Red Desert, Un Homme et une Femme,* and, more recently, *Les Biches* and *Je t'aime, je t'aime.* The screen at Le Biarritz is particularly vast.

A quelques pas derrière les Champs-Elysées (avec néanmoins une entrée vers le milieu de cette large avenue) le Biarritz est une salle U.G.C. de première exclusivité, offrant des places extrèmement confortables à 9F et 10F. De nombreux films importants ont donné leur première présentation française au Biarritz — VIRIDIANA, ELECTRE, LE DESERT ROUGE, UN HOMME ET UNE FEMME, et plus récemment, LES BICHES et JE T'AIME, JE T'AIME. L'écran du Biarritz est particulièrement vaste.

★ ★ ★ ★   **LE VENDÔME, 32 avenue de l'Opéra, Paris 2.** Only a few steps from the Opéra, Le Vendôme is a luxurious cinema screening new films in their original language. From the many successful first-run seasons at this world-famous cinema, one can cite titles such as *Miss Julie, Rashomon, The Medium, La Strada, Les Amants, Wild Strawberries, 8$^1/_2$, The Umbrellas of Cherbourg, Le Vieil Homme et l'Enfant,* and *In the Heat of the Night.*

Au centre de Paris, à quelques pas de l'Opéra, Le Vendôme, luxueuse salle d'exclusivité, projete tous ses films en version originale. Parmi les succès qui ont donné au Vendôme, depuis 1950, sa réputation mondiale, nous pouvons citer: MADEMOISELLE JULIE, LOS OLVIDADOS, RASHOMON, LE MEDIUM, LA STRADA, LES AMANTS, LES FRAISES SAUVAGES, L'AVVENTURA, HUIT ET DEMI, LES PARAPLUIES DE CHERBOURG, JULIETTE DES ESPRITS, FAHRENHEIT 451, PERSONA, LE VIEIL HOMME ET L'ENFANT, DANS LE CHALEUR DE LA NUIT.

★ ★ ★ ★   **STUDIO DES URSULINES, 10 rue des Ursulines, Paris 5.** The Ursulines cinema is internationally celebrated, cited by writers from Alexandre Arnoux to Cyril Connolly, and has a remarkable history. It began as a piano factory, then became a theatre; and finally a cinema — the first art cinema in the world — in January 1926. The Ursulines was founded by the late Armand Tallier, first President of the CICAE. Madame Peillon, the present director, continues the good work. Few art cinemas radiate such sheer love of films and pride in their past. The Ursulines is, of course, a first-run theatre.

LE RACINE

Un des plus jeunes cinémas
dans la plus vieille rue de Paris

6 rue de l'Ecole de Médecine, Paris 6e. Tel: MED 4371

Le Studio des Ursulines, de réputation mondiale, et cité par des écrivains tels qu'Alexandre Arnoux et Cyril Connolly, a une histoire remarquable. Il a débuté comme usine de pianos, pour devenir théâtre et enfin en janvier 1926 cinéma, le premier cinéma d'art et d'essai au monde. Le Studio des Ursulines fut lancé par feu Armand Tallier, premier Président de la CICAE. À sa mémoire un prix annuel est décerné au meilleur livre sur le cinéma. Madame Peillon, l'actuelle directrice, a donné à la salle un décor nouveau et charmant dans les tons crème, or et brun, avec fauteuils bleu clair. Il y a peu de cinémas d'où rayonne un amour aussi authentique pour les films et une telle fierté de leur passé.

✳✳✳✳ **LE RACINE, 6 rue de l'Ecole de Médecine, Paris 6.** Although it was at the geographical focus of the student riots earlier this year, Le Racine is still one of the most attractive and imaginative cinemas in Paris. On Fridays and Saturdays there are midnight matinées of horror films under the title "Sadistically yours", and when *Le Mur* was screened Jean-Paul Sartre joined in discussions with the audience. Then Keaton's *The Cameraman* was revived here, while difficult new films like *10,000 Suns*, *Terre en Transe*, and *Anita G.* were premiered.

STUDIO GIT-LE-CŒUR

un des plus jeunes cinémas de Paris

12 RUE GIT-LE-COEUR — PARIS VI

TEL. 326-80-25   METRO: SAINT-MICHEL

Bien que situé au centre géographique des émeutes estudiantines il y a quelque temps, le Racine reste l'un des cinémas de Paris les plus attrayants et imaginatifs. Les vendredi et samedi, on y passe, à minuit, des films d'horreur, portant par exemple le titre de "Sadiquement vôtre". Lorsqu'on y projeta LE MUR, Jean-Paul Sartre lui-même se joignit aux discussions engagées avec le public. Après cela, on y reprit LE CAMERAMAN de Keaton, tandis que de nouveaux films difficiles, comme 10.000 SOLEILS, TERRE EN TRANSE et ANITA G. étaient montrés en première exclusivité.

✳✳✳   **STUDIO GIT-LE COEUR, 12 rue Gît-le-Coeur, Paris 6.** Almost opposite the offices of our colleagues at "L'Avant-Scène", the Studio Git-le-Coeur opened less than two years ago with Rohmer's *La Collectionneuse*. But it is now firmly established as a first-run cinema of stature, and it pioneered the showing of American "underground" films in Paris. Unusual successes have included *Daisies*, Ivens's *The 17th Parallel*, and Christensen's *Witchcraft through the Ages*.

Presque en face des bureaux de nos collègues de "L'Avant-Scène" s'ouvrait, il y a moins de deux ans, le Studio Gît-le-Coeur, avec la présentation de LA COLLECTIONNEUSE de Rohmer. Maintenant, il est bien établi comme cinéma de taille passant les films en première. Il a d'ailleurs encouragé la représentation, à Paris, des films américains dits "souterrains". Parmi les succès inhabituels, on compte LES PETITES MARGUERITES, LE 17ÉME PARALLÈLE d'Ivens et LA SORCELLERIE À TRAVERS LES AGES de Christensen.

✳✳✳   **LE RANELAGH, 5 rue des Vignes, Paris 16.** Le Ranelagh is among the most enchanting of all art cinemas, its origins as a music room in the Château de Passy, and as an opera house, still being manifest in the oak panelling in Flemish Renaissance style. Monsieur Henri Ginet, who is also Secretary-General of CICAE, always has unusual ideas for his cinema. There are regular art exhibitions of quality at Le Ranelagh.

Le Ranelagh est parmi les plus ravissants de tous les cinémas d'art et d'essai. Les panneaux de chêne en style flamand de la renaissance témoignent de son origine comme salle d'opéra et de musique dans le château de Passy. Monsieur Henri Ginet, qui est, bien entendu, le secrétaire général de la CICAE, a toujours des idées inhabituelles pour son cinéma. Il y a souvent des expositions de qualité au Ranelagh.

✳✳✳   **STUDIO 28, 10 rue Tholozé, Paris 18.** What cinema outside Paris could claim to have shown art films for over 40 years? The Studio 28, praised by Jean Cocteau and others, has just celebrated its 40th

301

anniversary under the direction of the Roulleau family, and the policy continues. *Un Chien Andalou* and *L'Age d'Or* had their controversial premières here in the late twenties, and so did Gance's *Magirama* in the fifties. Now the Studio 28 is familiar to visitors to Montmartre for its repertory programmes. On to the 50th anniversary!

Quel cinéma en dehors de Paris pourrait revendiquer avoir mis à l'affiche des films d'art pendant plus de 40 ans? Le Studio 28, loué par Jean Cocteau et d'autres, vient de célébrer son 40ème anniversaire, sous la direction de la famille Roulleau, et la même ligne de conduite continue. UN CHIEN ANDALOU et L'AGE D'OR eurent, ici, des premières controversées dans les dernières années vingt; il en fut de même pour "Magirama" de Gance dans les années cinquante. A l'heure actuelle, les visiteurs de Montmartre connaissent le Studio 28 pour les programmes de son répertoire. Son 50ème anniversaire est en vue!

✳︎✳︎✳︎ **STUDIO 43, 43 rue du Fbg Montmartre, Paris 9.** In view of the increase of art cinemas in Paris, some degree of specialisation is necessary if a "salle" is to attract customers from all parts of the city. Studio 43 lays emphasis on the Eastern countries in its programmes, and the visitor is more than likely to find a Czech, Polish, Russian, Hungarian, Yugoslav, or Japanese film being screened. Under the title "Cinéma National Populaire", MM Rochman and Lichtiger have introduced *hommages* to the work of Roberto Rossellini and other radical directors.

Etant donné l'accroissement des cinémas d'art à Paris, un certain degré de spécialisation est nécessaire, si une salle veut attirer des clients de toutes les parties de la ville. Le Studio 43 met l'accent, dans ses programmes, sur les pays orientaux. Aussi, il est plus que probable que les visiteurs y voient un film tchèque, polonais, russe, hongrois, yougoslave ou japonais. Sous le titre "Cinéma National Populaire", MM. Rochman et Lichtiger ont rendu hommage à Roberto Rossellini et à d'autres réalisateurs, aux idées originales, pour leur oeuvre.

✳︎✳︎✳︎ **CINEMA DES CHAMPS-ELYSEES, 118 avenue des Champs-Elysées, Paris 8.** For year after year, this stalwart repertory cinema has catered for tourists, students and shoppers with its weekly revivals of film classics, at extraordinarily low prices too (2.50 F until 1.30 p.m., and 3.75 F thereafter): *Vie Privée, A Blonde in Love, Le Jour et l'Heure, Morgan* etc. Leaflets are issued giving details of programmes for two months ahead. Real enthusiasts should note that the first performance of the day starts at 10 a.m.

Pour des années et des années ce cinéma au répertoire vigoureux a fourni, chaque semaine, aux étudiants, aux touristes, et aux acheteurs, ses reprises de films classiques à un prix extraordinairement bas (2,50F, jusqu'à 13h.30, puis 3,75F ensuite): VIE PRIVEE, LES AMOURS D'UNE BLONDE, LE JOUR ET L'HEURE, MORGAN, etc. Des imprimés donnant les détails des programmes pour deux mois, paraissent régulièrement. Un avantage, disent de vrais enthousiastes, est que la première présentation est à 10h. du matin.

✳︎✳︎ **STUDIO LOGOS, 5 rue Champollion, Paris 5.** No street in the world has quite the same density of art cinemas as the narrow, steep rue Champollion, leading off the rue des Ecoles. Madame Villeneuve's Studio Logos is a comfortable haunt for the film enthusiast visiting Paris, and the stimulating programmes include films like Dreyer's *Vampyr, Drôle de Jeu*, the Greek picture *Jusqu'au Bateau*, and Jancsó's *Reds and Whites*. There are programmes every two hours from 2 p.m. onwards, and quality shorts are screened in place of advertising films or newsreels.

Dans la rue étroite et raide qui mène à la rue des Ecoles et qu'on nomme rue Champollion, les cinémas d'art et d'essai foisonnent comme nulle part ailleurs au monde. Le Studio Logos de Madame Villeneuve est un repaire accueillant pour le cinéphile de passage à Paris. Parmi ses programmes stimulants on pourrait citer VAMPYR de Dreyer, LES DESARROIS DE L'ELEVE TOERLESS, de Schlöndorff, et ROUGES ET BLANCS, de Jancsó, des films qui tiennent parfois l'affiche pendant des semaines. Programmes toutes les deux heures à partir de 14h. On remplace des films de réclame et les actualités par des courts métrages.

✶ ✶ **LE BONAPARTE, 76 rue Bonaparte, Paris 6.** Opposite Saint-Sulpice and close to Saint-Germain-des-Prés, this cinema enjoys a similar reputation to that of Le Vendôme. There is a special tariff for students, and among films screened recently have been *My Sister My Love*, *Ulysses*, and *I Am Curious*, all in their original version of course.

En face de Saint-Sulpice, tout près de Saint-Germain-des-Prés, cette salle a une réputation qui s'apparente à celle du Vendome. Un tarif spécial est consenti aux étudiants. Parmi les dernières oeuvres présentées: JEUX DE NUIT, MADE IN USA, ULYSSES, et JE SUIS CURIEUSE. Tous ces films en version originale.

Les **3** Luxembourg

Trois nouvelles salles d'art et d'essai

67 rue Monsieur-le-Prince (angle bd. St-Michel) Paris 6.

Tél. MED 97-77.

——————— *Sous la même direction* ———————

DOMINIQUE   STUDIO 43

Cinémas d'art et d'essai

99 rue St. Dominique Paris VII. Tél: INV 0455.   **43 rue du Faubourg Montmartre Paris IX.** Tél: PRO 6340.

✳✳   **STUDIO SAINT-SEVERIN, 12 rue Saint-Séverin, Paris 5.** Now firmly established in the front rank of Left Bank cinemas, Le Saint-Séverin both launches new films and revives classics (such as the James Whale-Elsa Lanchester *Bride of Frankenstein*). Seats cost 8F, with a reduced rate for bona-fide students. Our recommendation.

Le Saint-Séverin se trouve maintenant fermement établi au premier rang des cinémas de la Rive Gauche. Il lance des nouveautés et des reprises de films classiques (tels que BRIDE OF FRANKENSTEIN de James Whale, avec Elsa Lanchester). Places à 8F, tarif réduit pour les étudiants.

✳✳   **LES 3 LUXEMBOURG, 67 rue Monsieur le Prince, Paris 6.** This astounding complex of three art cinemas, built one upon another, is a welcome arrival on the Paris film scene. Air conditioned, and with luxury seating, all three auditoriums offer revivals and first-run films at reasonable prices. Closed circuit television in the foyer shows extracts from the films being played, and publicity shorts and "confectionery intervals" are deliberately avoided by MM Rochman and Lichtiger. Space prevents us from listing more than a handful of the different programmes that have distinguished "Les 3 Luxembourg" since their inauguration in December 1966. But *Vera Cruz, Genevieve, Two-faced Woman* and *Force of Evil* should be sufficient to whet the appetite.

Cet étonnant complexe de trois cinémas d'art et d'essai bâtis l'un sur l'autre est un nouveau-venu sur la scène du Paris-Cinéma qu'on est très heureux d'accueillir. Chacune des trois salles a l'air-conditionné et des sièges luxueux. Une télévision en circuit fermé montre au foyer des extraits des films en train de passer à l'écran. MM Rochman et Lichtiger évitent exprès films publicitaires et entr'actes avec vente de bonbons. La mention de VERA CRUZ, GENEVIEVE, LES SANS-ESPOIRS, et FORCE OF EVIL devraient suffir à nous allécher.

✳✳   **STUDIO RASPAIL, 216 Bd Raspail, Paris 14.** This is an intimate little cinema, halfway down the Boulevard Raspail, in the very centre of Montparnasse. The programmes are aimed at a mainly student audience and consist of revivals of classic films and recent pictures of quality, all shown in their original version. Performances begin at 9 p.m. every weekday evening, and are continuous on Saturday and Sunday.

Salle intime de 250 places, située au coeur du Montparnasse, sur le Boulevard Raspail, le Studio Raspail présente à sa clientèle, composée au majorité d'étudiants, des films d'avant-garde et certaines ré-éditions de films de qualité, comme JEUX INTERDITS. Tous les films sont présentés au version originale. Le spectacle est permanent et un tarif spécial est consenti aux étudiants.

✳✳   **LE CASINO SAINT-MARTIN, 48 Fbg Saint-Martin, Paris 10.** Monsieur Hatchuel and his wife continue to offer a repertory programme at this cinema that for sheer quality can compare with any in the city. The Casino Saint-Martin was originally a theatre, where singers and dancers would congregate. Revivals this season have included *491*, *Le Viol*, *O Salto*, *Giulietta degli Spiriti*, *A Bout de Souffle*, *I Am Curious*, *Prima della Rivoluzione*, and *The Seventh Seal*.

Monsieur Hatchuel et sa femme continuent à offrir, à ce cinéma, un répertoire de programmes qui, pour sa réelle qualité, peut se mesurer avec tout autre de la ville. Le Casino Saint-Martin était, à l'origine, un théâtre où se réunissaient des chanteurs et des danseurs: Cette saison compte, parmi les reprises, 491, LE VIOL, O SALTO, JULIETTE DES ESPRITS, A BOUT DE SOUFFLE, JE SUIS CURIEUSE, PRIMA DELLA RIVOLUZIONE et LE SEPTIÈME SCEAU.

✳✳   **STUDIO VAL DE GRACE, 30 rue Henri Barbusse, Paris 5.** Towards the southern end of the student quarter, the Val de Grâce is a repertory cinema that often manages to revive an unusual title like *Cry the Beloved Country*, *Man of Aran*, or *Sunset Boulevard*. Other successes during the 1967-68 season comprise *The Man who Shot Liberty Valance*, *The War Game*, *La Prise de Pouvoir par Louis XIV*, and *Chimes at Midnight*. Prices of admission, including weekends, are 5F and 4.25F for students and ciné-club members. Note that the Val de Grâce opens at 6 p.m., but that it is closed on Tuesdays.

Situé dans la partie sud du quartier latin, la Val de Grâce est un cinéma de reprise qui réussit souvent à faire revivre un titre inhabituel comme CRY THE BELOVED COUNTRY, MAN OF ARAN ou SUNSET BOULEVARD. Les autres succès de la saison 1967-68 comprennent L'HOMME QUI TUA LIBERTY VALANCE, THE WAR GAME, LA PRISE DE POUVOIR PAR LOUIS XIV et FALSTAFF. Le prix des entrées, le week-end y compris, est de 5F, 4,25 F pour les étudiants et membres des ciné-clubs. Notez que le Val de Grâce ouvre à 18 heures, mais qu'il est fermé le mardi.

✳✳   **STUDIO BERTRAND, 29 rue Bertrand, Paris 7.** Now that Monsieur J.-L. Cheray, one of the founder members of AFCAE, has joined Studio Bertrand, the double bills for which this cinema has long been known have taken on a new lease of enthusiasm. On Tuesday evenings there are discussion sessions and "Jeux de Questions" after the performance (and visitors will testify to the alertness of mind and stores of film knowledge required to survive at these meetings!). Recent programmes have coupled *Some Like it Hot* with *Julius Caesar*, and *Le Mani sulla Città* with *O Salto*.

        La double présentation pour laquelle ce cinéma a longtemps été renommé vient de connaître un renouveau d'enthousiasme depuis que Monsieur J-L. Cheray, un des fondateurs de l'AFCAE, s'est joint au Studio Bertrand. Les mardis soirs il y a des discussions et des "Jeux de Questions" après la séance (et les visiteurs pourront témoigner de la vivacité d'esprit et des connaissances en films nécessaires pour survivre à ces réunions). Parmi les excellents programmes des mois derniers on a pu voir: L'INVASION DES PROFANATEURS DE SÉPULTURES avec LA BATAILLE DE LA VALLEE DU DIABLE, CERTAINS L'AIMENT CHAUD avec JULES CESAR, et MAINS BASSES SUR LA VILLE avec O SALTO.

✳✳   **LA PAGODE, 57 rue de Babylone, Paris 7.** Madame Terme was well known for the cartoon programmes she arranged at the Studio Universel some years ago. Now she directs La Pagode, that most unusual and atmospheric of Paris cinemas, built as an exact facsimile of a Japanese pagoda. Only films of considerable quality are shown here, titles such as *Shakespeare-Wallah*, *Barrier*, and *Voyage Surprise*. Madame Terme will also introduce programmes of animation whenever possible. Performances are continuous from 2 p.m. until midnight.

        Il y a quelques années, Madame Terme s'était fait un certain renom pour les programmes de dessins animés qu'elle établissait au Studio Universel. A présent, elle dirige la Pagode, le plus inattendu des cinémas de Paris, avec énormément d'ambiance, qui est construit à l'image d'une pagode japonaise. Seuls les films de bonne qualité y sont montrés, avec des titres tels que SHAKESPEARE-WALLAH, BARRIÈRE et VOYAGE SURPRISE. Madame Terme introduira également des programmes d'animation, lorsque ce sera possible. Les séances sont permanentes à partir de 14 heures jusque minuit.

✳   **ARC-EN-CIEL, 154 rue Saint-Charles, Paris 15.** In a comparatively short time Monsieur Charles Bakouche (now assisted by Monsieur Philippe Joyeux) has raised the prestige of the Arc-en-Ciel, midway down the rue Saint-Charles and accessible on the Métro

307

direct from Odéon. Comfort and quality are the watchwords of this cinema, and one senses the enthusiasm at each evening performance. Leaflets with full details of every films are offered to patrons; there is a requests and "comments" book in the foyer; much care is devoted to the choice of shorts to complete a programme.

Dans un temps relativement court Monsieur Charles Bakouche (maintenant assisté par Monsieur Philippe Joyeux) a élevé le prestige de l'Arc-en-Ciel, à mi-chemin dans la rue Saint-Charles et accessible par le métro directement de l'Odéon. Confort et qualité sont les mots d'ordre de ce cinéma et on sent l'enthousiasme à chaque projection. Des imprimés avec tous les détails concernant chaque film sont offerts aux habitués de la salle. Il y a un livre de requêtes et de critiques au foyer; le choix des courts métrages, pour complèter un programme, est fait avec beaucoup d'attention.

Germany

✷✷✷   **ALLEGRO FILMBUHNE, Bismarckstr. 69, Berlin-Steglitz.**
Although it is situated to the south of the city centre, the Allegro
maintains an excellent reputation for Berlin premières. The management issues approximately 20,000 programmes every month. Visitors
should note that buses A2, A25, A68, A75, A76, A81, and A83 all
pass by, or nearby, the Allegro, and that the nearest S-Bahn station
is Feuerbachstrasse. The Adria Filmbühne, not far away at Schlossstr. 48, is good for revivals.

*Trotzdem es südlich vom Stadtzentrum gelegen ist, hält das Allegro
seinen ausgezeichneten Ruf für Berliner Premieren. Die Geschäftsleitung druckt monatlich ungefähr 20,000 Programme. Besucher sollten
notieren, dass die Busse A2, A25, A68, A75, A81, und A83 alle direkt
am oder nahe dem Allegro vorbeifahren. Die nächste S-Bahn Station ist
Feuerbachstrasse. Die Adria Filmbühne in der Nähe (Schlossstr. 48)
bringt Repertoire Filme.*

✷✷✷   **WOKI am Bahnhof, Bonn.** The Woki has been playing quality
films for nearly fifteen years, and attracts a high attendance from
Bonn University and from the diplomatic and civil service circles in
the city. Since January 1967 the Woki has become a repertory cinema,
changing its programme each evening (performances at 7.15 and
9.15 p.m.) Detailed leaflets are issued by Herr Zimmermann every
two months, and there are reduced prices for students. Most of the
films are screened in their original version.

*Das Woki zeigt nun schon fast seit 15 Jahren Filmkunst und zieht
seine Besucher von der Bonner Universität und aus Diplomatenkreisen.
Seit Januar 1967 ist Woki ein Repertoire-Kino mit täglichem Programm-
wechsel (Vorführungen um 19.15 und 21.15 Uhr). Ausführliche Pro-*

Oldest Association of Independent Art Houses

Geschäftsstelle:
68 Mannheim, Viktoriastr. 33. Tel. 44 o 86
Informationszentrale:
8 München 23, Unertlstr. 1. Tel. 33 1 o 86

grammhefte werden jeden zweiten Monat von Herrn Zimmermann herausgegeben. Für Studenten sind die Preise reduziert. Die meisten Filme werden in Ihren Originalfassungen gebracht und stammen von einem Dutzend verschiedener Länder. Eine besondere Empfehlung.

✳ ✳ ✳   **STUDIO FUR FILMKUNST, Occamstr. 8, Munich 23.** This cinema is situated in the student quarter (Schwabing) of Munich. It was founded in 1951 by Fritz Falter, Walter Talmon-Gros, and Werner Zurbuch (who is now responsible for preparing the programme leaflets). The Studio is virtually as active as the Cinémathèque Française or the National Film Theatre, and its management also screens rare films at the sister cinemas, Isabella and Türkendolch. This latter specialises in Westerns and thrillers. No visit to Munich would be complete without a glimpse of the Studio, however.

Das Studio für Filmkunst liegt direkt in Münchens Studentenviertel Schwabingen. Gegründet wurde es von Fritz Falter, Walter Talmon-Gros, und Werner Zurbuch (Letzterer ist verantwortlich für viele der Programme). Das Studio ist fast so aktiv wie die Cinémathèque Française oder das National Film Theatre. Ebenso zeigt die Geschäftsleitung seltene Filme in den Schwestertheatern Isabella oder dem Türkendolch, welcher speziell Westerns und Krimis bringt. Die Programmhefte, herausgegeben vom Studio, sind wohl die besten in Deutschland: ausführlich, regelmässig und begeistert.

✳ ✳ ✳   **ALSTER-LICHTSPIELE, Viktoriastr. 33, Mannheim.** Since it opened on December 20, 1948, with the original version of *The Red Shoes*, the Alster-Lichtspiele (under the direction of Dr. Bernhard Künzig) has been recognised as the leading art cinema in Mannheim. From 1951 until 1961 it was the venue of the Mannheim Film Festival, and it is closely associated with the "Alster-Abendstudio im City". Dr. Künzig is also President and Treasurer of the German Guild of Art Cinemas.

Seit ihrer Eröffnung am 20. Dezember 1948 mit der Originalfassung von THE RED SHOES haben sich die Alster-Lichtspiele unter der Leitung von Dr. Bernhard Künzig als das führende Filmkunsttheater an Mannheims eleganter Geschäftstrasse durchgesetzt. Von 1951 bis 1961 waren sie Schauplatz der Filmwoche Mannheim." Sie sind in Verbindung mit dem Alster-Abendstudio im City. Dr. Künzig ist ausserdem Präsident und Schatzmeister der Gilde deutscher Filmkunsttheater.

Alster-Lichtspiele

Mannheim

studio für filmkunst

Vorbildliche Filmkunst-Pflege seit 1948

Netherlands

✳ ✳ ✳   **DE UITKIJK, Prinsengracht 452, Amsterdam.** Mr. D. Vriesman, former President of the CICAE, has directed De Uitkijk in Amsterdam for over 27 years, and in fact the cinema is the oldest art house in the Netherlands, founded by Mannus Franken in 1928. Only films of the highest quality are shown here, and nearly all of them are new to the Netherlands when they appear. *A Funny Thing Happened on the Way to the Forum*, *What's New Pussycat?*, *Il Demonio*, and especially *Un Idiot à Paris* have been the principal successes of the 1967-68 season.

✳ ✳ ✳ ✳   **KRITERION** and **STUDIO K, Roetersstraat 34-36, Amsterdam.** This unusual pair of cinemas in the eastern part of Amsterdam are among the best in Holland at the moment. The auditorium of the large Kriterion is skilfully shaped so that all seats enjoy an ideal view of the screen. The leaf-green décor and upholstery give a serious tone to the cinema, and there is a coffee lounge in the foyer. Stairs at the side lead to Studio K, a small but extremely popular cinema directly above the Kriterion, where films of more sophisticated appeal are shown. The Kriterion group is entirely staffed by students as a result of the postwar establishment of "Stichting Onderlinge Studenten Steun", whereby those attending University can pay for their studies by working at the cinemas in their spare time.

✳ ✳ ✳ ✳   **LEIDSEPLEIN THEATER, Leidseplein 12, Amsterdam.** At the heart of the student quarter of Amsterdam, and only a stone's throw away from De Uitkijk (under the same management), the Leidseplein Theater has managed to build up an audience of its own since

☐ ☐

INTERNATIONAAL VERB. v. FILMKUNST THEATERS
AFDELING NEDERLAND

Secretariaat: Leidseplein 12, Amsterdam.
Tel. 24 76 06

☐ ☐

1958, and to present it with a series of excellent new films. These are screened in their original language, in an elegant auditorium holding 400 seats (all of which are reasonable in price and are bookable in advance). Performances begin regularly at 2,30, 7.15, and 9.30 p.m. Readers will notice the display of INTERNATIONAL FILM GUIDE and other film publications in the foyer!

* * * *　　**STUDIO 2000** and **DE UITKIJK, Churchillplein 7, The Hague.** In the magnificent new Congress Building, designed by the famous architect Oud, Mr. D. Vriesman has established two cinemas. One is really De Uitkijk, which was formerly in the Municipal Museum, but the other, Studio 2000, is a splendid addition to the ranks of Dutch cinemas. Before each performance, patterns of coloured light play harmoniously over the screen. Seats are in a tasteful grey, with ample leg-room. The décor as a whole is influenced by the paintings of Mondriaan. Both projectors are fully automatic, and there is also first-class 16mm equipment at Studio 2000. Among the first programmes were *A Man for all Seasons*, *Le Scandale*, and *The 10th Victim*.

In the smaller, no less attractive Uitkijk (which has already screened Makavejev's *Love Dossier*, Godard's *Made in USA*, and the Swedish *Stimulantia*), the auditorium is flanked by aisles where photographic and art exhibitions can be mounted. There is a bar

The sumptuous and restful décor of Studio 2000, on the outskirts of The Hague, Holland.

which serves both cinemas, and which has film magazines and books for sale. As the Congress Building is to the west of The Hague, on the way to Scheveningen, there are ample parking facilities. Further details can be obtained from N.V. Maatschappij voor Cinegrafie, Leidseplein 12, Amsterdam.

✳ ✳ ✳ **KRITERION, Westeinde 15, The Hague.** The Kriterion in this city was launched 17 years ago, as a branch of the non profit-making organisation, "Stichting Onderlinge Studenten Steun", whose guiding spirit is Mr. P. A. Meerburg. The formula is simple: good films *of their type*, whether they be gangster dramas or Bergman chamber cinema, are given fair coverage. The Kriterion has 225 seats at moderate prices.

✳ ✳ **STUDIO, Hereplein 73, Groningen.** Recently Groningen has developed into the cultural centre of the northern Netherlands, and the Studio cinema has played a useful role in promoting interest in fine films. Premières, late night performances on Fridays and Saturdays, and the local film society programmes, make up an interesting regular schedule. Screenings begin at 2.45, 7, and 9.15 p.m. daily, and there is an extra matinée on Sundays. Prices are reasonable.

DE AFSTAND TUSSEN U EN EEN FIJNE FILM IS NOOIT MEER DAN 50 KILOMETER

STUDIO UTRECHT ★ **STUDIO GRONINGEN** ★ **CAMERA TILBURG** ★ **STUDIO HAARLEM**

IF YOU CAN'T READ DUTCH, JUST REMEMBER THE NAMES OF THE CINEMAS

✷✷   **STUDIO, Grote Markt 25, Haarlem.** Bioscooponderneming A. F. Wolff, N.V., the organisation responsible for art cinemas in Utrecht, Tilburg, and Groningen, also arranges the programmes for the Studio in Haarlem. All films are presented in their original version with sub-titles, and include the best new productions from many countries. Performances commence at 2.15, 7, and 9.15 p.m., with an extra matinée on Sundays.

✷✷   **KRITERION, Stationsplein 45, Rotterdam.** Now 8 years old, the Kriterion in Rotterdam is perched high above the city. The box-office is downstairs, and lifts take patrons up to the auditorium, with its attractive cerise-coloured seats and its screen that draws apart to reveal an imposing view over Rotterdam. Performances start at 2.30, 7, and 9.30 p.m., with an extra matinée on Sundays. All features and shorts are projected in their original language with sub-titles.

✷✷   **'T VENSTER, Gouvernelaan 129, Rotterdam.** Since Mr. P. A. Meerburg assumed the direction of 't Venster in December 1965, the receipts have more than doubled, and the programmes have also improved enormously in quality. The cinema provides a much-needed second outlet for art films in Rotterdam, and it is often the centre for discussions and "teach-ins" on cinema topics.

✷✷   **CAMERA, Willem II-straat 29, Tilburg.** Like its *confrères*, Studio Utrecht and Studio Groningen, the Camera in Tilburg is an up-to-date art cinema whose programmes reflect the latest trends in the film world. Every September, the Camera holds an "International Film Week", which attracts much support and recognition. There are late night performances on Fridays and Saturdays, and an extra matinée each Sunday. Prices are modest.

✷✷✷✷   **STUDIO, Oude Gracht 154, Utrecht.** Standing beside the old canal in the centre of the ancient University town of Utrecht is the Studio art cinema, the venue for the 1968 "Cinemanifestatie, Première Nederland", an important festival organised by Huub Bals and better in many ways than more famous European events. One of the biggest successes at the Studio in 1968 has been the Makavejev film, *Love Dossier*, and the Studio is also good in promoting the new Dutch cinema, giving first-runs to local films that might otherwise not be shown properly. Write for details of the Studio to Bioscoop-onderneming A. F. Wolff N.V. at the above address.

Scandinavia

✳✳✳✳　　**PUCK, Sibyllegatan 26, Stockholm.** All films presented at Puck are premières for Sweden, and under the enthusiastic guidance of Wilmar Andersson (with Ragnar Erixon as head of Svensk Film-industri's import dept.), the programmes this year have included *Il Vangelo Secondo Matteo*, *The Round-Up*, *Don't Look Back* (the documentary on Bob Dylan by D. A. Pennebaker), and *Weekend*. There was also a remarkable Yugoslav Film Week, with several directors and stars present in Stockholm. There are late night shows on Saturdays (*Chappaqua*, *Judex*, *Mon Oncle*, *La Battaglia di Algeri*, *Le Caporal Epinglé*, etc.) Programme leaflets, in Swedish, are issued for each new film. Puck has 408 seats and its attendance figures reached over 60,000 between August 1967 and April 1968.

✳✳✳　　**SMULTRONSTÄLLET, Kungsgatan 31-33, Göteborg,** and **Gustav Adolfs Torg 45, Malmö.** These two "branches" of Puck enable the other major cities of Sweden to see the best of the new continental and American cinema (although a notable summer season at Göte-borg was devoted to the vintage American cinema), and programmes change usually once a week. All films are screened in their original versions with Swedish sub-titles. Times of evening performances at both cinemas are 7 and 9 p.m.

✳✳✳　　**GIMLE CINEMA, Bygdøy Alle 39, Oslo.** Situated in the West End of the city, the Gimle is Norways' principal art cinema, known as the venue of film festivals, international film weeks, and for pre-mière runs of new foreign films, which are all shown in their original version. Titles screened this year include *Ulysses*, *The Round-Up*, *Abschied von gestern*, *Une Femme est une Femme*, *Closely Observed Trains*, *Persona*, *Es*, *La Fuga*, and *La Guerre est Finie*. Performances start daily at 5, 7, and 9 p.m.

✳✳　　**CARL JOHAN TEATRET, Karl Johansgt. 39, Oslo.** This cinema is also part of the Oslo municipal film enterprise, but it is basically a repertory ("Kavalkaden") theatre. Programmes change twice a week, and there are two films shown alternately each evening. Among the more significant revivals this season have been *Rope*, *Eve*, *Kattorna*,

Marie Walewska, *The Fifth Rider is Fear*, and *So Close to Life*. There is a bar for light refreshments, and copies of the quarterly brochure listing the "Kavalkaden" can be obtained from Oslo Cinemas, Stortingsgaten 16, Oslo.

✶✶✶ **REPRISETEATRET, Øverødvej 12, Denmark.** Although it is half an hour's ride by train from the centre of Copenhagen, the Repriseteatret has become known and respected all over Denmark. Ulrik Uhrskov's formula for success springs from his own enthusiasm, his imaginative selection of films, and inventive exhibition techniques. Coffee and film books are on sale in the foyer; magazines are provided free for consultation; and the interior is immaculately decorated, with paintings hung along the inside walls. A recent innovation has been the screening of silent films with piano accompaniment, works like *The Black Dream*, starring Asta Neilsen, Clair's *An Italian Straw Hat*, and Benjamin Christensen's *The Evil X* and *Haemnens Nat*.

✶✶✶ **CAMERA, Sønder Boulevard 81, Copenhagen.** Peter Refn, also a film director, has now firmly established the Camera as both art cinema and specialised distribution company. There are 440 seats and projection is fully automatic. The programmes are extremely varied and always rewarding. Recent revivals and Danish premières have included *The Flim-Flam Man*, *Le Départ*, *A Fine Madness*, *Der junge Törless*, *Salvatore Giuliano*, *Le Journal d'un Curé de Campagne*, *Seven Samurai*, *The Maltese Falcon*, and even *Häxan*, Christensen's masterpiece of 1922. The Camera distributes some of these titles in Denmark, and Mr. Refn is always interested in adding to his repertory.

REPRISE THEATRE
Holte, Copenhagen
Cinema d'Art et d'Essai
Tlf. 42 00 09

✳ ✳ ✳   **PICCADILLY, Mühlebachstr. 2, Zurich 8.** The Piccadilly Cinema was opened in 1927 and has had a faithful student audience right to the present day. Until 1949 it was a high-class repertory cinema and since 1950 it has screened new films from England, Sweden, Japan, and the U.S.A. It has presented the great English comedies with Alec Guinness etc., the major Bergman films, and the best pictures from Japanese directors. The owner and directress, Frau Dr. Erika Kaestlin, plays only carefully-selected films, which please her personally, so that the Piccadilly has maintained a consistently high level of programmes these past 17 years. During 1967-68 the cinema screened *Accident, Persona, Georgy Girl*, and *Här har du ditt liv* among others.

Das Cinema Piccadilly wurde 1927 eröffnet und wandte sich von Anfang an an die Studenten, die ihm bis heute treu bleiben. 1931 auf Tonfilm umgestellt, pflegte es bis 1949 vor allem gute Reprisen, um von 1950 an als Boudoir-Theater umgebaut, sich dem künstlerischen Film aus England, Schweden, U.S.A., und Japan zu widmen. Es zeigte die grossen englischen Komödien mit Alec Guinness etc., alle Bergman Filme und die grossen japanischen Filme. Die Besitzerin und Leiterin, Frau Dr. Erika Kaestlin, spielt nur einzeln ausgewählte Filme, die ihr persönlich gefallen und ein überaus gepflegtes Publikum folgt treu ihrem Geschmack, sodass das Cinema Piccadilly seit 17 Jahren ein konsequent hohes Programm-Niveau führte. Neben Premieren wurden gegentlich klassische Reprisen vorgeführt. Für 1967/8 hatte das Piccadilly folgende Filme programmiert: ACCIDENT, PERSONA, GEORGY GIRL, HIER IST DEIN LEBEN.

Cinema Piccadilly

Mühlebachstr. 2, Zürich 8

Tel. 32-81-30　　　　*15h./17h./19h./21h.*

"Das gepflegte Kunstfilmtheater in dem jeder Regisseur, der künstlerische Filme schafft, ein Heim findet."

✳✳✳ **CINÉ BELLEVUE, Bellevueplatz, Zürich.** For several years the Ciné Bellevue has been known to Zürich residents for its excellent film programmes. It is one of the oldest theatres in this largest Swiss city, and was completely refurbished in 1966. Programmes now consist almost exclusively of première runs of major films. In the summer months there are outstanding seasons of genre-films (Westerns, for instance). There are special performances for children, and the major programmes take place at 7 p.m. Monday to Friday, when new and old classics are screened.

Das Ciné Bellevue gehört seit einigen Jahren zu jenen Züricher Lichtspieltheatern, die ein besonders ausgewähltes Programm für den Studiofilm-Freund spielen. Als eines der ältesten Kinos der grössten schweizer Stadt überhaupt, wurde das Bellevue 1966 vollständig umgebaut. Der Spielplan ist jetzt vor allem auf Premièren grosser, internationaler Meisterfilme ausgerichtet. In den Sommermonaten werden besondere Zyklen (Western-Filme etc.) gezeigt. Auch dieses Jahr zeigt das Ciné Bellevue wiederum ein Programm mit international berühmten Filmen. Ebenso werden die beliebten Kindervorstellungen weitergepflegt. Montag — Freitag, jeweils 19,00 Uhr, sind im "Sonderprogramm" ausgewählte, neue und alte Spitzenfilme zu sehen.

✳✳✳ **MASCOTTE, nr. Railway Station, Basel** is one of two art cinemas in Basel. Apart from a few first-class reissues during summer, the cinema shows mainly interesting studio films for a discriminating audience. *Masculin-Féminin, Ulysses, Kuckucksjahre, Falstaff, Trans-Europ-Express,* and *Tätowierung* have been screened these past few months. The Mascotte always shows an interesting cartoon in place of the conventional newsreel. In co-operation with the Royal Cinema (owned by the same company), the Mascotte organises each summer a programme of successful revivals. It is just near the railway station in Basel.

Das Ciné Mascotte ist eines der beiden Filmkunsttheatern Basels. Das Theater zeigt nebst einigen wenigen erstklassigen Reprisen (im Sommer in Form von Zyklen) vor allem gute und interessante Studiofilme für ein anspruchsvolleres, aufgeschlossenes Publikum. Das Programm der letzten Monate umfasste unter anderem folgende Filme: GEORGY GIRL, ULYSSES, TÄTOWIERUNG, KUCKUCKS-

Bellevueplatz Zurich
Tel. No. (051) 32'25'45

Cinéma **bio**
Neuchâtel
Faubourg du Lac 27

Mascotte Cinéma
d'art et d'essai

Basel near Railway Station SBB
Tel. (061) 24'64'62

JAHRE, MASCULIN-FEMININ, FALSTAFF, TRANS-EUROP-EXPRESS ... Als besondere Attraktion zeigt das Mascotte anstelle der üblichen Wochenschau jeweils einen interessanten Zeichentrick-Film. Zusammen mit dem der gleichen Gesellschaft gehörenden Cinema Royal organisiert das Mascotte jeden Sommer einen Zyklus mit erfolgreichen Reprisen. Der von den beiden Verleihfirmen Columbus-Film KG und Rialto-Film AG im Mascotte begonnene Zyklus "Filme für Film Freunde" wird im Herbst 1968 unter dem Patronat der Basler Filmkritiker, der Studentenschaft und anderer Organisationen täglich (Montag bis Freitag 19.00 Uhr) im Cinema Royal weitergeführt.

✳✳✳   **CINÉMA DU BOURG, 51 rue du Bourg, Lausanne.** Visitors to Lausanne will know the best shopping street in the town, the rue du Bourg. Here Monsieur Walter Beck runs one of the best art cinemas in Switzerland, and among its recent programmes have been *Persona*, *Accident*, *Face to Face*, *Cul-de-Sac, The Face*, *Morgan*, and *My Sister My Love*. The Bourg is fully air-conditioned, and one of the four daily performances begins usefully at 7 p.m.

Les visiteurs à Lausanne doivent connaître la rue du Bourg, où se trouvent les meilleurs magasins de la ville, et devraient noter que le meilleur cinéma d'art et d'essai du Vaud est située en haut de la butte. Depuis l'année dernière on y a passé LES AMOURS D'UNE BLONDE, CUL-DE-SAC, LE VISAGE, MORGAN, FACE A FACE, PERSONA, ACCIDENT, et MA SOEUR, MON AMOUR. Parmi les films à passer à présent ou prochainement, LES CENDRES de Wajda, ROUGE ET BLANC de Jancsó, L'ÉTÉ CAPRICIEUX de Menzel, et plusieurs reprises excellentes. Le Bourg a l'air conditionné, et Monsieur Beck en a établi la renommée, et la clientèle pendant ces dernières années. Une des séances de chaque jour commence à propos à 19h.

✳ ✳ ✳   **CINÉMA BIO, Faubourg du Lac 27, Neuchâtel.** Michel Schwob has established a splendid art cinema in one of western Switzerland's most secluded and attractive towns, Neuchâtel. During 1968 he has screened a selection of new films including *A Ciascuno il Suo, Happy Gipsies, Hunger, La Chinoise, La Mariée était en noir, I Am Curious* (a 5 week run and then banned by the authorities!), *Le Viol, The Whisperers*, and revivals of Russian classics such as *Mother Ivan's Childhood* and *Quiet Flows the Don*. Prices start at 2,50 Swiss francs per seat. On weekdays there are performances at 6.40 p.m. and about 8.30 p.m. with slightly different times at weekends.

Michel Schwob a créé un splendide cinéma d'art dans une des villes de Suisse les plus écartées et les plus jolies, à savoir Neuchâtel. Au cours de 1968, il y a mis à l'écran toute une sélection de nouveaux films, dont les suivants: TO EACH HIS OWN, HAPPY GIPSIES, HUNGER, LA CHINOISE, LA MARIÉE ÉTAIT EN NOIR, I AM CURIOUS, LE VIOL, THE WHISPERERS; il y a aussi fait revivre des classiques soviétiques, tels que Schors, La Mère, L'Enfance d'Ivan et L'Histoire du Don. Le prix des places est de 2,50 francs suisses et plus. En semaine, il y a une séance à 18.40 heures et une autre à environ 20.30 heures; ces heures varient légèrement le week-end.

✳ ✳ ✳   **L'ÉCRAN, 6 rue Bartholoni, Geneva.** Four programmes daily are held at this specialised cinema in the students' quarter of Geneva, and all films are screened in their original version with French subtitles. Foreign pictures of quality are sought eagerly by Monsieur Chasalle, who has been involved in the theatre and cinema world for close on half a century. He is interested to hear from foreign producers who would like their films marketed in Switzerland, and he is also the proprietor of another theatre, Ciné 17, in the Corraterie. *Woman of the Dunes* has been the major success of the past year.

Dans ce cinéma spécialisé, situé dans le quartier latin de Genève, on tient quatre programmes par jour et tous les films sont mis à l'écran dans leur version originale, avec sous-titres français. Les films étrangers de qualité sont fort recherchés par Monsieur Chasalle, qui s'occupe de théâtre et de cinéma depuis près d'un demi-siècle. Il s'intéresse notamment à ceux que les producteurs étrangers, invités à le contacter, voudraient lancer sur le marché suisse. Il est aussi propriétaire d'un autre cinéma, le Ciné 17, dans le Corraterie. LA FEMME DU SABLE a été le plus grand succès de la saison dernière.

U.S.A.

✶✶✶✶ **NEW YORKER THEATRE, 2409 Broadway, New York 10024.** During the past 8 years Daniel Talbot has launched over 30 new pictures at his cinema on Broadway, titles like *La Terra Trema, Boudu saved from drowning, Pickpocket, Gertrud, Mr. Arkadin, Echoes of Silence . . .* His basic policy is one of "total cinema" — embracing every conceivable category from early silents to current underground movies. In the past year, the emphasis has shifted more to neglected works like *Les Carabiniers.* The New Yorker has also run dozens of retrospectives (Griffith, Ford, von Sternberg, Belmondo, Fields, Rossen, etc.) Mr. Talbot relies heavily on his own idiosyncratic judgement, not on audience demands, and the cinema has proved an outstanding success, well worth visiting while in New York.

✳✳✳✳ **THE BIOGRAPH, 2819 M Street N.W., Washington.** Washington's newest and liveliest art house, The Biograph in Georgetown, was founded in 1967 by 5 young film buffs who converted a disused car salesroom into a 280-seat intimate theatre. The spacious, high-ceilinged lobby serves as a gallery for changing exhibitions of modern paintings, and a bulletin board displays film news clippings, and notices of cultural and political happenings. Lawyer-manager David Levy and his 4 partners have livened up the capital's film scene with imaginative programmes, including the local premières of 3 Godard features. First-run films alternate with double-bill revivals, and the cinema also extends a standing invitation to guest pianists to accompany their silent movie programmes.

Canada

✳✳✳ **VERDI, 5380 St. Lawrence Blvd, Montreal 14.** The Verdi is the first and only repertory cinema in Montreal. Roland Smith, the proprietor and programmer, has presented nearly 400 films (in double bills) since he opened the Verdi in December 1966. Works by American masters such as Hawks, Boetticher, Ray and Welles have been shown alongside films by Resnais, Truffaut, Renoir, Kurosawa, Eisenstein, and Bunuel. There have also been a few first runs *(El, Chafed Elbows, The War Game, Intimate Lighting* etc.), and a Week of Political Films was another exciting piece of initiative. The Verdi has the largest selection of film periodicals on sale anywhere in the city.

Cinema Directory

THIS LIST OF ART CINEMAS IS CAREFULLY REVISED EACH YEAR.
THOSE HOUSES MARKED WITH AN ASTERISK ARE MEMBERS OF
THE INTERNATIONAL CONFEDERATION OF ART CINEMAS.

AUSTRALIA
Savoy, Bligh Street, Sydney.

AUSTRIA
*Burg-Kino Opernring 19, Vienna.
Studio 1 ("Studio Avant"), Vienna.

BELGIUM
*Avenue, 4 Av. de la Toison d'Or, Brussels 5.
*High-Life, 35 Av. Louise, Brussels 6.
*Studio, 5 Av. de la Toison d'Or, Brussels 5.
*Vendôme, 35 Av. Louise, Brussels 6.

BRITAIN

ABERDEEN
Cosmo, 2 Diamond Street.
ALDEBURGH
National Film Theatre, Tel. 2347.
BATH, Somerset
Little Theatre.
BELFAST
Classic, College Square East.
BRADFORD
Classic, Manningham Lane.
BRIGHTON
Curzon, Western Rd.
BRISTOL
National Film Theatre, Tel. 45008.
CAMBRIDGE
Arts Cinema, Market Passage. Tel. 52001.
CHESTER
Classic, Foregate St. Tel. 21354.
COLCHESTER
National Film Theatre. Tel. 72939.
EASTBORNE
Classic, Seaside. Tel. 0323.20043.
EDINBURGH
Cameo, Home St., Tollcross. Tel. Fountain-
    bridge 6822.
EXETER
National Film Theatre. Tel. 77911.
GLASGOW
Classic, 15 Renfield St., C.2. Tel. Central 3400.

Cosmo, 12 Rose St., C.3. Tel. Douglas 7679.
Curzon Classic, 520 Sauchiehall St. Tel.
    Douglas 1298.
HATFIELD
Classic, St. Albans Rd. Tel. 456.2001.
LEICESTER
Classic, Baxter Gates, Loughborough.
LONDON
Academy Cinemas, 161-7 Oxford St., W.1. (Un-
    derground: Oxford Circus): **One** (Tel. GER
    2981), **Two** (Tel. GER 5129), and **Three**
    (separate performances) (Tel. GER 8819).
Cameo, 152 Victoria St., S.W.1. Tel. VIC
    6588. (Underground: Victoria).
Cameo-Poly, Oxford Circus, W.1. Tel. LAN
    1744. (Underground: Oxford Circus).
Classic, 96-98 Baker St., W.1. Tel. WEL 8836.
    (Underground: Baker St.).
Classic, 148-150 King's Road, Chelsea. Tel.
    FLA 4388. (Underground: Sloane Sq.).
Classic, Brighton Road, S. Croydon. Tel.
    688 6655.
Classic, Pond St., N.W.3. Tel. 794 4000. (Un-
    derground: Hampstead).
Classic, 405 High Road, N.W.6. Tel. 624
    6767. (Underground: Kilburn).
Classic, Notting Hill Gate, W.11. Tel. PAR
    5750. (Underground: Notting Hill Gate).
Classic, Piccadilly Circus. Tel. GER 2380. (Un-
    derground: Piccadilly Circus).
Classic, Stockwell. Tel. 274 2513. (Under-
    ground: Stockwell).
Curzon, Curzon St., Mayfair, W.1. Tel. GRO
    3737 (Underground: Green Park).
Everyman, Hollybush Vale, N.W.3. Tel. HAM
    1525. (Underground: Hampstead).
Globe, Upper Richmond Rd., S.W.15.
Institute of Contemporary Arts, Nash House,
    The Mall, S.W.1.
National Film Theatre (members only), South
    Bank, S.E.1. (Underground: Waterloo).
New Cinema Club, 122 Wardour St., W.1. Tel.
    734 5888.
Paris Pullman, Drayton Gardens, S.W.10. Tel.
    FRE 5898. (Underground: South Kensing-
    ton or Gloucester Rd.).

Starlight Club, May Fair Hotel, W.1. Tel. MAY 7777.
MALVERN
National Film Theatre. Tel. 3377.
MANCHESTER
Classic, Oxford Road Station. Tel. Central 6015.
National Film Theatre, 16 Oxford St. Tel. Central 0497.
MIDDLESBROUGH
National Film Theatre. Tel. 85181.
NEWCASTLE
People's Theatre Arts Centre/Tyneside Film Society (members only), Stephenson Rd. Heaton. Tel. 655020.
NEWPORT (Mon.)
National Film Theatre. Tel. 63670.
NORWICH
National Film Theatre. Tel. 26402.
NOTTINGHAM
Classic, Market St. Tel. 0602.44749.
National Film Theatre. Tel. 46094.
OXFORD
Scala, 58 Walton St., Tel. 54909.
PETWORTH
National Film Theatre. Tel. 2327.
READING
Glendale Cinema, Caversham.
SHEFFIELD, Yorks
Classic, Fitzalan Square. Tel. 25624.
National Film Theatre. Tel. 78771.
SOUTHAMPTON
Classic, 98 Above Bar.

CANADA
MONTREAL
*Verdi, 5380 St. Lawrence Blvd, Montreal 14.
QUEBEC
Le Studio, 9 rue Saint Louis.
TORONTO
Cinecity.

CORSICA
Empire Cinema, 30 cours Napoleon, Ajaccio.

DENMARK
COPENHAGEN
Alexander Teatret, Gammel Torv 8, Copenhagen K.
Camera, Sønder Blvd. 79-81, Copenhagen V. Tel. Central 5577.
HOLTE
*Reprise Teatret, Øverødvej 12. Tel. 42-00-09. (S-Train from Copenhagen).

FRANCE
ABBEVILLE
*Le Ponthieu, rue des Minimes.

AIGLE
*Aiglon, rue du Dr. Rouyer.
AIX-EN-PROVENCE
*Le Club, 21 rue Goyrand Prolongée.
AMIENS
*Le Club, 10 rue Ernest Cauvin.
ANGOULÊME
*Le Valois, 35 rue de Saintes. Tel. (45) 95.16.15.
ANNONAY
*Alhambra, 29 bis, rue Sadi Carnot.
ARBOIS
*Vox, 72 Grande Rue.
ASNIÈRES
*Alcazar, 1 rue de la Station, Tel. 473.02-13.
AUBERVILLIERS
*Théâtres de la Commune, rue E. Poisson.
AULNAY-SOUS-BOIS
*Le Prado, 26 rue J. Princet.
AUTUN
*Vox.
AUXERRE
*Casino, 1 Blvd. du 11 Novembre.
BEAUVAIS
*Le Paris, 6 rue Dobos.
BOIS COLOMBES
*California, 19 rue Raspail.
BOIS GUILLAUME
*Coucou, 154 rue du Champs des Oiseaux. Tel. (35) 71.54.09.
BORDEAUX
*Etoile-Palace, 133 Cours Victor Hugo.
*L'Intendance, 59 cours de l'Intendance. Tel. (56) 48.72.79.
*Victoria, 35 rue René Roy de Clotte. Tel. (56) 92.47.30.
BOUGIVAL
*Grenier, 7 rue du Mal Joffre.
BOULOGNE
*Pathé-Palace, 149-151 Bd. Jean-Jaurès.
BOURG-LA-REINE
*Regina, 3 rue René Roëckel.
BOURGOIN-JALLIEU
*Royal,5 rue de Charges.
BREST
*Theatre Comoedia, Place Wilson.
BRUNOY
*La Palace, rue de la République.
CAEN
*A.B.C., 56 rue de la Falaise. Tel. (31) 81.62.45.
Lux, Avenue Ste Thérèse.
CANNES
*Le Français, Traverse Marceau.
CARIGNAN
*Vox, Route de Blagny.
CHALON S/SAONE
*Le Paris, 1 rue Fructidor.
CHAMPIGNY
*Centre Cultural "Les Loisirs" 4 rue Proud'hon.

CHARENTON
*Le Celtic, 29 rue Gabriel Péri. Tel. 368.25.76.
CHARLEVILLE
*Le Palace, 19 cours A. Briand. Tel. (24) 22-30-88.
CHARTRES
*A.B.C., 10 Avenue Jean de Beauce.
*Majestic, 12 rue du Gal Patton.
CHATENAY
*Rex, 362 Avenue de la Div. Leclerc.
CLERMONT-FERRAND
*Ambiance, 7 rue St. Dominique.
*L'Essai, 16 rue Torrilhon. Tel. (73) 93.77.73.
*Le Mozart, 35 rue Blatin.
COMPIÈGNE
*Nouveau-Théâtre, 1 bis, place St. Jacques.
CONFLANS
*Palace, 5 rue Arnoult-Crapotte.
CORBEIL ESSONNES
*Eden, 29 rue de Paris.
COURBEVOIE
*Le Paris, 1 avenue Château du Loire. Tel. 333.33-59.
CRETEIL
*Le Courteline, 12 rue Monfray. Tel. 207.19-50.
DIJON
*Le Paris, 13 rue de la Liberté.
DINAN
*Familia, 27 rue Leconte-de-l'Isle.
ENGHIEN-LES-BAINS
*Hollywood, 21 rue du Gal de Gaulle. Tel. 964.05-94.
EVREUX
*Rex, 3-5 rue Saint Pierre.
FECAMP
*Palace, 36 rue Théagène Boufart.
GAP
*Le Club, rue Bon Hôtel.
GARCHES
*Select, 3 Avenue H. Bergson.
GENNEVILLIERS
*Maison pour Tous, 1 rue Pierre Curie.
GONESSE
*Théâtre La Fauconnière, Place Marc Sangnier.
GRENOBLE
*Apollo, 18 Blvd. Edouard Rey.
*Le Club, 9 bis rue du Phalanstère. Tel. (76) 44.53.24.
HOSSEGOR
*Bengali.
ISSY-LES-MOULINEAUX
*Casino du Parc, 9 avenue V.-Cresson.
IVRY
*Luxy, 77 rue Joseph Staline.
LA FLECHE
*Eden, 22 rue St. Jacques.
LAGNY
*Majestic, 26 rue du Chateau Fort.

LA ROCHELLE
*Rex, 12 rue Chef de Ville.
LAVAL
*Variétés, 14 rue Jules Ferry.
LAVAUR
*Rex, Allées Ferréol-Mazas.
LE BOURGET
*Aviatic, 26 rue de la Div. Leclerc.
LE HAVRE
*Le Grillon, rue Edouard Herriot.
*Normandy, 387 rue Aristide Briand.
LE MANS
*Eden, 21 rue Beauverger.
*Le Patis, 38 rue d'Eichtal. Tel. (43) 28.30.91.
LE RAINCY
*Le Sévigné, 20 Blvd. de l'Ouest. Tel. 927.25-71.
LE VESINET
*Le Médicis, 20 Avenue Galliéni. Tel. 966.18-15.
LILLE
*Bellevue, 17 pl. du Gal de Gaulle. Tel. (20) 54.72.93.
LIMOGES
*Lido, 1 bis avenue de la Gare. Tel. (55) 32.52.17.
LYON
*Aiglon, 2 rue Stella.
*Le Duo, 98 rue du Pt. Herriot. Tel. (78) 37.05.55.
MALAKOFF
*Palace, 2 place du 11 Novembre.
MANTES-LA-JOLIE
*Normandie, place de Lorraine.
MARSEILLE
*Festival, 26 quai du Port. Tel. (91) 20.28.77.
*Le Paris, 29 rue Francis Davso. Tel. (91) 33.15.59.
MEAUX
*Varietes, 16 place Henri IV. Tel. 934.11-28.
METZ
*Pax, 31 rue de Verdun. Tel. (87) 68.62.68.
MONDEVILLE
*Studio 14, Avenue Emile Zola.
MONTARGIS
*Alhambra, 56 place de la République.
MONTLHERY
*Casino, 18 rue de la Chapelle.
MONTMORENCY
*Eden, 1 bis Rue de Pontoise.
MONTPELLIER
*Lynx, Blvd. Victor Hugo. Tel. (67) 62.86.94.
*Royal, 13 rue Boussairolles. Tel. (67) 72.48.87.
MONTREUIL
*Normandy, 83 rue Victor Hugo.
MONTROUGE
*Palais des Fêtes, 93 avenue de la République.
MORANGIS
*Le Morangis, Avenue de la République.
MULHOUSE
*Corso, 55 rue du Sauvage. Tel. (89) 45.43.08.

MULHOUSE BOURTZWILLER
*Pax , 54 rue de Soultz.
LES MUREAUX
*Familia, 71 Avenue Paul Doumer.
NANCY
*Cameo, 16 rue de la Commanderie. Tel. (28) 53.35.68.
*Le 7ème Art , 63 rue Jeanne d'Arc.
NANTES
*Rex , 16 rue Racine.
*Versailles, 15 Quai de Versailles.
NEUFCHATEAU
*Scala, 3 rue de la Comédie.
NICE
*Ritz, 33 rue Masséna. Tel. (93) 88.66.43.
NOGENT S/MARNE
*Royal, 165 Grande Rue.
NOISY-LE-SEC
*Rialto, 109 rue de Paris.
ORLEANS
*Rio, 191 rue de Bourgogne.
OYONNAX
*Rex, 64 rue Anatole France.
PARIS
*Arc-en-Ciel, 154 rue St. Charles, Paris XVème. Tel. 828.94.47. (Métro: Ch-Michels or Lourmel).
*Arlequin, 76 rue de Rennes, Paris VIème. Tel. 548.62.25. (Métro: St.-Sulpice).
*Biarritz, 22 rue Quentin Bauchart, Paris 8ème. Tel. 359.42.33. (Métro: George-V).
*Le Bonaparte, 76 rue Bonaparte, Paris 6ème. Tel. 326.12.12. (Métro: St.-Sulpice).
*Calypso, 27 avenue des Ternes, Paris 17ème. Tel. 425.10.68 .(Métro: Ternes).
*Casino St.-Martin, 48 Fbg. St. Martin, Paris 10ème. Tel. 208.21.93. (Métro: Strasbourg St. Denis).
*Celtic, 5 rue d'Arras, Paris 5ème. Tel. 033.47. 62. (Métro: Cl-Lemoine).
*Champollion, 51 rue des Ecoles, Paris Vème. Tel. 033.51.60. (Métro: Odéon).
*Cinéma des Champs-Elysées, 118 avenue des Champs-Elysées, Paris 8ème. Tel. 359.61.70. (Métro: George-V).
Cinémathèque, Palais de Chaillot, angle des avenues A.-de-Mun and Président-Wilson, and Institut Pédagogique, 29 rue d'Ulm. Tel. 704.24.24.
*Cujas, 20 rue Cujas, Paris 5ème. Tel. 033.89.22. (Métro: Odéon).
*Dominique, 99 rue St. Dominique, Paris 7ème. Tel. 468.04.55. (Métro: Latour-Maubourg).
*Dragon, 24 rue du Dragon, Paris 6ème. Tel. 548.54.74. (Métro: St.-Germain-des-Prés).
*Hollywood, 4 rue Caumartin, Paris 9ème. Tel. 073.28.03. (Métro: Madeleine).
*Jean Renoir, 43 Bd de Clichy, Paris 9ème. Tel.

874.40.75. (Métro: Pigalle or Blanche).
*Luxembourg I, II and III, 67 rue Monsieur le Prince. Tel. Méd. 97.77. (Métro: Odéon).
*Le MacMahon, 5 avenue Mac Mahon, Paris 17ème. Tel. 380.24.81. (Métro: Etoile).
*Marais, 20 rue du Temple, Paris 4ème. Tel. 272.47.86. (Métro: Hôtel-de-Ville).
Le Mayfair, 90 avenue Paul Doumer, Paris 16ème. Tel. 523.36.40 (Métro: Muette.)
*Napoléon, 4 avenue de la Grande Armée, Paris 4ème. (Métro: Etoile).
*Les Noctambules, 7 rue Champollion, Paris 5ème. Tel. 033.42.34. (Métro: Odéon).
*La Pagode, 57 bis rue de Babylone, Paris 7ème. Tel. 468.12.15. (Métro: St. F. Xavier).
*Panthéon, 13 rue Victor Cousin, Paris 5ème. Tel. 033.15.04. (Métro: Odéon).
*Le Passy, 95 rue de Passy Paris 16ème. Tel. 288.62.34. (Métro: Muette).
*Publicis Elysees, 131 avenue des Champs-Elysées, Paris 8ème. Tel. 225.76.23. (Métro: Etoile).
*Publicis St.-Germain, pl. St. Germain, Paris 6ème. Tel. 222.72.80. (Métro: St. Germain-des-Prés).
*Quartier Latin, 9 rue Champollion, Paris 5ème. Tel. 326.84.65. (Métro: Saint-Michel).
*La Racine, 6 rue de l'Ecole de Médicine, Paris 6ème. Tel. 633.43.71. (Métro: Odéon or St. Michel).
*Le Ranelagh, 5 rue des Vignes, Paris 16ème. Tel. 288.64.44. (Métro: Muette or Passy).
*Les Reflets, 27 avenue des Ternes, Paris 17ème. Tel. 425.99.91. (Métro: Ternes).
*Septième Art, 9 rue de la Pépinière. Tél. 387.42. 90. (Métro: Saint-Lazare).
*Studio Acacias, 45 bis rue des Acacias — avenue MacMahon, Paris 17ème. Tel. 425.97.83. (Métro: Ternes or Etoile).
*Studio Action, 9 rue Buffault, 9ème.
*Studio Alpha, 25 rue de la Harpe, 5ème.
*Studio Bertrand, 29 rue Bertrand, Paris 7ème. Tel. 783.64.66. (Métro: Duroc).
*Studio du Dragon, 24 rue du Dragon, Paris 6ème. Tel. 548.54.74. (Métro: Sèvres-Baby-lone St.-Germain-des-Prés).
*Studio-Etoile, 14 rue Troyon, Paris 17ème. Tel. 380.18.93. (Métro: Etoile).
*Studio Git-le-Coeur, 12 rue Git-le-Coeur, Paris 6. Tel. 326.80.25. (Métro: St. Michel).
*Studio de la Harpe, rue de la Harpe, Paris. Tel. 033.34.83. (Métro: St. Michel).
*Studio Logos, 5 rue Champollion, Paris 5ème. Tel. 033.26.42. (Métro: Odéon).
*Studio Médicis, 3 rue Champollion, Paris 5ème Tel. 633. 25.97. (Métro: St. Michel).
*Studio Parnasse, 11 rue Jules Chaplain, Paris 6ème. Tel. 326. 58.00. (Métro: Vavin).

*Studio Raspail, 216 Blvd. Raspail, Paris 14ème. Tel. 326.38.98. (Métro: Vavin).
*Studio Saint-Germain, 53 rue de la Harpe, Paris 5ème. Tel. 033.42.72. (Métro: St-Michel or Odéon).
*Studio Saint-Lazare, 101 rue Saint-Lazare, Paris 9ème. Tel. 874.77.44. (Métro: Saint-Lazare).
*Studio Saint Séverin, 12 rue Saint Séverin, Paris 5ème. Tel. 033.50.91. (Métro: Saint-Michel).
*Studio du Val de Grâce, 30 rue Henri Barbusse, Paris 5ème. Tel. 326.03.36. (Métro: Port Royal).
*Studio 28, 10 rue Tholozé, Paris 18ème. Tel. 606.36.07. (Métro: Blanche or Abbesses).
*Studio 43, 43 rue du Faubourg-Montmartre, Paris 9ème. Tel. 770.63.40. (Métro: Montmartre).
*Théâtre de l'Est Parisien, 17 rue Malte-Brun, Paris 20ème. Tel. 636.79.09.
*Ursulines, 10 rue des Ursulines, Paris 5ème. Tel. 033.39.19. (Métro: Luxembourg).
*Le Vendôme, 32 Avenue de l'Opéra, Paris 2ème. Tel. 073.97.52. (Métro: Opéra).

PAVILLONS S/BOIS
*Gaîté, 58 Avenue Victor Hugo.
LE PERREUX
*Palais du Parc, 39 avenue Ledru Rollin.
POISSY
*Rex, 6 Bd de la Prix.
PONICHET
*Le Paris, Place du Mal. Foch.
PONTOISE
*Royal, 16 rue A. Prachay.
PRIVAS
*Le Royal, 9 Avenue de Chomirac.
PROVINS
*Rexy Cinéma, 11 rue du Ct Genneau.
PUTEAUX
*Lido, 35 rue Eichenberger. Tel. 506.03-35.
QUIMPER
*Cap Horn, 3 rue du Pt l'Abbé
LE RAINCY
*Sevigné, 20 Bd de l'Quest.
*Casino, I Rond Point de la Station.
REIMS
*Le Studio, 5-7 rue d'Ormesson.
RENNES
*Français, 5 rue Poulain-Duparc.
RETHEL
*Rex, 5 rue Marie-Feuillet.
REVIN
*Rex, rue Waldeck Rousseau.
ROANNE
*Le Zed, 80 rue Jean Jaurès. Tel. (77) 71.32.15.
ROUEN
*Studio 34, 75 rue du Gal Leclerc.

REUIL-MALMAISON
*Imperator, 99 avenue Paul Doumer. Tel. 967.25-00.
*Malmaison, Lot. no. 32, rue d'Estiennes d'Orves. Tel. 967.00-81.
RUMILLY
*Rex, Grande Rue.
SAINT-CLOUD
*Le Régent, 11 rue Gaston Latouche.
ST. ETIENNE
*Lux, 6 Place de l'Hôtel de Ville.
STE GENEVIEVE DES B.
*Le Perray, 44 avenue Gabriel Péri.
ST. FARGEAU PONTHIERRY
*A.B.C., 10 avenue A. Beaufils.
SAINT GERMAIN
*Majestic, 1 rue de Pologne.
ST. MANDE
*Rexy, 19 Avenue Joffre.
SAINT-MAUR
*Eden, 116 Blvd. de Champigny.
*Horloge, 2 av. du Général LeClerc.
SAINT NAZAIRE
*Trianon, 8 avenue de la Republique. Tel. (40) 70.04.79.
SARCELLES-LOCHERES
*Ravel, Blvd. Maurice Ravel. Tel. 21-77.
SAUMUR
*Le Palace, 13 Quai Carnot.
SAVERNE
*Lux, 35 Grande Rue.
SAVIGNY S/ORGE
*Excelsior, 78 Avenue Roger Salendro.
SCEAUX
*Trianon, 3 rue Marguerite Renaudin. Tel. 702.20-52.
SEDAN
*L'Excelsior, 13 bis avenue de Verdun.
SENLIS
*Le Valois, 5 bis rue de Beauvais.
SETE
*Rio, 7 Quai Noël Guignon.
STRASBOURG
*Studio Kléber, 31 Place Kléber.
STRASBOURG-NEUDORF
*Lido, 60 rue du Polygone. Tel. (89) 34.06.77.
TALENCE
*Idéal-Ciné, Place de l'Eglise.
TOULON
*Comœdia, 10-12 place Orves, Le Mourillon.
*Le Grillon, 3 rue d'Antrechaus.
TOULOUSE
*A.B.C., 13 rue Saint Bernard.
*Le Paris, 7 rue Lapeyrouse.
TOURS
*Mexico, 24-26 Bd Thiers.
*Studio des Ursulines, 2 rue des Ursulines.

VAUCRESSON
*Normandy, 72 Bd de la République.
VERSAILLES
*La Tannerie, 73 bis, rue du Maréchal Foch. Tel.
950.36-72.
*C.2 L (centre culturel et de loisirs), 2 rue Jean
Houdon.
VIGNEUX
*Bijou, 55 avenue Jean Corringer.
VILLEJUIF
*Théâtre Romain Rolland, 18 rue Eugène Varlin.
VILLENEUVE-LE-ROI
*Royal, 55 rue du Gal De Gaulle.
VIROFLAY
*La Cigale, 9 Avenue G. Boisier.
VIRY CHATILLON
*Calypso, 38 rue Victor Basch. Tel. 921.85-72.

GERMANY

ALSFELD/HESSEN
*Bambi-Filmtheater, Marburgerstr. 11. Tel. 401.
BAMBERG
*Bambi Im Luli, Luitpoldstr. 17.
BERLIN
Adria-Filmbühne, Schlossstr. 48, Berlin-Steglitz.
*Allegro Filmbuhne, Bismarckstr. 69, Berlin-
Steglitz. Tel. 7 96 55 00.
*Atelier am Zoo, Kurfürstendam.n 153, Berlin-
Halensee. Tel. 134075.
*Capitol-Lichtspiele, Thielallee 36, Berlin-
Dahlem. Tel. 765327.
Filmkunst Olivaerplatz am Kurfürstendamm,
Olivaerplatz 15, Berlin-15. Tel. 881 1170.
*Filmbühne am Steinplatz, Hardenbergstr. 12,
Berlin-Charlottenburg. Tel. 327100.
*Die Lupe, Kurfürstendamm.
*Studio-Filmtheater, Kurfürstendamm 153,
Berlin-Halensee. Tel. 8873315.
BIELEFELD
*Kamera, Am Berliner Platz, Tel. 64370.
BOCHUM
*Capitol-Studio, Kortumstr. 51. Tel. 66652.
BONN/RHEIN
*Woki, Gangolfstr. 1-5. Tel. 52225.
BRAUNSCHWEIG
*Studio für Filmkunst, Gördelingerstr. 7. Tel.
24711.
BREMEN
*Studio für Filmkunst, Herdentorsteinweg 39.
Tel. 313212.
DUSSELDORF
*Atelier im Savoy, Friedr. Ebert-Str. 59-61.
Tel. 28060.
*Bambi-Filmstudio, Klosterstr. 78. Tel. 353730.
ERLANGEN
*Schauburg, Friedrichstr. 1. Tel. 3060.
ESSEN
Filmstudio "Gluckauf", Rüttenscheiderstr. 2.

FLENSBURG
*Holm-Lichtspiele, Holm Nr. 47. Tel. 3444.
FRANKFURT
*Atelier am Zoo, Pfingstweidstr. 2. Tel. 491725.
FREIBURG/BR
*Die Kamera, Sedanstr. 1. Tel. 47145.
*Kandel.hof-Lichtspiele, Kaiser-Joseph-Strasse
268-270. Tel. 46480.
GOPPINGEN
*Stauffen-Theater, Poststr. 36. Tel. 73620.
GOTTINGEN
*Cinema, Weenderstr. 58. Tel. 41483.
*Studio fur Filmkunst, Hospitalstr. 1. Tel. 55867.
HAMBURG
Filmkunsttheater Dammtor, bei der Staatsoper.
Tel. 340706.
*Filmtheater "Gondel", Sierichstr. 97, Hamburg
39. Tel. 470795.
*Liliencron-Theater, Beselerstr. 21, Hamburg-
Grossflottbek. Tel. 895005.
*Studio an der Binnenalster, Post Str. 10.
HANNOVER
*Hochhaus-Lichtspiele, Goseriede 9. Tel. 14454.
HEIDELBERG
*Die Kamera, Brückenstr. 26. Tel. 23902.
INGOLSTADT
*Filmstudio im Roli, Roseneckstr. 2. Tel. 2581.
KARLSRUHE/RHEIN
*Resi-Filmtheater, Waldstr. 30. Tel. 26585.
Studio 3, Kaiser-Passage.
KIEL
*Studio im Capitol, Holstenstr. 62. Tel. 42727.
KOLN/RHEIN
Film-Casino, Hohe Str. 128-132. Tel. 212340.
*Filmkunsttheater die Lupe, Zülpicherstr. 24.
LUBECK
*Lichtspiele "Hoffnung", Hüxtertor Allee 23a.
Tel. 29418.
MAINZ/RHEIN
*Cinema, Bahnhofstr. 4-6. Te!. 28850.
MANNHEIM
*Abendstudio im City, B 1, 6. Tel. 44086.
*Alster-Lichtspiele, Viktoriastr. 33. Tel. 44086.
MARBURG/LAHN
*Capitol-theater, Biegenstr. 8. Tel. 2552.
*Rex-Filmtheater, Biegenstr. 8. Tel. 2552.
MONCHEN-GLADBACH
*Bambi, Hindenburgstr. 170. Tel. 22900.
*Filmstudio, Hindenburgstr. 170. Tel. 21005.
MUNCHEN
*Isabella-Lichtspiele, Neureutherstr. 29, Mün-
chen 13. Tel. 347401.
Lenbach Film Theater, Lenbach Platz.
Film Casino, Odeonsplatz.
*Rex-Filmkunst im Westen, Agricolaplatz, Mün-
chen 42. Tel. 12500.
*Sollner-Filmtheater, Sollnerstr. 43, München-
Solln. Tel. 796521.

*Studio für Filmkunst, Occamstr. 8, München
23. Tel. 347401.
*Theatiner Filmkunst, Theatinerstr. 32, München
2. Tel. 223183.
Tivoli, Neuhauserstr. 3.
MUNSTER/WESTF.
*Schloss-Theater, Melcherstr. 81. Tel. 22579.
OLDENBURG
*Studio Z im Ziegelhof, Friedhofweg 15. Tel.
80123/80333.
PADERBORN
*Studio im Universum, Postfach 908. Tel. 2984.
PFORZHEIM
*Cinema, Jägerpassage. Tel. 6200.
RECKLINGHAUSEN
*Studio 63, Marktstr. 2. Tel. 23420.
SAARBRUCKEN
*Camera, Berliner Promenade.
SCHWABISCH-GMUND
Turn-Theater, Pfeifergasse. Tel. 3040.
STUTTGART
Difia-Filmkunst-Studio, Königstr. 68. Tel.
90404.
TUBINGEN
*Studio Hirsch, Grabenstr. 2. Tel. 3661.
ULM/DONAU
*Filmtheater "Lichtburg", Frauenstr. 91. Tel.
65400.
WIESBADEN
*Atelier, Vereinigte Filmtheater Erich Ewert,
Moritzstr. 6.
Filmkunst Bühne im Thalia, Kirchgasse 72.
Tel. 27964.
WUPPERTAL-BARMEN
*Studio im Fita-Palast, Concordienstr.
WUPPERTAL-ELBERFELD
*Studio, Neumarkstr. 14. Tel. 591043.

ITALY
BOLOGNA
Apollo.
Fulgor, Via Montegrappa 2.
FIRENZE
Arlecchino, Via dei Bardi 47.
MILANO
Arti, Via Conservatorio 9.
Orchidea, Via Terragio 3.
Ritz, Via Torino 21.
ROMA
Nuova Olympia, Via in Lucina 16.
Rialto, Via IV Novembre.
Salone Margherita, Via Duo Macelli 75.

JAPAN
KOBE
Sky Cinema.
NAGOYA
Theatre Meiho Bunka.
OSAKA
Kitano Cinema.

TOKYO
Theatre Nichigeki Bunka.
Theatre Shinjuku Bunka.

LEBANON
BEIRUT
Studio Clemenceau.

NETHERLANDS
AMSTERDAM
*Kriterion, Roetersstraat 34-36.
*Leidsepleintheater, Leidseplein 12.
*Studio K, Roetersstraat 34-36.
*De Uitkijk, Prinsengracht 452.
ARNHEM
*Studio A, Langewal 35.
BREDA
De Beyerd, Boschstraat 22.
GRONINGEN
*Studio, Hereplein 73.
DEN HAAG
*Bijou, Spui 27.
*Kriterion, Westeinde 15.
*De Uitkijk, Churchillplein 7.
*Studio 2000, Churchillplein 7.
HAARLEM
*Studio, Grote Markt 25.
HILVERSUM
*Bijou, Luitgardeweg 2.
LEIDEN
*Studio, Steenstraat 39.
NIJMEGEN
*Studio, Bloemerstraat 113.
ROTTERDAM
*Kriterion, Stationsplein 45.
*'t Venster, Gouvernelaan 129.
TILBURG
*Camera, Willem II-straat 29.
UTRECHT
*Studio, Oude Gracht 154.

NORWAY
OSLO
Carl Johan Teatret, Karl Johansgaten 39, Oslo
1. Tel. 41 74 90.
Gimle Cinema, Bygdøy Alle 39. Tel. 41 39 95.

POLAND
GDANSK
Zak, Waly Jagiellonskie 1.
KRAKOW
Sztuka, Sw. Jana 4.
LODZ
Stylowy, Kilinskiego 123.
NOWA HUTA
Swit, Osiedle C 1.
POZNAN
Muza, Armii Czerwonej 30.
SZCZECIN
Delfin, Mariana Buczka 40-41.

WARSZAWA
Bajka, Marszalkowska 136.
Polonia, Marszalkowska 56.

SPAIN
MADRID
Alexandra, San Bernardo 29.
Galileo, Galileo 100.
Goya, Goya 22.
Infantas, Infantas 15.
Palace, Plaza de los Cortes 7.
Rosales, Quintana 22.
BARCELONA
Arcadia, Tuset 14.
Maryland, Plaza Obispo Urquinaona 5.
Publi, Paseo de Gracia 57.
Rialto, Plaza Calvo Sotelo 3.
Studio Atenas, Balmes 365.

SWEDEN
GOTEBORG
*Smultronstället, Kungsgatan 31-33.
MALMO
*Smultronstället, Gustav Adolfs Torg 45.
STOCKHOLM
Eriksberg, Birger Jarlsgatan.
*Puck, Sibyllegatan 26.
Studio Lumière, Kakbrinken 5.

SWITZERLAND
BASEL
Mascotte, Elisabethenanlage 7. Tel. 246462.
*Zentral Kino.
BERN
A.B.C., Moserstr. 24.
GENEVA
*L'Ecran, 6 rue Bartholoni. Tel. 240511.
LA-CHAUX-DES-FONDS
Palace, Avenue L. Robert 78.
LAUSANNE
*Cinéma du Bourg, Rue du Bourg. Tel. 228622.
LOCARNO MINUSIO
*Bruno Dinkelspuhler (Villa Nice).
LUCERNE
Kino Moderne, Pilatusstr. 21.
NEUCHATEL
*Cinéma Bio, Faubourg du Lac 27.
SAINT-GALL
Studio Hecht, Hechtplatz.
ZURICH
Ciné Bellevue, Bellevueplatz. Tel. 322545.
*Cinema Piccadilly AG, Mühlebachstr. 2.
*Studio 4 AG, Pelikanstr. 19.
*Studio Nord-Sud, Limmatquai 16. Tel. 243575.

TUNISIA
TUNIS
7e Art Cinarès, 14 rue de Marseille.

YUGOSLAVIA
BELGRADE
Kino Kulturnog Centra, Terazije.
ZAGREB
Jadran Kino, Ilica.

U.S.A.
ATLANTA
Festival, 142 Spring St. N.W.
BALTIMORE
Charles.
Five West.
Seven East.
BOSTON
Exeter.
Kenmore Square.
Paris.
Park Square.
West End.
CHICAGO
Cinema.
Clark Theatre, 11 N Clark St.
Playboy, 1204 N Dearborn St.
CINCINNATI
Esquire.
Guild.
CLEVELAND
Continental Art.
Heights Art.
Westwood Art.
DENVER
Vogue.
DETROIT
Studio.
Studio 8.
Studio North.
KANSAS CITY
Kimo.
Rockhill Theatre.
LOS ANGELES
Cinema Guild, 263 Hillcrest Road, Berkeley 5.
Tel. OL 8-7035.
Four Star.
Los Feliz Theatre, 1822 N. Vermont Avenue
Tel. 664.2669.
Lido.
Music Hall.
LOUISVILLE
Crescent.
MINNEAPOLIS
Walker Art Museum.
Westgate.
NEW YORK
Art 38 E. 8th. Tel. GR 3-7014.
Baronet, 3rd Ave. at 59th. Tel. EL 5-1663.
Beekman, 2nd Ave. at 66th. Tel. RE 7-2622.
Bleecker St. Cinema, 144 Bleecker St. at W.
Broadway. Tel. OR 4-3210.

Carnegie Hall Cinema, 7th Av. at 57 th. Tel. PL 7-2131.
Cinema II, 3rd Ave. at 60th. Tel. PL 3-0774.
8th. St. Playhouse, Ave. at 60 th. Tel. PL 3-0774.
8th. St. Playhouse, 52. W. 8th. Tel. GR 7-7874
Festival, 6 W. 57th. Tel. LT 1-2323.
5th. Ave. Cinema. 5th Ave. at 12th. Tel. WA 4-8339.
Fine Arts, 130 E. 58th. Tel. PL 5-6030.
Gallery of Modern Art, 2 Columbus Circele (daily 3 and 5.30 only; Sunday 2 and 4).
Lincoln Art, 225 W. 57th. Tel. JU 2-2333.
Little Carnegie, 146 W. 57th. Tel. CI 6-5123.
Midtown, Broadway at 99th. Tel. AC 2-1200
Murray Hill, 160 E. 34th. Tel. MU 5-7652.
Museum of Modern Art, 11 W. 53rd. (Sun.-Fri. 2 and 5.30, also Thurs. at 8; Sats. 11.30, 3 and 5.30).
New Yorker, Broadway at 88th. Tel. TR 4-9189
Paris, 4 W. 58th. MU 8-2013. Tel.
72nd St. Playhouse, 1st Ave. at 72nd.

Tel. BU 8-9304.
Thalia, Broadway at 95th. Tel. AC 2-3370.
34th. St. East, 241 E. 34th. Tel. MU 3-0255.
Tower East, 3rd Ave. at 71st. Tel. TR 9-1313
York Cinema, 1st Ave. at 64th. Tel. TR 9-2717.
PHILADELPHIA
  Bryn Mawr.
  Lane, Broad St. at 67th. Ave.
  World, 1830 Market.
  Yorktown.
PITTSBURGH
  Encore / Forum / Manor.
ST. LOUIS
  Apollo Art / Shady Oak.
SAN FRANCISCO
  Bridge / Larkin / Music Hall / Presidio.
SEATTLE
  Uptown.
WASHINGTON
  Biograph, 2819 M St. N.W., Georgetown. Tel. FE 3-2696.
Janus One / Janus Two.

London School of Film Technique

THE DIPLOMA COURSE concentrates into 2 years an intensive study of professional film making.

During that time students must work on a minimum of six films, at least two of them in 35 mm.

Only those who complete the first year satisfactorily are allowed to continue into the second.

THE THIRD YEAR COURSE is for 'honours' Diploma students who will normally be required to work for some time 'out' in the industry before re-enrolling.

QUALIFICATIONS

This course — like the profession it leads to — requires talent, artistic sensibility, technical aptitude, business ability and stamina.

Residents in Great Britain should either be graduates of a university, art school or technical college or should have at least 5 passes at 'O' level and 2 at 'A' level: experience of film making is also taken into consideration: all such residents are required to attend for at least one interview.

Candidates are never accepted immediately they complete their secondary education but would be wise to make their first application and obtain advice from the school.

Students resident abroad and unable to attend for an interview must be University Graduates. All applicants are required to submit an illustrated script.

London School of Film Technique is a company limited by guarantee and is registered as an educational charity with the Department of Education and Science.

Full details from:

The Registrar, London School of Film Technique, 24 Shelton Street, London W.C.2.

Vibeke Lökkeberg, the attractive star of Norway's first important feature film of the sixties, LIV, directed by her husband Paul Lökkeberg. We hope to devote a specific section to the young Norwegian cinema industry next year.